Under the Green Tree

By

Clayton Brown

ISBN: 1-4033-1026-2 (e-book)
ISBN: 1-4033-1027-0 (Paperback)
ISBN: 1-4033-1028-9 (Dustjacket)

This book is printed on acid free paper.

1stBooks - rev. 08/02/02

ACKNOWLEDGEMENTS

I thank God almighty first of all, and also thanks to:

My wife and daughter for putting up with me during the times I sat at the computer for hours, and still maintained a family life; your patience has been greatly appreciated.

All of my family and friends that believed in me, your support and inspiring motivation, gave me the strength to keep trying to fulfill my dream. I deeply appreciate everything you have done for me.

My mother, whose tremendous support and love can never be measured.

Maria and Duane Thompson whose continuous opinion of the novel, I absorbed and embraced with gentle thoughts.

Kimberly Martin: for doing the first editing from front to back, and endlessly proving to be a true friend.

Last, but for sure not the least: the lady that has taught me so much. I would like to say thanks to my editor; Susan Kaney *(The author of Angel Crossing)*.

Thank you for believing in me and most of all believing in the potential of **'Under The Green Tree,'** and helping me to bring it to life. Without you there is no way I could have possibly be where I am now. Thank you for the endless hours of editing, layers at a time, and helping me to create a redeemable character. It's been a long year, but I thank God for bumping into you.

To some, dreams are something that may never come true; to others dreams are a vision of what will soon be reality. With prayer, and the support of family and friends, obstacles and barriers that hinder a person from being what he wants to be can be moved. Life hasn't been easy for me, but these elements have eased the pain. Thanks to all, if I missed your name, know that you are in my thoughts with a smile. Clayton.

TABLE OF CONTENTS

PREFACE

During the course of my life I've met so many different people of various life styles, curious if their personalities or role in society will play a major part in my own struggling theatrical fantasies. There have been times when people or things would enter my path of life and become a barrier or deterrent to the goals I set for myself in life. These obstacles amazed me with their immoral or illegal values, but I didn't care about the consequences.

Since I've grown older and gained more experience, knowledge and wisdom, I've learned that many of the things that I thought were necessities aren't really necessary. Furthermore, the things in life that were once important in my past are now irrelevant. For years, I've considered myself to be a dynamic individual. My friends, the few that I have, often criticize the unconscious meticulousness that exists within my personality. Nevertheless, I concur with their criticism. Often I'm guilty of seeking perfection even when pursuing some of the simplest tasks in life.

It's difficult to describe this behavior that consistently drives me to create something positive of myself. I enjoy the gratification of completing projects that others may find difficult. I believe that there are people who share similar views as I do, especially when a situation prevails that has an enormous possibility to off set my equilibrium. Like most Libras, my life has to be balanced.

Often I have asked myself if my perception of life is normal. My answer was merely another question; what is normal? It's for certain that if the desire to excel in life is abnormal, then I choose to be a part of the abnormal clan. Keeping things in order is the type of teachings that were instilled into me through my family upbringing. I now realize that some things aren't going to be impeccable. With the aid of time, I've learned to balance my life by expressing thoughts and ideas on paper.

Unlike some of my incarcerated comrades, I have managed to squeeze through the doorway of rightful citizenship. Choosing the pen has enriched my soul. Writing has become a major factor in the construction of my self-esteem. Before, I didn't have the slightest clue that positive self-esteem and self-confidence are essential to the uniqueness that I now possess. Prior to believing in myself, the idea of writing a novel was absolutely ludicrous; I feared failure and numerous rejections.

Accepting constructive criticism pertaining to my intense endless hours of work wasn't my idea of being an artist. The people that knew me best thought that my education level was substandard for being a writer. I asked myself if I would have to wear those thick bifocal glasses, and be disassociated from the male society? What if my vocabulary wasn't extensive enough to be an author, what shall I do then? All of my friends will be partying and having a good old time, while I'm struggling to compose a marketable manuscript. After all of the negative, stereotyping and limited mind setting came to pass, it was then I had to figure out what to write about.

I decided to write someone else's story. Doing so would give me the chance to implement a new writing style; my own. Writing a novel was in my heart; it was my destiny. Figuring out a subject or person to write about was another problem. Fortunately, with determination, I was able to convince myself that I could do it. Somehow, I knew that, with perseverance, any goal could be achieved.

'Under the Green Tree' has become my life. Although, it's the story of someone else's life, I'm the creator of the transformation of Cleabo Jones' story to paper. I had the opportunity to meet this dynamic inmate, a native of the Big Apple who possessed an unusual personality. His thoughts and ideas about his life were fascinating and how he lived was even more exciting. From the first moment I laid eyes on him, I knew there was a tremendous story of his life style. Certainly he wasn't ready for the life that awaited him. From the time he stepped off the bus at the facility he seemed disarranged. It was easy to assume that this place was going to be difficult for him. Confinement for most military soldiers was difficult as they were punished and tormented on a daily basis.

INTRODUCTION

Throughout the latter nineteen fifties, a majority of the African-American population migrated to the north from the south. They were in-search of a new life, a life that would perhaps provide a lucrative income, more than the poor wages received in the cotton fields. Their objective was to segregate themselves from the croak sack bag that carried the four dollars per hundred pounds of cotton. The bag was straddled across their shoulders and hips, as it dragged the dirt of the narrow rows of the endless fields during the course of the day.

The sunrays beamed on the straw hats of the workers, the drips of their sweat crept from underneath their bandannas and thumped the blazing hot soil. Their hands were swollen and their fingers bled from the pointed end of the cotton boll, due to the indignities of picking the soft white substance that supplied our nation with fabric. Some of them finally realized the possibilities of a better life and they sought refuge in the north; others stayed and settled for less.

It was a period of time when racial and cultural issues were on the rise. African-Americans discovered the need to educate themselves. While being submerged into a dead end life, and swinging from a tree with a rope wrapped around their necks, the African-Americans finally realized that migration was their only alternative. Society of the past truly demonstrated what happened to *uppity* or *out of line colored folks* in a primitive but effective manner. The treatment towards the African-Americans in the south was effective enough to accelerate the migration to the north. Sara Jones and her family traveled the path to a better life in the north. *"Under the Green Tree,"* delivers the difficulties and hardship they encountered, while continuously surviving in a cruel suppressed situation.

CHAPTER I

THE BIRTH OF CLEABO

The wind blew the snow in a sweeping motion on a cold November night, while pedestrians hailed taxicabs on the streets of downtown Rochester, N.Y. Cold winters weren't uncommon, most of the children enjoyed building a snowman or having snowball fights. The older generation preferred the other three seasons and impatiently waited for spring. The elderly would complain about their arthritis or *rheumatism* during the cold season; the majority of them stayed inside and hibernated.

On this particular night the snow was about a foot deep and the melted snow had turned into slush. The gutters were clogged, making it difficult for the liquefied snow to drain. Water flooded the streets while the wind made things miserable for the people that were downtown.

Three winos had a fire blazing from a fifty-five gallon steel drum at the corner of one block. They kept themselves warm by holding their hands over the fire and taking an occasional sip out of the bottle disguised in a brown paper bag. The winos had long coats and hand-me-down clothes on. Dirty scarves were wrapped around their necks to protect their ears, and their fingers poked out of holey gloves.

An ambulance sped down the street flashing its lights and blasting the siren; clearing a path to the hospital. Some of the cars on the street didn't give the ambulance due respect by pulling to the side. Steering the ambulance onto the sidewalk was the only choice the driver had to get around the cars. As he made his turn to get back onto the street, he hit the steel drum that the winos were using to keep warm. The winos were startled as they watched their drum tumble into the street. The slushy snow prevented a fire from starting and the ambulance continued its high-speed journey.

The ambulance arrived at the hospital. Security guards cleared the entrance of the emergency room, while the ambulance crew brought a woman in on a stretcher. Paramedics forcefully opened the doors and perspiration dripped from the woman's face, as she burned with the intense pain of her labor. She grabbed the arm of one of the paramedics and began to squeeze while her moaning became louder. The agonizing pain was unbearable!

The doctor on duty was calm; it seemed like this was the millionth time he had delivered a baby. After putting on his rubber gloves he instructed the paramedics where to take the woman. He tried to console her during his examination, but she was close to ten centimeters, so he immediately came to the conclusion that it was time to deliver the baby.

A smack on the butt and a baby's scream filled the delivery room. The woman exhaled, displaying relief now that her son had exited her womb. The doctor handed the baby to the nurse; she began to clean the after-birth from the infant's body. He explained to the woman that everything went well and she should try to get some rest. While walking away he displayed the attitude of just having another day on the job, however; the glow on the woman's face expressed how happy and relieved she was. The doctor stopped at the door; he turned around and smiled at the woman, saying "congratulations." His smile was evidence that he was proud to have been a part of the miraculous work of God.

Returning the smile, the new mother said "Thank you." Then she turned to her side, positioning herself to receive the infant from the nurse. She could hardly wait to hold the baby that had been doing somersaults inside of her for the past eight months. After cleaning the after-birth from the newborn, the nurse handed him to the woman. It seemed like she was trying to eliminate any doubts to the infant's fresh mind who his mother was. The woman smiled as she gazed into the eyes of her newborn son. His round brown eyes stared back at her, watching her lips move, but unable to comprehend.

"You look so clean and pure," she said. "You are a clean looking baby boy. I don't think Clean Boy would be a good name for you; the kids in school will just *pick* at you. Perhaps if I write the two words together it will sound better?" The woman reached over to the nightstand at the side of the bed to get a pen and a piece of paper. She then started to write other names for the baby; however, Clean Boy was the name with the most significant impact to her.

Taking the first four letters of the word 'clean' and the first two letters of the word 'boy,' she formed the name Cleabo. Cleabo Jones was the baby's name. It was an unusual name, but to the woman it was a good name because it had meaning. Names like Larry, Tom or Dick were ordinary and the woman preferred something different for her child. Perhaps she felt that with a different name a different life would accompany the infant. The woman wanted her infant son to have a life unlike her own, which had been filled with pain, sorrow and regrets. She was the owner of a life that explained why she was all alone in the hospital, with no family or friends to share the glorious event of childbirth.

Sara Jones was the woman's name; she was young and attractive. Her brown eyes and beautiful creamy complexion made her irresistible to men. She was five foot ten, rather tall for a woman. She knew some men found her height to be intimidating, but she felt her height was an advantage. In the nineteen fifties it was typical for a young black woman to have a gold crown on her tooth, and Sara's left front tooth was no exception.

She turned the heads of many men with her long straight hair and brown eyes. She wore her hair up with a small hat pinned to it; it was the norm for a woman in the fifties. Sara looked polished and glamorous in her business suits. Although this was Sara's second baby, she still had a beautiful figure. She had a small waistline and a figure eight, or Coca-Cola bottle shape.

Men, congregating like a pack of wolves, couldn't help themselves from watching Sara when she walked by. Just to tease them, Sara would cross her left foot over her right as she walked and swish her perfectly round rear end. She could always feel their eyes watching her everywhere she would go; everyone would stop and stare. She felt that being attractive could have its rewards and difficulties, and she knew how to handle either.

Most of the women she met displayed signs of being intimidated or jealous of her. When women would compliment her, she was unaware if they were making a pass at her or just being friendly when they said, "Oh, you are so beautiful." She was a proud, positive thinking woman whose goal in life was to be the best mother she could possibly be to her children.

Sara left South Carolina at the age of seventeen, after her parents learned that she was pregnant with her first child. Sadie Bell, her mother, was sympathetic about the pregnancy; but her father wasn't. He couldn't handle the fact of his little girl being pregnant. James, her father, stood about six foot four. He was dark as the night, sometimes called charcoal black. His deep, rich, shiny black eyes had the gloss much like a pearl. On the other hand, the tiny veins in the whites of his eyes were always blood shot red, probably from the alcohol he kept in the kitchen cabinet.

He was as mean as a bull and whenever he spoke people listened; the three-inch scar by his ear intimidated people that didn't know him. James had the facial features of a slave from Africa; he walked with a slight limp resembling a captured runaway slave with an amputated foot.

James had been stabbed in the leg when he was caught cheating in a card game at one of the local juke joints. He worked for the city driving a backhoe. Most of the time when he arrived home he was tired, exhausted and covered with mud. His normal routine was to grab his bottle of vodka from the cabinet and have a drink while he sat on the porch in his rocking chair. From his pocket he would extract a brown leather pouch that looked like it had been in a World War II battle. It was filled with tobacco; he would stuff his pipe as he sat in his rocking chair and have a smoke with his drink.

After a few drinks, supper would be waiting for him inside on the small wooden table in the kitchen. Sadie Bell knew his routine and she did everything to comply with his needs. When James finished eating he would go to Brown's store and sit around with his friends and drink some nasty corn liquor. He did this every night and would return home at around ten thirty. Sadie Bell had some idea that he was seeing another woman at the store, but it didn't seem to bother her. Her main concern was keeping her family together. Back then women expected that a man wasn't going to be faithful. They believed that a piece of a man was better than being alone.

Sara's relationship with her father changed after she saw him with another woman at Brown's store. James was sitting on a wooden milk crate while a woman was rubbing his shoulders and kissing him on the neck. Sara immediately ran home and told her mother. Sadie Bell was angry and didn't want to believe Sara, but she knew there was a possibility that Sara was telling the truth.

When James arrived home he knew that Sadie Bell was going to be angry with him. He recalled the look on Sara's face when she saw the woman kissing his neck.

"Damn! What was she doing at the store?" James thought.

James entered the house, and Sadie Bell began throwing things at him as she yelled.

"You son of a Bitch! What the hell you doing with some other woman!"

"I wasn't with another woman, that was just old Jessie Bell. You know her, Clim's cousin. I don't know what Sara told you, but it sure ain't true."

Sadie Bell didn't want to believe a thing he said, so they began to fight. A physical fight between married couples was normal in the fifties. Police seldom came to the aid of the female. Society understood what happened when they saw a Negro woman wearing a pair of dark shades to cover up her black eyes from a dose of physical abuse. James and Sadie Bell fought for about an hour and a half, then they went into the bedroom and made love. Sara could hear her mother and father making love and it upset her. She thought her mother was being foolish for making love to her father after he had beaten her up and was seeing another women. She began to hate him.

She hated him for who he was and the things that he would do to her, and her mother. Although she had four younger siblings, their father treated none of them like her. Being the oldest child, her chores of cooking, cleaning and being responsible for her siblings' actions were a tremendous responsibility for a fifteen-year-old. Whenever her mother and father decided they wanted to go out for the weekend with friends, Sara had to take care of her brothers and sisters, as well as the children of her parents' friends.

She would baby sit them from Friday until late Sunday night. If things went wrong while her parents were gone, she would be responsible and her father would beat her when they returned.

After James and Sadie Bell finished making love that night, James came into Sara's bedroom and shook Sara's shoulders. "Get up, get up you little lying ass wench! Get your ass up!" Before Sara could open her eyes, a belt that was used to sharpen the razors in the barbershop came smashing across her face. In terrible pain and only seeing stars, she heard his voice, but she couldn't see him as she tried to protect herself from the belt that was continuously swatting her. Her siblings stood watching, too scared to say anything to their father. Besides, he didn't beat them; he would only beat Sara. Sara grew to hate her father; she didn't understand why her mother stayed with him.

Sadie Bell was around five foot nine, bowlegged, with long black hair. She was a woman of fair skinned complexion. Her skin color, as she would say on numerous occasions, *"Was not derived from the mixture of slaves and their masters."* Sadie Bell's ancestors were Native American, that later mixed with those of African-American blood. She would tell Sara a lot of Native American stories that were told to her by her grandparents.

Sadie Bell had a green thumb; she had no problem growing any kind of vegetables in her garden in the back yard, and her garden was beautiful. Some of the neighbors thought that Sadie Bell was mean, but in reality she was a sweetheart. She received a reputation of being mean when one day she was talking to a neighbor, and the neighbor's kid was looking at her in the face as she spoke, so she spit in the kid's face. Sadie Bell's form of discipline was crazy to the neighbors, and her actions spread like a wild fire within the neighborhood.

Sara loved her mother, she was her mother's right hand. The day she had to tell her mother she was pregnant was the saddest and most disappointing day in her life. "Momma, can I talk to you for a minute?" she asked.

"What, Sara, can't you see I'm trying to clean these greens before your dad gets home?" said Sadie Bell impatiently.

"Momma, I really need to talk to you."

Sadie Bell stopped cleaning the collard greens and wiped her hands off on her white apron. "What's the matter honey? What is it you want to talk about?"

"Momma, I don't know how to tell you this but…Oh Momma please don't be mad! Momma, I've been trying to do good. You know I have," Sara said, as she started to cry.

"Child, say what you need to say and get it over with," Sadie Bell insisted.

"My thing hasn't come for two months now and I'm scared."

"Scared, why in the world would you be scared when you ain't doing anything, are you?"

"One weekend when y'all went off, and I had all those kids, I did something with that old boy name Benny. I didn't know what I was doing and he was showing me how. All the kids in school talked about how good it would feel. But Momma it hurt, and I started bleeding like I was having my thing. Momma I was scared and I tried to push him off of me. But Momma he wouldn't let go. He held me tight and was just'a panting and a moaning. I was getting so scared, Momma, and he was still humping me; it hurt, Momma. He didn't stop until he did his business inside of me! I hate him, Momma. Just like I hate Daddy. But I never did it again, Momma, so help me; it was just that one time!" Sara said, as tears ran down her face.

Sadie Bell grabbed Sara and held her in her arms, rubbing her hair, trying to comfort her. She knew that James would be upset and all hell would break loose once he found out. Sadie Bell tried her best to ease her daughter's mind.

"I'm going to take you to the doctor tomorrow so that we can be sure. We don't want to jump to conclusions, so let's just wait until then. Remember, this will just be our secret until we know for sure."

"Yes, Momma," Sara lifted her head, then placed it on Sadie Bell's chest.

Sitting in the doctor's office was like waiting in a cell on death row, Sara thought. It seemed like it took forever for the doctor to come out of his office. Sara and her mother sat impatiently in the lobby for the test results. Finally he came out of his office, telling Sadie Bell and Sara the test results were positive. They gathered up their things and cried the entire way home. Once they were home, Sadie Bell greased Sara down with some lard. She knew that when James arrived home he was going to have Sara strip down to her bra and panties and give her a good beating. Sara's father normally arrived home around five thirty, the wait was long and she was tired of waiting. "The doctor's office was enough for one day!" she thought.

When her father came home, Sadie Bell, being the faithful wife she was, had no choice but to tell her husband. James was so upset he brutally whipped Sara with the extension cord. She thought he was trying to beat the baby out of her; perhaps this was his intention. Sara had welts from the cord and blood dripping down her fragile body; all she could think about was running away, as far away from her father as possible. The next day she ran away to New York and eventually had the baby.

Now, here she was again, giving birth to another child. Her father was always abusive to her and she promised herself she would never go through that again. The abusiveness had turned her into a strong woman, but when she would think about her family she'd feel depressed.

At feeding time, little Cleabo had no problem finding his way to Sara's perfectly round breast. Babies can smell milk and he just wrapped his little mouth around one of her breasts and began to suck. Breastfeeding Cleabo was painful to Sara. Although she went through this ordeal with her other son Barry a year ago, she had somehow forgotten how painful it was.

Barry stayed with the neighbor Julie while Sara was in the hospital. Sara considered her to be an associate, she didn't know if she could trust her to be a friend. Sara needed her to look after Barry while she was in the hospital. Julie was out going and sometimes loud. She acted like she had just come off the streets. The way she talked made a person think she was a retired hooker. Julie was about five foot six inches tall with short hair that had a blond streak; a popular style at the time. Julie was pretty and like Sara, she had a body that would turn heads. Sara thought that Julie's attractiveness was all she really had going for herself.

Julie's house was always a mess and she was a terrible cook, unlike Sara, who kept a clean house and could cook some good southern style meals. Julie was a northerner; she kept a drink in her hand and a cigarette in the corner of her mouth throughout the day. She loved to party and have a good time. She had plenty of money, her husband had died mysteriously in his sleep one night and Julie was living off of his pension.

Sara and Julie would go out to the Cafe 260 nightclub on Saturday nights sometimes. They would have a good time partying, but they wouldn't pick up any men. They would just come back to Julie's house and have a couple of drinks, while they talked about how much money foolish men spent on them. Together they felt like they were two precious jewels that knew how to work a nightclub. It wasn't unusual to have men hovering over them at the bar, trying to get to know them, in order to sleep with them.

After sucking Sara's breast dry, Cleabo fell into a deep sleep. Sara was a little tired and was ready to fall asleep too. While trying to position Cleabo underneath her armpits to a comfortable position in the tiny hospital bed, the nurse walked into the room.

"Here, let me have him so you can get some rest. I know you're tired. We'll change his diapers, but you'll have to feed him. Get as much rest as you can; he might be a greedy little fellow."

"Thank you, I sure can use a little nap. It's been a long time since I had a baby yanking on my breast like this little fellow," Sara said as she picked up Cleabo and handed him to the nurse. The nurse received Cleabo and cuddled him in her arms as if he was a fragile doll baby. Rocking him like she was a human cradle, she turned her head away from the baby to say goodbye to Sara.

"I'll bring him back in a couple of hours. Say goodbye to Momma."

"Bye sugar, Momma will see you later," said Sara.

The nurse turned around at the door with the baby in her arms, "Oh yeah, have you decided on a name? We need to get his birth certificate ready and put his nametag on his crib," she said.

"Yes, I decided his name will be Cleabo, it means a Clean Boy."

"Cleabo, that's different, but you know it sort of fits him." The nurse looked at Cleabo, then turned her head back to Sara. "Okay. Get some rest now and I'll see you after a while."

Sara finally had a chance to get some rest. It had been a busy night for her. She knew that in a few hours one of her breasts would be sucked dry again. Breast feeding a baby was something she didn't look forward to. Sara closed her eyes and fell into a deep sleep. She managed to rest that night; she only had to feed Cleabo twice and there was long interval between feedings. Sara's vital signs were back to normal, so she was able to sleep until morning after Cleabo's last feeding.

The next morning she woke up feeling as though she had been hit by a truck. Her body was sore and it was hard for her to sit up in bed. After inhaling and slowly exhaling for a repetition count of thirty, she was able to sit up. Sara used this breathing exercise every morning. She believed that if people stepped out of bed and started their normal activities it would shorten their life span. Sara felt that her breathing techniques prepared her body for her daily activities. She thought breathing in deeply and exhaling slowly in the mornings helped her body walk in unison with her mind. This, she thought was a way to nurture her body in order to sustain her beauty.

After exhaling the last breath Sara rotated her head attempting to loosen up her neck muscles. She looked at the window and observed the battle the morning sunrays were having with her closed blinds. She immediately stopped her neck rotations and stepped out of the bed to open the blinds. While walking to the window she didn't think about what she was wearing. Sara was wearing a hospital gown that had the tie straps in the back and it exposed all of her rear end. Forgetting that all of her ass was exposed, she opened the blinds to get some morning sunshine. After she opened the blinds she began to stretch, as she stood on her toes the hospital gown lifted while she reached for the ceiling; exposing her backside further. Sara had no idea that her privacy would be invaded. When she stopped stretching and was flatfooted again, she was startled by a voice.

An orderly had walked into her room while she gazed out of the window. He stopped and stared at Sara in total admiration as he held her breakfast tray in his hands. Sara stood at the window as a strip of the sunrays diagonally rippled across her gown and her exposed ass. The light from the sun just intensified her beauty. The orderly was hypnotized as he watched her run her hands through her hair, lifting the gown higher and exposing more of her.

"They told me that I would have to leave New York to find the perfect peach. But, from where I'm standing I can see perfection." The voice of the orderly startled Sara. She quickly turned around to see who had entered her room. She instantly noticed how handsome the orderly was. She was impressed and immediately physically attracted. After catching her breath she was able to respond to his smart 'come on' remark, one that could only be delivered by someone who possessed confidence.

"Are you just going to stand there looking at the view, or are you going to put my food down?"

"Oh yes, if I can manage to take my eyes off of you for a moment, I guess I can find somewhere to put this tray. I'm sorry for staring, but I'm sure that if you were in my shoes you would have done the same. They told me that when I brought your breakfast to you I would be impressed. That was an understatement, I'm more than impressed!

The way you look, it's hard to believe that you are in here for having a baby. You look so nice, even in the morning."

"Thank you for the compliment," said Sara humorously. Then she glanced down at her hospital gown. "But I know that I look terrible. Just look at me, I'm a mess! Here I am looking like 'Who did it and what for,' and you are still trying to come on to me, probably because my entire ass is hanging out."

"No, no, I wasn't trying to come on to you because of your ass. Awe...I mean...I was just merely trying to say how beautiful you are."

"Once again thank you, and thank you for bringing my food. What's your name?" Sara responded with a smile.

"My name is Jonah, Jonah Walker and it's a pleasure to meet you Miss." He then tilted his head down to read the name card on the tray. "Miss Jones, or may I call you Sara?"

"No, Miss Jones will do, and once again thank you."

"Miss Jones, I would really like to get to know you. Maybe we could have lunch, or dinner, or something sometime? I know that you just had a baby and you may be involved in a relationship already. But if you're not, I would like to be given the opportunity to become a friend of yours."

"That sounds nice, Jonah, and you really know how to come on to a lady. I gathered you have a lot of experience with women by the way you talk. Unfortunately, I'm involved with someone and he's the father of my newborn child."

"I understand," Jonah answered but persisted, "But there's one thing I need to know. Are you happy with him all of the time or some of the times?"

"I would have to say most of the time if you must know. Why are you asking me that anyway? Is this part of your 'player's rap' or something?"

"I just wanted to know in a nonchalant way, if there's any room in your life for me. You see, Sara, if I may say so, I'm a firm believer that there are two types of relationships in the world. The first is when a person has someone and the other is when he or she has someone in mind. They have that person in their mind because they can't feel or touch them, maybe because of distance or wrong timing? So based on my little theory, can you tell me your situation?"

"He is with me for the time being, but if things would ever go sour I will be sure to keep you in mind! That is, if you are still available at the time. I know a man of your caliber probably has women standing in line."

"No, it's not like that at all, but you do that. You know where to find me. Maybe we can go out and shake a tail feather or something. Bye-bye for now and you take care of yourself. I hope to see you soon." Jonah walked to the door while smiling at Sara with his pearly white teeth. She turned the table by leaning her head to the side and glancing at his lower posterior as he exited. He noticed that she was looking at his behind so he laughed while he walked away.

After exchanging their views of each other's "fineness," Sara was able to continue on with her morning activities of eating breakfast and preparing herself to receive Cleabo from the nursery. Breakfast was filling; however, being delicious was another question. It served the purpose despite the fact that it had become a little cold while she was having the flirtatious conversation with Jonah.

Sara pushed the tray of food away from her and wiped her mouth with a napkin. While wondering why the nurse hadn't brought Cleabo to her, impatiently she began to try to find something to do. She went into the bathroom and started putting her make up on and fixing her hair. "Fifty strokes on one side and fifty on the other side with the brush will do," she thought. After brushing her hair she then rolled it into a bun and pinned it up. Lipstick, eyelashes and powder were an easy task. Within five minutes Sara was looking glamorous even with the hospital gown on.

Just as she left the bathroom, the nurse entered her room. Surprised to see one another they exchanged morning greetings.

"Hi, good morning to you. I've got some good news for you. The doctor has decided we can release you and little Cleabo. He's such a cute little thing," she added cheerfully. "Do you want us to give someone a call to pick you up?"

"Good morning to you too. Yes, you can call my friend Julie; I put her on the paper work as next of kin. How is my son doing and when will you be bringing him to me?"

"He's doing just fine! You'll be able to see him as soon as I can get back. It's time to feed him and that will take a mother's touch. I'll be giving you some bottles to take home with you and a breast pump. I hope these items will help you."

"I sure do thank you! Anything to stop that little fellow from yanking on me will be a great help. Let me prepare myself for him; this is one ordeal I really don't look forward to."

"I'll be back in a minute, oh yeah," the nurse said hastily before walking to the door. "Hospital rules say that you have to be taken to the car in a wheelchair. I'll let your friend know where to park."

The good news of going home made Sara happy instantly. She wanted nothing more than to get out of the hospital. One more day there would have been too much, she thought. Sara never did care for the hospital and she was beginning to miss her other son, Barry. Barry was a busy little tot; like most kids he was mischievous and a bit hyperactive. He was born the year before Cleabo. More than likely he would be jealous of the newborn, especially if Sara had any intention of giving all of her time to the new intruder. The transition of relinquishing the role of being the baby over to a newborn is always difficult for a child.

Sara began to think about how Cleabo's father June Smith would feel when she returned home. From the time she told Cleabo's father that she was pregnant, there was nothing but trouble between the two of them. Sara could remember him saying, "Woman, I don't want no damn baby!"

She thought the name June was an unusual name for a man. It was understandable to her that a female could have a name like May, April or Julie, which she thought stood for the month of July. But when it came to naming a boy after a month of the year, it was a little ridiculous she thought. Sara would sometimes tease him by calling him December.

June was a tall, handsome ladies man; he had no problem sweet talking women into anything he wanted them to do. He always walked like he was taking a stroll in the park. It was called a "Diddy Bop" walk back then. His hair was processed straight and his skin was completely unblemished. He was attractive to women, as Sara was to men. Like her father, he too was a womanizer and a beater. He would constantly physically abuse Sara for some of the pettiest things.

At one point in her life, wearing a pair of dark shades to cover up her black eyes, was a standard part of her wardrobe. The black and blue bruises on her body were covered up with her clothing. When he choked her she would wear a turtle neck sweater to hide the prints of his fingers that were squeezing the breath of life out of her. Though Sara swore that she would never put herself in a position as her mother had been with her father, June had managed to sweet talk his way into her life. Love has a strange way of making people blind.

Despite the fact that when he got liquored up and would beat the crap out of her, she wasn't ready to give up on him. Although she would have had no problem finding another man, Sara was obsessed with this man and she loved June dearly. When she told him that she was pregnant, he insisted that she get an abortion, but she refused and the argument escalated into a fight. June started punching Sara like she was a punching bag. He had been drinking and the thought of having a baby was the last thing he wanted to hear. June felt that having a baby would seriously interrupt his player status. That was just one of the fights Sara amazingly survived without severe damages. She still felt that she was fortunate to have a so-called family life. Little did she know this type of occasional abuse was far from being any kind of a life.

Sara was afraid to give birth to her new child with June acting this way. She didn't have a clue as to what he might do to it. She thought about having an abortion, but it was definitely out of the question. Her family values were totally against early pregnancy, but an abortion was taboo and unheard of. Sara finally rationalized with the fact that June wasn't her soul mate, but she still put forth the effort to make things work.

When it was time for Sara to go to the hospital, June made it clear, "I'm not going to be watching no kid," and then he went to the bar. June was a cold-hearted player. He only wanted to be with the finest women in town and dog them royally. He made his money on the streets and would never look for a job. Perhaps he was into some illegal activities, Sara didn't know. One thing was for sure; she feared this cold-hearted gangster type of a man, almost as much as she loved him.

Julie understood the situation between June and Sara and she was willing to assist Sara in her time of need. Julie feared for Sara's life because of the situation she was in. She disliked June and she would let Sara know it almost everyday. "I would only trust him as far as I could see him." Julie would say.

"Every man deserves a chance; maybe things will work out for us." Sara would respond. Sara always defended her man when Julie would talk about him. She would tell her it was her problem and she would just deal with it. Knowing the position she was in, Sara wondered if she would really be happy returning back to her home. She was appreciative of Julie taking care of Barry, but the idea of confronting June with the new kid was indeed intimidating.

The nurse finally returned to the room with Cleabo; it seemed like it took forever. The hospital had Cleabo dressed in a cute little outfit with a hat over his head. He was staring at Sara with the *"I want milk look,"* written all over his face. Cleabo began to cry and the nurse said, "I guess you know what time it is; it's time to feed him again."

"Yeah, I guess so; come here little fellow; let me give you some milk." Sara said as she pulled out one of her breasts and placed it into Cleabo's mouth.

"Your friend is on her way, when you're finished you can leave. Just make sure you stop by the outpatient's desk and sign out okay?"

"Okay, I'll make sure to do that," Sara added sincerely. "Once again thank you very much for everything you have done for us."

"Oh, you're quite welcome," the nurse said as she was walking out of the door. "It's been my pleasure. Now you take it easy and don't rush back to work; good luck."

Sara finished feeding Cleabo and gathered up her things as another nurse brought in a wheelchair to take her out of the hospital. Sara and Cleabo were on their way home. She could hardly wait to get out of the hospital and see her son Barry.

Sara held Cleabo in her arms and they rode the elevator down to the first floor; the nurse was at her side with her bags. The elevator door opened and the cold air from the lobby froze her face. Quickly she covered Cleabo's little head with the blanket, and the nurse wheeled them to the outpatient's desk to sign out. After signing out, she noticed that Julie was there, her car was parked in front of the entrance door. Julie came running after she saw Sara and the baby.

"Hey Sara, how you doing? It's good to see you girl," Julie said as she reached for Cleabo. "Let me hold the little fellow." Cleabo looked at Julie wondering whom this stranger was. Barry saw Sara and he followed Julie, then he tried to climb into Sara's arms.

"Sara, I'm glad everything went well and he came out healthy. Look at him, just as handsome as he wants to be!" Julie said as she held the baby while Sara climbed into the back seat. "Sara he looks so clean." She handed the baby to Sara and buckled Barry up in the front seat.

"I sure am glad to get out of there girl." Sara sighed deeply, leaning her head back against the car seat.

"I know you are," Julie agreed, nodding her head emphatically.

"Hey, Julie, what's been going on, girl?" Sara asked, interested in catching up on the latest news.

"Oh, nothing much, Barry has been keeping me busy, and that turkey I met last week called a few times. You know, I introduced you to him at my place one time. The construction dude that owns his company, remember?"

"Yeah, I remember him." Sara nodded, "So how is it looking for him? He was kind of cute; does he have a chance?"

Julie shook her head. "I don't know, Sara. He seems to have it going on and everything, but I'm just not ready to settle down with just one man. You know, I want to explore and not be tied down. I definitely don't want to run into a Dr. Jekyl and Mr. Hyde, like that *'fool of a man'* you have. Damn girl!" she emphasized her words by thumping the steering wheel with her palm. "I've been trying to tell you for the longest that your man is no good! That man will try to screw a squirrel if it opened up its legs too wide."

"Now, Julie, what I tell you about going there? Me and June just have some things that we are going to have to work out."

"Yeah, work out alright," Julie rolled her eyes, "I'll tell you what, if a man hit me the way he has hit you, he'll be working it out in his grave, six feet under!"

"Don't worry about me, I'll be all right!" Sara responded, lifting her chin with disdain. "I've got my boys now and I don't think that I will be tolerating any more of his shit. Besides, I can do bad by my damn self. If he put his hands on me again, he is going to be in for a rude awakening!" she added emphatically.

When the car arrived at the two-story home, Sara expressed contentment; she was glad to be home. Sara's home was connected to other houses, similar to the way townhomes are. Next door was where Julie lived and the entire block was filled with what was called 'private houses' of this type. Sara loved her little house. She had never lived in a house that had a basement in it before; she thought it was huge and beautiful.

A barbershop and the neighborhood grocery store was at the corner; Sara did most of her shopping there. She had established herself well enough at the grocery store to receive an account, or tab, from the storeowner Mr. Sam. It was an unusual name for an Italian, but he was a nice man who was sympathetic towards the single parents that frequently visited his store. Barry had received his first haircut at the barbershop next to the grocery store. It seemed like Barry cried for days while he was sitting in the chair; he almost made Sara cry, but she knew that this was something a mother had to endure with boys.

The car stopped and Julie came to Sara's door to assist her out of the car. After opening the door, Sara managed to get situated with the kids. Little Cleabo had fallen asleep and Barry just went into his own little world playing with his toys. Once again Sara thanked Julie. Julie just said, "That's what friends are for." Sara looked at her and smiled, still feeling suspicious all the while.

"Sara, I'll see you later," Julie waved as she sat behind the wheel, "I've got a million and one things to do. Let me get out of here before that *'fool of a man'* of yours comes home."

Sara watched Julie drive away before taking a deep breath. Joyfully she walked her family up the steps to their home. After her day of playing the motherly role, the sun began to set. Sara walked over to the curtain to observe the view. Such a pretty sight she thought; to her there was nothing more beautiful than watching the horizontal plane of the sun as it diminished into the earth, while its rays reflected off the sparkling soft white snow. Sara always tried to watch the sunset.

Sara felt that night time was generally when all bad things would happen and she knew in a little while her *'fool of a man,'* as Julie would put it, would be coming home. Sara didn't look forward to this; she wasn't in the mood for his *'sugar honey ice tea.'* She had a lot of things on her mind, like going back to work, her bills and taking two kids to the daycare. Fortunately, the daycare was down the street in route to her bus stop to work. That eased some of the stress of being without a driver's license or a car.

Around eight o'clock she heard a key fumbling at her door. She knew it had to be June, he was the only one that had a key. Usually she could determine the level of intoxication he was in by the way he came into the house. Sara could assume that from the difficulties he was having getting the key into the keyhole, he was approximately three-quarts full of alcohol. Sara had her own theory of using quarts to determine his comprehension level after he had been drinking. One quart or half, June could have been tolerable. At three-quarts or full, she didn't want to deal with him at all.

June entered the house reeking like he'd been drinking all day, with the noxious fumes of alcohol seeping through the pores of his skin. He staggered his way to Sara; she had a look of disgust written all over her face, but she managed to smile. After all, he was the father of her child, though, "Such an unfortunate mistake!" she would think at times.

"How are you, Sara? I hope that everything went well?" June made an attempt at pleasantry then went straight to the defensive. "Now, woman, don't be mad at me, I wanted to be there; I truly did, but I couldn't get myself up to it. I know I haven't been the man you wanted, but I told you a long time ago I didn't want no damn kids! You already had one and that was fine, he wasn't mine, so it was cool. But then you had to go off and get yourself pregnant. Baby, I can't be tied down; you know who I am. Shit woman, I think I love you and all, but I be damn if you think that I have time to be playing some fatherly game. That's just not me; that kind of game is for the birds. I'm a street man! I was born to the streets and I'll die in the streets."

Looking at his figure and smelling the rankness of his stumbling body was like setting a torch to her anger. "June, I'm not asking you for a thing! Shit, you can go back to the streets if that's where you belong! We will be fine with or without you. I'm just thankful that you didn't drop him in a napkin and flush him down the toilet after jerking off that's all! He's a beautiful kid and I'm sure that he will have a good life, one hopefully far different than yours!"

"Woman, who the hell you think you're talking to, don't you know I will slap the shit out of you for talking to me like that?" June moved closer to Sara threatening her with the force of his large body.

"You forget who you talking to! You better mind yourself before I walk all over your ass." Abruptly he turned and looked into the kitchen. "What the hell you cook in here today anyway? I'm hungry!"

Sara knew she should've kept her mouth shut, but she couldn't stop her words. "Me and the boys already ate; you should've got something to eat while you were out in those streets. I just got out of the hospital, and I don't feel like standing over a stove today, not for you or anybody else!" she said it firmly, but before she could close her mouth after completing her last sentence, June swung his fist across the side of her face, knocking her to the floor.

Sara was on the floor curled up defensively as he continued to punch her. "Woman, I told you not to be sassing me! Bad enough you done went off and had this kid; now you trying to have a smart ass mouth! Woman, don't you know I'll kill you?" June continued punching Sara in the head and all over her body. Sara continued to hold the shielding fetal position on the floor. She was trying to protect herself the best she could, but his cruel blows continued to rain on her delicate body.

Sara managed to roll away from June, then stumbling to her feet, she ran into the kitchen. Barry began to cry as he watched June chase Sara. The only man he knew of as a father was brutalizing his mother. Sara reached the counter and fumbled through the drawer that contained the silverware to get a butcher knife. June was quicker though, grabbing her and wrapping his arms around her in a bear hug fashion. He began dragging her out of the kitchen as blood ran down the side of her face.

While being dragged, one of her arms was free from the elbow joint to her fingertips, she managed to pick up the cast iron frying pan that was lying on the stove. Sara bent over, hiding the pan from his sight, while June was on her back holding her. Then, erecting herself back to the standing position, she swung the frying pan towards his head. Whack!

The backside of the frying pan connected to his head and his arms released her as he fell to the floor unconscious. Sara stood over him for a moment observing his chest rising. This was a good indication that she hadn't killed him. Wearily, she placed her arms on the stove and rested her head near the burners, tears and blood from her bruised lip dripped to the floor as she cried and moaned her misery and discomfort.

"You motherfucker, die! I hope you die and leave us alone! I made a promise to God that if you ever put another hand on me I would send you to your maker." She paused and peered at him again to make sure he was still unmoving.

"Look at you; just look at you now. June, if you ever try this shit again so help me I will kill you! I took enough shit off of my father and I ran away. This is my house and my kids and I be damned if I'm going to run or take anymore shit off of you!" She ended her tirade with a kick to his ribs, then dragged his limp body into the spare bedroom and somehow managed to throw him on the bed. He was still breathing, and Sara gave him a hard look then she closed the door. Then she went into the bathroom to clean herself up.

Sara wiped the blood from her face and thought about the .38 caliber she had to protect herself in the event of an intruder. She thought about picking it up and just shooting June and getting it over with. She liked that thought, but Sara was smart in some aspects and she knew that she would have to serve time if she killed him; and that wouldn't work for her kids. She loved her children and no man was going to interfere with their life.

All of the commotion must have awakened Cleabo; he was screaming. Sara knew this was a good indication that it was time for his feeding, so she put one of the bottles that she had filled earlier into his mouth. Little Cleabo was content and fell fast asleep. Barry went into his room after everything had quieted down and fell asleep on his bed. Sara went into the room and tucked him in. After tucking Barry in Sara fell to her knees to say her prayers, asking God to watch over Barry while he slept. She finished saying her prayers and stood next to Barry's bed staring down at him.

"Look at my big baby, sleeping all by himself like a big man. Don't worry, baby, I know that if you were a little older you would have kicked his ass for me. But Momma's going to be all right."

She walked out of the room and began preparing herself and Cleabo for bed. Sara felt that the newborn was too young to sleep by himself in his crib, so she had him sleep with her. Sleeping with the infant was somewhat uncomfortable for her. She had to hold him and that meant positioning herself on her back. Sara wasn't used to sleeping on her back; she would always have nightmares. After tossing and turning she came to the conclusion she needed to put Cleabo on one side of the bed, and herself on the other side in order to get some sleep. The new sleeping arrangement didn't wake Cleabo up; he was totally exhausted and full of milk. He probably could've slept through an earthquake.

Sara finally went into a deep sleep; it had been a strenuous day for her. She was at peace in her sleep as her body drifted into her dreams while lying on her side. Around three o'clock in the morning, she felt a breeze blowing over her body. With her eyes closed Sara pulled the blanket up to her shoulders and ensured the cover was on Cleabo. While pulling the covers over Cleabo, Sara felt a presence in the room with them. She felt someone standing over her and she could feel the person's breath falling upon her. She quickly sat up in the middle of the bed and opened her eyes.

It was June; he stood at the side of the bed where Cleabo was sleeping. Sara gasped at the sight of the butcher knife he was holding; June's right hand was tightly clenched around the handle. He held the wicked blade at his shoulder level, and it seemed as though he was ambivalent of what was going on. Sara quickly grabbed Cleabo and screamed. "June! What the hell are you doing with that knife, are you going crazy?"

"Don't worry," June told her, lowering his arm. "If I wanted to kill the little crumb snatcher he would've been dead by now." He gave her a knowing look. "Especially with how hard you sleep!" He put the knife down on the dresser and began to walk out of the room.

"June, I really think that you are going fifty-one fifty. Man, you need some help!" Sara shouted. "Stay the fuck away from my baby, you hear me? If anything ever happens to him, you will wish you would have never known me, so help me, June!"

Sara was too frightened to sleep; she sat up in the bed holding Cleabo in her arms the remainder of the night. Sara waited for daylight to come, because she knew that like a vampire with the arrival of the sun, June would disappear and maybe then she could get some rest.

Finally the morning sun came shining across her living room floor, and just as Sara predicted, June left the house without saying goodbye. Sara's normal routine was to go get the morning newspaper after June's departure; however, this particular morning, she didn't care about the newspaper. She felt what had happened last night should have been headline news.

Sara worked at a law firm as an administrative assistant. Early on, she bought a typewriter to teach herself how to type; filing and the other duties she learned studying at the library. Most of the time she would always be running late to work. Getting herself ready and Barry in the mornings were indeed challenging. Whenever she needed June to take Barry to the day care for her, he wouldn't comply.

"That's not my damn baby," he would say. That was the reason she had to have Julie watch Barry while she was in the hospital.

Cleabo didn't walk until he was eighteen months old; he was a heavy little round boy. He was a lazy little fellow because his mother would always hold him, fearing for his life whenever June was around. Although June never put his hands on her again after that day she returned from the hospital, she couldn't forget him standing over Cleabo with the knife. Most relationships have their ups and downs, but since Cleabo's birth, Sara and June's seemed to be on the downhill.

Sara would never leave Cleabo alone with June; Cleabo would always be saddled on her hip. He was on her hip when she cooked, cleaned, or even when she went to the bathroom. Finally, with the help of the day care, Cleabo began to walk. His first steps were a joyous occasion for Sara; she was so happy that her little boy had finally started walking despite how much she had held him back. Sara was pleased to see that her son didn't develop any type of abnormalities because of his father. Most of the time when June was around, he just played with Barry; he had a better relationship with Barry than he did with his own son. Sara was always around protecting Cleabo from him. Barry wasn't his kid so Sara knew that he wasn't going to hurt him.

One Saturday morning after Cleabo starting walking, Sara stepped out of the bed to retrieve the newspaper off the steps of her front door. Wearing only her night gown and robe, she opened the front door and squatted down to pick up the paper. While trying to remain covered without exposing her undergarments, she picked up the paper and the thought of her *'fool of a man'* June, came rushing across her mind. She hadn't seen him all day Friday and now it was Saturday morning.

Still squatting, she looked to her left toward Julie's house. A smile lit her face as she recalled all the noise Julie was making while she was having sex last night. Their walls were connected, so when Julie made love, it wasn't hard to listen to the screaming and moaning sounds. Julie's door opened and a man came out of the house with a long coat on. Julie was with him at the door and she delivered a long juicy French kiss to him. A smile came across Sara's face as she awaited the opportunity to see the man.

After their lips separated and their eyes opened, both Julie and the man's heads turned toward Sara. Sara stood up, her mouth opening wide. To her amazement, the man that was kissing her so-called best friend was June! Both Julie and June were startled and surprised. Sara dropped the newspaper and ran down the steps after them. June jumped over the hand railings and began to run faster than a track star. Sara took the garbage can top and threw it like a Frisbee, hitting June on the head, but it didn't stop his stride. Knowing she couldn't catch June, Sara then turned to Julie to give her a good beat down. Julie quickly ran inside and shut her door, while Sara yelled, kicked and beat on the door.

"Bitch! Open up this door, you little ten cent tramp! I had a feeling something like this was going on! Open this damn door! Okay, that's all right, you don't have to open the door, I'll get you later, your ass is mine! I don't know how you think you can still live here, there will be no more peace in this valley. You little whoring ass wench, I will kill you!" To her embarrassment, Sara noticed that a number of people had gathered on the sidewalk watching the spectacle. She composed herself and went inside her house. Once inside, knowing that Julie could still hear her, she continued her rant, yelling at the top of her lungs.

"You motherfucking bitch; you know that's good! It's good because you two deserve each other! Two pieces of shit! You're nothing but a whore! Forget you and forget him! I'm moving on!" it was at that time that Sara decided that it was best for her to move back down south and remove her children from the dog eat dog environment. She thought that it would be best for her family to be close to family instead of being in the midst of strangers she couldn't trust. Sara knew that even though her family didn't always approve of the things she had done, there was still that unconditional love that

23

prevailed. This event helped Sara realize and appreciate the unconditional love her family had for her. Despite the beatings she received as a kid, her parents never stopped loving her, nor did she them. The type of love she had for Julie and June was truly conditional; they weren't her blood relatives and her love for them was set on the condition that they treated her right, and they didn't comply.

CHAPTER II

THE TRANSITION BACK TO REALITY

Sara was upset and disoriented for the next couple of months, then she began to prepare herself to move back to South Carolina. She contacted a realtor to sell her place and submitted her resignation at work. Sara was fed up with New York. She wanted to get as far away as possible from June.

The movers came to pack Sara's household goods, their belongings were packed in suitcases waiting on a cab. The cab arrived the same time the last box was being put on the truck. Her furniture was heading down south and she was on her way to the bus station. Moving can be expensive, but fortunately for Sara, she had saved her money for such an emergency. She knew that when her savings depleted, she would be able to rely on the equity from the sale of her house which would later be sent to her.

Although this was only her second time at the station, Rochester's bus terminal seemed to be a familiar place to Sara. Sara knew that it was time to get the hell out of New York before she hurt someone. The majority of the buses were clean and the restrooms weren't filthy. Bus stations can be kind of scary with all of the *hooligans* around, but Sara was prepared for it. She figured that if she was approached by a stranger in an unusual way, all she would have to do was pretend she was just as crazy as they were. Most of the time this behavior worked for her.

Sara patiently waited for the bus going to South Carolina. It was going to be a long ride she thought as they stood in line. She realized how much she was going to be losing, she only wished that she could regain her family's love and be able to start a new life. It seemed like it was only yesterday when she traveled this long road from South Carolina to New York. She was a child then, but now she was returning, a woman with two kids.

Sara didn't let her parents know she was coming home, she figured she would just surprise them. Sara wondered how her father would react when she arrived, she hoped he had changed since she ran away. She was also hoping that unconditional love would bring forgiveness to her father's heart. Sara was ready to rely and depend on her family. "That's what family is for," she thought. She no longer feared her father; now that she was a woman. She felt she could communicate with him better and was willing to do anything to get away from June.

The trip to South Carolina took a total of twenty two hours. Sara had a long old fashioned dress on and a scarf wrapped around her hair. She dressed herself to blend in with her surroundings. Knowing that she would be going through a figurative time warp, she was prepared for it.

Drizzling rain fell as the bus entered the terminal of Orangeburg, South Carolina. Sara gathered her things and held Cleabo and Barry's hands as they exited the bus. After getting their luggage, she realized that there was no one waiting for them.

The telephone number to the cab station was posted on the wall outside of the bus terminal. Sara and the two boys walked in the rain to the telephone that was about twenty feet away from the terminal. While holding the umbrella underneath her chin and shoulder, her raised leg held the pocket book steady in order to find change to call a cab. Cleabo and Barry stood patiently observing their surroundings as the rain momentarily soaked them, while their mother held the umbrella over her. She finally found the correct amount of change and the boys were happy to have the umbrella returned to its rightful position.

After dialing the number the telephone rang until finally someone answered. The lady that answered the telephone didn't say the name of the taxi cab place, she merely said hello. Sara thought she'd mistakenly dialed someone's home or perhaps received the wrong number, however, the fact of needing a cab still remained.

"Hello?" said the person at the cab station.

"Hello," Sara said quickly, "Yes, could you send a cab to the bus station please?"

"Where you going, honey?" the woman answered.

"I'm going up 601 to Golf street."

"Hold on a minute and let me see if Ned is driving today. Wait a minute, I'll be right back. He's taking a nap. He love to sleep in the rain, *you know*," the lady said.

Sara could hear the woman as she walked away yelling Ned's name, trying to wake him up. Sara took the phone away from her ear while the woman went to wake up Ned, and looked at the receiver in disgust.

"Damn! Here I am back again in primitive land. Wake Ned's ass up. He likes to sleep in the rain *you know*. Hell no, I didn't know until you told me!" Sara shouted while the lady was away from the telephone.

"Hello? Hello, you still there, honey?" said the old lady at the cab station or house. "Ned's going to come and get y'all, he said it will be fifty cents though."

"That's okay, ma'am." Sara answered, relieved to hear the low cost. "Did he say how long it will be? I have two kids with me and they are kind of wet from the rain."

"Shouldn't take that long," the strange woman responded, then began rambling. "All Ned have to do is get dressed and take his medicine. Yeah, he been my man for forty-five years now. Poor thing still sleep in the bare *you know*. I still don't know why, can't get nothing from me, don't have the feeling for it no more. I wonder sometimes what he's doing sleeping in the raw this time of the day? Maybe he be dreaming or something, 'cause he sure ain't had a boner in a good fifteen years, *you know*."

Sara didn't know and she didn't care, but she answered politely. "No, I didn't know. Sorry about that lady."

"Y'all just go sit inside and I'll tell Ned you'll be waiting. Go and get them chillins out of the rain. Ned will be on his way."

"Yes Ma'am, and thank you." Sara said, preparing to hang up.

"And you know what else, honey?"

'Click!' Sara hung up and marched her two boys into the bus terminal to wait on the cab and to stay dry. Unlike other terminals, Orangeburg had an old fashioned country atmosphere. There was a small dining area and the smell of cheesy grits, bacon and eggs filled the small three-lane bus station. It was clean, too, with no homeless people hanging out. After about thirty minutes, Ned peeped through the glass door looking for Sara and her kids. He approached Sara slowly, as most old men do.

"You called for a cab, lady?"

27

"Yes, I did, thank you for coming. I spoke to your wife. She seems to be so nice. Thanks for stopping your sleep to come and get us. Your wife sure is lucky."

"Oh shucks," Ned shuffled a bit, appearing embarrassed. "That old bag of wind. She just talks, and always talking about me. I would get rid of her, but we've been together too long. She's a bag of wind alright, but she's my bag of wind," he added as he bent down to pick up some of Sara's bags.

Sara smiled in total admiration. She thought to herself that it must be nice to have someone to share that many years with and still be together through thick and thin. "Now where 'bout you going?" Ned asked as he put the bags in the trunk of the car.

"Golf street, right up 601, you know where that is?"

"Now sweetie," Ned answered. He was somewhat annoyed that she'd think he didn't know. "There ain't a spot in Orangeburg I don't know. You just tell me where you want to go and I'll take you there. I've been driving a cab for, let me see, forty-two, no it's been forty-one?" he stopped a moment in concentration, then continued. "No, it has been forty-four years now. I can remember just like yesterday, it was right before Maryland and me, that's my wife you know…right before we…"

"Look Mr. Ned," Sara interrupted, "I just had a long trip and I don't mean to be rude, but can we just go please? I want to get the kids out of these wet clothes. You do understand don't you?" she asked in exhausted zeal.

"Yeah, I understand," he nodded vigorously as they approached his ancient rusty cab. "You know how old people just love to run off at the mouth, come on get in." He opened a rear door. "Let the boys ride in the back and you ride up front with me. Maybe some of my friends might see me and think I hit the jackpot with a young pretty thing like you in my cab." He laughed at his joke as he walked to the driver's side.

"Yeah, right gramps," Sara laughed with him. "You know you are a little too old to be talking like that, and besides your wife is going to kill you for even thinking about talking like that." Sara winked and Ned laughed louder.

"Yeah, you right!" he cackled, slapping a thigh. "Now I was a fool! Wild as a bat in the old days. She made me slow down. Yeah, especially after she threw them hot collard greens on me for cheating. I had to go to the hospital for third degree burns! Yeah, but she stuck by me, took me to the hospital and everything. That's one good woman, my Maryland is. Got a pretty good aim, too!" Ned finished as he and Sara laughed heartily together.

The cab arrived at Sara's destination and they exited the cab as the rain began to pour on them again. She paid Ned and told him that she would try to come by to see them one day. She waved goodbye to Ned and attempted to open the small umbrella, unfortunately it was broken. Sara and her two boys walked up to the little wooden house with their bags in their hands and the weight of fatigue written all over their faces.

Stopping at the steps to the front porch, she slowly raised her head as the heavy rain soaked her and the boys. Grandpa James was on the porch rocking while the rain continued to drench their bodies and flow down the sides of their faces. Since she had run away, Sara knew she had to get permission before she could ever enter again; Sara didn't know how to set her pride aside to do so. Grandpa James held his head up and looked Sara in the eyes.

"You done come back from up that road, ain't ya?" he turned in the rocker and called through the front door. "Sadie! Sadie Bell! Come here and see why we got all this here rain."

"What James? I'm trying to cook!" Grandma Sadie Bell hollered back.

"Woman, you better come out here, 'fore I drag your ass out here, now look over there!" he pointed at Sara.

Grandma Sadie Bell came to the porch and saw Sara and the boys. Quickly she ran down the steps and hugged Sara, then she picked up Cleabo and Barry, joyfully holding them.

"How y'all doing? Come on in out of the rain!" she exclaimed, hurrying everyone in. "Are y'all right? Y'all ain't got to go nowhere now, do you? You's home and you're going to stay here with us!"

Grandpa James said, "Damn! That just makes more mouths to feed! Look at them two boys. Them damn chillins look like they'll eat us out of house and home, specially that old big head one right there!" he said, pointing at Barry. "Come here boy." He gestured to Barry, then picked the boy up experimentally. "Let me see how much you weigh. It look like you hungry anyway. Them young folks been starving you?"

Sara looked over at her mother and said, "He ain't changed a bit, has he Momma?"

"No, he hasn't," Sadie Bell agreed, "James is just set in his ways, and it's so hard for him to forget. He never did go for the idea of you running off like you did."

"Momma, I was grown then and I'm grown now, and I won't be depending on you for long."

"Child, stay as long as you please, we missed you so much. James don't show it but he couldn't wait to see his grands."

"Yeah I know Momma, and it sure is good to see y'all again."

"Hey, Sadie Bell!" James called, interrupting the two women. "I'm going to take these chillins down to the store, now that it done stop raining. They look like they hungry. Hell, they probably ain't eat in weeks! They're a little wet but that's alright. It's probably their first time having clothes dry on their asses, but it won't be the last." Grandpa said as he started preparing himself and the boys to go.

Grandma Sadie Bell and Sara started laughing because they knew that he was going to show off his grandkids to the rest of his friends that hung out at the corner store. Grandpa James had been waiting for the day when he could take his own grandkids to the corner store and brag on them. It seemed like this was a common ritual while they drank their moonshine liquor.

The men would bring their grandkids and all of their friends would have to give the kids some money the first time they were at the store. By the time the kids would leave, their pockets would be fat with money. Grandpa James knew the tradition well and he could hardly wait until it was his turn to play the game with his grandkids. Every time someone new came into the store he would say proudly, "These here my grands' first time here at the store, from up north you know." When grandpa said 'first time at the store,' the tradition was for the men folks to reach inside their pockets and give money to the kids. Grandpa recalled all the money he had given to his friends' grandkids, and he felt proud to be able to get some of it back. He was happy the boys could have a little money in their pockets.

Cleabo's grandparents were happy to see him and his brother. Somehow, grandchildren are easier to face than a pregnant daughter.

The anger James had felt when Sara was pregnant was long gone and he didn't want to hit her anymore. He felt that since she had moved away and survived, she had become an adult and he had more respect for his oldest daughter now. In his own old fashioned southern way, he would sometimes show his affection to Sara. Although the words, "I love you, Sara," never came out of his mouth, Sara realized how much her father loved her, and she managed to stop hating him. Sara had forgiven her father for what he had done to her in the past.

After being back for a few days, Sara decided that she would prepare her father's lunch. At five o'clock in the morning, Sara was up stirring around in the kitchen. She had told her mother the day before that she would be fixing her dad's lunch, so she could get some rest for a change. "Child you don't have to do that," Sadie Bell told her. "I've been doing that for years, I don't know what rest is."

"You will know what rest is tomorrow, when you get some Momma, 'cause I'm fixing Daddy's lunch." Sara responded determinedly.

"Okay," her mother gave into Sara's will. "If that's the way you want it, but you ain't got to, you know."

Sara could smell her Daddy's stinky smelling shaving cream. She knew that he would use a butter knife to shave with, but the aroma of the shaving cream really turned her stomach. Smelling her father's shaving cream in the morning time was something she hadn't missed. Although she knew it was the only kind of shaving cream he could use to prevent his smooth face from bumping, she thought the smell of it was revolting.

Grandpa James had finished shaving and was ready for work. Sara met him in the living room. Her father had a surprised, but sad look on his face when he saw that it was Sara with his lunch in her hands. He looked at her, wishing that he could turn back the hands of time and change the way he had treated his oldest daughter. Sara, with her pretty round brown eyes, returned his look, her eyes alone telling him everything was okay. The expression on her face let her father know that she understood, and forgave him for making one of the most important times of her life so miserable.

Without saying a word to each other, they both knew that they shared mutual feelings. At that moment, they shared the feelings that only a father and a daughter could possibly share. It was a sign of true regrets and the sad but hopeful indication of a new beginning with each other. "Here's your lunch Daddy." Sara said handing the bag of food to him.

"What a surprise, thank you for fixing my lunch Sara," he said uncomfortably.

Sara attempted to put her father at ease. "Oh, you're welcome, now don't you work too hard today. Those grandkids of yours will be waiting on you."

He nodded, then repeated, "Yeah, yeah, I know. They are real special, thanks for giving them to me."

Sara smiled, feeling genuine warmth, "You're welcome Daddy and you have a nice day." She paused for a moment, then added, "I love you Daddy."

Grandpa James was stunned. He never heard those words before from his oldest daughter. He didn't know how to respond. He was completely speechless, which was totally unusual for him, then he managed to find his tongue. "You have grown up to be one fine woman, haven't you? I'm proud of you. I'm just disappointed in myself that I had nothing to do with it."

"Oh, Daddy you had plenty to do with it," Sara disagreed cheerfully. "You gave me life, kept clothes on my back and you just wanted me to do well. But, most of all you made me have a mind of my own, just like you and Momma, now go on." She said, while making him take the lunch bag and giving him a gentle push towards the door. "Get out of here before you be late for work."

"Okay, you just like your Momma. I'll see you later."

Grandpa James closed the door behind him and walked to the car. Sara watched from the window as he drove away. When she turned around to go clean up the kitchen, her mother startled her. Sadie Bell was standing in the doorway, rubbing her eyes and smiling.

"Momma, what are you doing up?"

"Girl, you know I can't sleep with all that noise going on. I'm glad you and your father made up. He's going to have a good day today. You're something special Sara, come give me a hug, baby." Sara and her mother hugged each other and they almost shed tears together again, just like the time she found out that she was pregnant. This time, however, Grandma Sadie Bell's stomach growled from hunger as they hugged. They smiled and laughed then they began to fix breakfast.

Cleabo's grandparents lived in a wooden house; the roof was made of tin. When it rained, you could hear the rain drops while sitting inside. They were poor, but they were happy most of the time. There were only two bedrooms in the little wooden house and Sara's two sisters also lived there. Things were a little crowded, but, they made room for family.

Sara and her two boys slept in one bedroom and Cleabo's grandparents took the other. His two aunts slept in the living room on the sofa. Cleabo's aunts were named Louina Mae and Dora Gene. Dora Gene was slim with a nice figure. She was dark as the night with a rich, smooth, black skin complexion like her father, James. Her skin was unblemished and it was complimented by her short hair style. Dora Gene was the youngest and like Sara, she was blessed with beauty. She was quite outspoken and had an active social life with the young men at her school.

Dora Gene would fight girls after school and most of the time the disputes would be about a boyfriend. She would change boyfriends like a person would change their socks. A few times, the fights would end up in front of the little wooden house, and Grandma Sadie Bell would have to come to Dora Gene's rescue.

Dora Gene stayed in trouble all the time. She would purposely hangout late at night with her friends at parties and juke joints, knowing that Cleabo's grandmother would be waiting up for her. When she finally made it home, Grandma Sadie Bell would be waiting behind the front door. At this point, Grandpa James had stopped being the disciplinarian. He felt bad for how he had treated Sara and he didn't want to run anyone else away from the family. His two sons were already out of the little house, one in the military and the other up north somewhere. Grandma Sadie Bell had taken over giving out the whippings when wrongdoing was done.

When Dora Gene stepped inside the house after missing her curfew, Grandma Sadie Bell would commence to whip her with that same heavy leather belt that Grandpa James used to use. Dora Gene stayed in trouble. She was considered to be fast, unlike her sister, Louina Mae. Dora Gene kept the excitement going; she was so funny! His grandparents didn't understand her generation at all; they never had as much trouble out of Sara like they did with Dora Gene. She was wild.

Louina Mae stayed around the house and out of trouble. She always helped with the work and didn't complain about anything. Louina Mae wasn't slim like Dora Gene, she was thick and big boned. Louina Mae had a boyfriend, but she wouldn't allow him to come to the little wooden house to court her. They would meet secretly after school and sometimes on the weekends at the picture show. She was ashamed of her family and the little wooden house, and she didn't want him to see how they carried on all the time.

Grandma Sadie Bell would clean the house, listen to the blues, and take a little nip during the course of the day. The toilet was outside in a little wooden outhouse. The toilet seat was also wooden, and you had to watch your rear for splinters. Cleabo never knew how they extricated the waste or whether they waited for it to dissolve. Maybe, he thought, there was a man called the Boo-Boo Man that came around collecting human waste for a living.

His grandmother washed their clothes in a hand cranked washing machine. It was the kind that used what looked like rolling pins. She would scrub them first by hand on a scrub board. The scrub board was made of wood and it had ridges that were made of tin. It was always strenuous work to wash clothes. Cleabo enjoyed his days in the little wooden house. It was exciting and there was always some sort of commotion going on.

Sara had developed her independence in New York and she knew that before long she would want to regain it and find a place to call her own. She received the equity from her home in New York and established a savings account. Then she managed to find her own little wooden house, right down the street from her parents. Cleabo spent most of his early years of life there.

It was difficult for Sara to find a decent job with only a high school education, despite the fact she was well qualified with secretarial skills. She finally found a better job to support her family and pay the twenty-five dollars a month rent for her little wooden house. Sara's new job was at a company called Deman's Moving and Storage. The office had a total of nine employees and they moved people and companies all over the U.S.A. In the south, it was unheard of having a colored woman in an executive secretarial position in the sixties, but Sara was exceptionally skilled from working in New York, and that had made the difference. Naturally, this was difficult for the white southerners to understand.

On the morning of her interview, Sara woke up feeling great. The wonderful smell of coffee filled all of the rooms in her little home. After washing up Sara sat at the table wearing her robe and she sipped her coffee, wondering how the interview for the new job was going to go. She realized that it was time to wake Cleabo and Barry up to drop them off at grandma's. Sara stepped into the boys room and turned their light on as she shouted, "Wake up! Wake up, you two!" she sounded like a drill sergeant. The boys wiped their eyes as they sat up in the bed wishing Sara would tell them to go back to sleep. Unfortunately, for Cleabo and Barry, that was never going to happen.

Sara was so excited about her job interview she was singing as she walked through the house. Cleabo and Barry just looked at each other with the expression, "We are up for the duration now, Momma is singing." By now, a few years had passed and Cleabo and Barry were able to dress themselves. Sara would put their clothes out the night before and the boys would get themselves ready.

It was six thirty, and she realized she was running late. She quickly ran into her room and hurried to get into her gray business suit she brought home with her from New York. She knew that particular suit would get her any job. It was a gray tweed, double-breasted and tight at the waist suit. The skirt hung just above her knees, it displayed every curve and roundness of Sara's luscious body.

Sara wrapped her hair up and pinned a hat on her head. The gloves and the small purse were definitely a northerner's touch. She wasn't sure how the southerners were going to respond to her dressing like she was in New York. She only hoped that she wasn't too stylish or flamboyant in her tweed suit. Most of all, she didn't want to have a 'nightclub's look' at an interview. Sara dropped the boys off at Grandma Sadie Bell's, they kissed each other on the cheek and Grandma Sadie Bell told her, "Good luck."

"Come on here girl," said Grandpa James as he walked to his nineteen fifty-seven Chevy to give Sara a ride to her interview.

"Okay Momma, Daddy's waiting. Bye boys!" Sara said, then she dashed out of the door. Grandpa James and Sara arrived at Deman's

Moving and Storage at 8:55 sharp. Sara was a little nervous at first, until her father began to talk to her. When the car stopped, he looked at her and noticed how nervous she was. James watched her intertwine her fingers and move her hands in a circular motion.

"You sure you're going to be all right walking home?" he asked.

"Oh, yes Daddy, I'm going to be all right."

He noticed Sara still twisting her hands out of nervousness. "Sara, don't be so damn nervous! You've handled more stressful situations than this little penny ass interview."

"I know Daddy," she said. "I don't know why I'm so nervous. I guess it's been a long time and I just got a serious case of the butterflies. I'll be all right once I get inside. No need to be this nervous anyway; the job only pays minimum wage."

"Just think of it this way Sara," James stated, giving her some philosophical advice. "You came here without a job, you can leave without one; nothing will change. And besides," he added proudly, "It's to their advantage to have my little girl working for them, so don't be so nervous over nothing." He patted one of her hands and continued. "Now when you get the job, be nervous then. That's when you will be wondering what to expect of the people that you are working with, or who you can trust. That's when you should be a little nervous."

"Oh Daddy," Sara said, looking at him in admiration, "In your own little world and the way you say things, your words do sometimes make a whole lot of sense." She picked up her purse and opened the car door. "Okay Daddy, gotta go. Wish me luck."

"Knock'm dead honey! Show them that Jones' spirit." Said Grandpa James enthusiastically.

After waving goodbye to her father, Sara walked into the office of Deman's Inc. There was a long counter in the middle of the large hall. It was a quiet but busy place, the people walked from one room to another; while the sound of elevator music played. Sara walked up to the counter and approached the receptionist sitting in her chair behind the counter. The receptionist spoke first.

"Hi, may I help you, hon?"

"Yes, I'm here for a job interview." Sara said, still feeling nervous, but hiding it well.

"Oh really?" the woman said sarcastically, "Who would you like to speak to?" she looked Sara up and down like Sara was a piece of dirt, let alone someone presenting herself in a professional manner for a job. The receptionist had, "I'm looking at a jigga boo," written all over her face and presented an ugly demeanor towards Sara.

Sara maintained her composure. "I'm here to see a Mr. Barnes. I have a nine o'clock appointment."

"Let me see here, hon." the receptionist said as she scrolled down the appointment book. She looked up at Sara, "What's your name, hon?"

"My name is Sara Jones." Sara said slowly and calmly, although mentally she was starting to lose her temper.

"Oh, I see it. Yep, there you are, nine o'clock." She gave Sara a pointed look. "Are you sure Mr. Barnes knows that you are colored?" she asked.

Sara looked at her strangely and said, "I don't know, my resume was printed in black ink on white paper. You think he can tell if I was from that?" Sara smiled coolly.

"Oh, so you're one of those uppity niggers aren't you?" the woman challenged Sara with a freezing stare.

Not wanting to make a scene as the people walked in and out of the different rooms, Sara leaned across the counter. She looked the receptionist in the eyes, and softly whispered to her. Her soft voice belied her furious anger.

"Look bitch, I didn't come here for trouble. Mr. Barnes has seen my qualifications, but as long as I'm in this office I'm not going to be nobody's Nigger. If you ever call me that again, I will beat the living shit out you. Believe that!" she stood up straight smiling sweetly again, "Now call Mr. Barnes and tell him his nine o'clock is here. Oh and honey, be nice about it okay?"

Sara sat down in the chair in the receptionist area, the receptionist picked up the telephone and called Mr. Barnes. Sara watched her closely, she was reading the receptionist' lips while she spoke. The receptionist returned the telephone receiver back to its base and kindly said to Sara, "He'll be right with you."

Sara, smiling to herself, began to read a magazine while she patiently waited for Mr. Barnes. After about ten minutes, a door opened and a short, stubby, middle-aged bald man stepped out of one of the offices. He walked into the receptionist area, looking over Sara as though she wasn't there. Sara noticed how he glanced at her, then looked away like she was made of air or was invisible. He then turned to the receptionist and asked, "Where is my nine o'clock?" The receptionist leaned to the side with a pencil in her hand, and pointed at Sara. Ensuring that Sara knew she was being nice, the receptionist said, "There is Ms. Jones, Mr. Barnes."

Mr. Barnes turned around trying to hide his stupidity and shallow mindedness. He had embarrassment stamped all over his face. "Ms. Jones! Hello, I'm Roger Barnes. It's a pleasure to meet you. I'm sorry that I'm a little late. I was tied up in the office."

"Oh that's fine." Sara rose, offering her hand to shake. "I understand how things can get sometimes. I was just enjoying some good old southern hospitality from the receptionist, she's such a nice person," she added, smiling at the woman.

The receptionist took her eyes off of Sara's mouth and lowered her head as Mr. Barnes turned around and looked at her and said, "Oh really." He gave his receptionist a thoughtful stare, then turned back to Sara.

"Come into my office so we can start the interview." He waved a hand at his office door indicating that Sara should go in. Sara agreed, "Okay," and she walked ahead of him into the room.

Mr. Barnes' office was quite dull looking. He was no interior decorator that was for sure. The pictures on his desk of his family were a painful sight to Sara. Mr. Barnes was indeed overweight, but his wife was twice his size. His three children looked like a horrid combination of them both. Their faces were round, puffy and looked like they had the mumps. Sara felt sorry for those poor children being born into obesity. His family pictures looked like two hogs with three little pigs. Mr. Barnes' desk looked like it hadn't been organized in years. There were piles of papers stacked up and an ashtray filled with cigarettes butts. "Surely he's overdue for a secretary," Sara thought.

She sat down and Mr. Barnes asked her the basic interviewing questions, like where did she receive her training, where was her last employment and how did she obtain her secretarial skills. Although the answers to all of his questions were on Sara's resume, she answered all of his questions, leaving Mr. Barnes impressed with her attitude and skills.

The south was still fairly primitive at that time. When he read Sara's resume and saw that she had secretarial skills, he had to interview her. Knowing that she was colored made no difference to him; he was overwhelmed. Sara was offered the double position of Secretary and Accounts Payable and Receivable. She was happy despite the fact that she would be the only colored person in the company. The important thing was, she had a job.

Sara knew that she would be able to deal with all of the racial negativity that would accompany the position and it didn't matter to her. Mr. Barnes told her she could start on Monday. He explained her duties and told her he thought that she would fit in nicely. Sara smiled and said thank you, as she thought about the small confrontation in the hall with the receptionist. "Yeah, if he only knew. I won't be taking any shit off of anybody here." She thought to herself.

"Thank you for coming Ms. Jones. We are glad to have you aboard. I bet you can't wait to start on Monday? Don't worry, we will still be here, and once again welcome to the company."

"Thank you Mr. Barnes," Sara gave him a genuine smile of pleasure. "You know it isn't often that a colored woman gets an opportunity to use her skills in today's society. I think you know what I mean."

"Yes, I know what you mean, but you don't have anything to worry about with your skills. A person would be a fool to hire someone else. Now, you let me know if you have any problems here. I think you'll work out just fine." He said as he offered his hand in parting.

Sara shook his hand and said, "Thank you again, I'll see you on Monday."

When Sara turned and walked out of the office, she could somehow feel his eyes watching her smooth, perfectly shaped body. She thought it didn't matter what it took to get the job, as long as her morals weren't compromised. She felt blessed to have such a beautiful body. She knew for sure she wasn't going to be anyone's concubine, slave girl or a bed warmer; she just wanted a job. Sara waved goodbye to Mr. Barnes and closed the door behind her. She walked down the hall into the receptionist area feeling confident, as though she were floating on air. Smiling like she had won a million dollars, she waved at the receptionist.

"Goodbye, I'll see you on Monday, hon."

"Oh, you got the job?"

"Yeah, and I hope that we don't have any hard feelings because we have to work together, you know?"

"Oh, no, I understand, I shouldn't have been so rude, hon. Sorry." The receptionist apologized.

"That's okay, hon, I think that everything is going to work out just fine. See you Monday."

"Okay, see you on Monday Ms. Jones. Have a good weekend."

Sara was suspicious of the receptionist's nice behavior, but she responded. "You too."

She closed the entrance door and began to walk her way home; she was on cloud nine. The receptionist held her head down and said, "That bitch, just who does she think she is? She won't last here long, I'm going to see to that!"

After walking for about three blocks or so and still feeling like she was floating on air; her feet started hurting. She took her heels off and threw her jacket across her shoulder, and walked the streets in her stockings. Sara couldn't help noticing guys turning their heads as she passed by. The desire in their hearts and the lust displayed on their faces was obvious as they looked at Sara.

Sara made it to Grandma Sadie Bell's house and shared the good news with her. The first thing that came out of her mother's mouth after she told her how her day went was, "Girl you better watch yourself, you know this is the south here. We don't want to find you hanging from a tree somewhere." Sara didn't care, she was happy with how everything had gone. Grandma Sadie Bell could've said whatever she wanted. Sara wasn't in the mood to let her mother, or anyone else for that matter, piss on her rainbow.

Sara took the kids home and began to cook for them. Cleabo and Barry were bored so she sent them outside to play for a little while. The Jefferson's who lived next door had a son named Derrick. Derrick and Cleabo were around the same age and they played together most of the time. The neighborhood was friendly and everyone knew each other. If a neighbor saw a child misbehaving, you could guarantee that they would tell the parents or whip the child's butt on the spot. It was more or less neighborhood implied permission to whip a neighbor's child if they were out of line.

At the end of the block lived a woman name Mrs. Garvis. She always had a lot of powder on her face and didn't say too much to anyone. Mrs. Garvis' granddaughters were beautiful. It was a treat for Cleabo to watch as they jumped rope inside their Grandmother's fence when they would come to visit her. Mrs. Garvis would always yell at the kids when they would go into the cornfield to steal corn. The cornfield was located across the dirt road next to Mrs. Garvis's house. 'Crazy Man Joe' owned the cornfield. He would shoot at kids that were in his cornfield with his shotgun.

Mrs. Garvis would merely try to warn the kids of the danger. One day, some of the kids were in the cornfield and the sound of a shotgun was heard. They immediately started running without looking back to analyze the life-threatening situation. They just sprinted their way to safety. If a person wanted some free corn there was definitely a risk factor involved. The field also had enormous pecan trees that increased the temptation of entering. Everyone in the neighborhood did it; fortunately no one was ever shot.

Most of the neighbors and friends all had specialties. If anyone needed anything they would come to one another for help or support. There were doctors, lawyers, nurses and other professional people in the neighborhood. These people weren't licensed but they serviced the neighborhood, and they were free. Payments were given by returned favors.

When a neighbor's house was on fire, everyone had to pitch in to put the fire out. Fire trucks weren't authorized, because of the location being out of the city limits. In the neighborhood, one neighbor was almost burned rescuing a child when a neighbor's house was on fire. Buckets of water were being passed from one neighbor to another to put the tremendous blaze out. It was always a sad day when a neighbor's home was burned to the ground. Within a few weeks everyone pitched in and cleared the land to build a new house. Clothes were provided for the homeless family and they moved in with Mrs. Carrington until their new home was built. Mrs. Carrington was the unlicensed nurse and the midwife. She was Grandma Sadie Bell's best friend. She delivered every baby in the neighborhood and she was everyone's Godmother. Mrs. Carrington also knew everyone's family tree or roots. She and Grandma Sadie Bell used to always talk on the front porch and watch the sun go down.

Clayton Brown

While sitting on the porch one day, Mrs. Carrington told Grandma Sadie Bell the story about Grandpa James' family.

"Your husband's family comes from down deep in the country. I used to know his people before they died off. His Momma died of some sort of disease when she was still young. She left James' father, Jim, with five kids. They lived on a farm and there was always a lot of work to do. It was kind of hard on the children. All of them were unable to go to school. They had to keep up the farm, *you know*. He kept mourning for his wife so much that he took up drinking and different women and he stayed in the juke joints. Didn't have time for the kids anymore. It was like they was on their own."

"One night he got liquored up and him and his buddies went to this party. Now, he had no business going to this party anyhow. You see, he was fooling around with the woman that was giving the party and she was married. Her husband had some idea about it, but could never prove it so he didn't like Jim. Jim didn't care once he got that liquor in him. He was determined to go to that party."

"Jim and his friends went to the party and started drinking some more. They got loud and acting like natural born fools. The husband was angry, but was quiet. Jim and his friends went into the kitchen where the food and the liquor were kept. He starting bragging about how good he was screwing the wife and how much he could do anything he wanted. One of his friends noticed a big pot of stone stew cooking on top of the stove. They made a nickel bet with Jim that he wouldn't spit in the pot. Now, the husband overheard this and told him he better not spit in his stone stew pot."

"Jim told the man that he couldn't tell him what to do and he brought some spit up from his throat and spit into the man's pot of stone stew. The husband went into the bedroom and returned with his shotgun and shot Jim in the face. Blood was everywhere and he had to have a closed casket funeral. He won the bet, but was unable to collect the nickel."

"That's sad," Grandma Sadie Bell responded, "You know I always wanted to know how to make that stew. James says he don't like it. Now I know why, but tell me how to make it anyway girl."

"Girl, it's made out of pig ears, pig stomach and pig feet. You must cut the ears into little squares which is hard to do with a knife, so most people use a sharp pair of scissors. Then cut the stomach into

42

the same dimensions as the ears. Season all three, then put them all into a pot along with some onions, ground red pepper, hot sauce and water. Boil it with vinegar until the pig feet meat falls completely off the bones. Keep adding water then add ketchup and stir. A few minutes later add potatoes to it. Not too soon, 'cause you don't want the potatoes to break. The combination of the pig feet bones and the potatoes is your stones."

"Hum, hum. Sounds like some good eatin'." Grandma Sadie Bell said.

"Oh, it is girl." Mrs. Carrington said, "Okay girl, now let me finish the story."

"Go ahead." Grandma Sadie Bell said, nodding her head.

"Now, the State took the children and put them in a home and had them up for adoption. They all were separated except for James and his sister. The last name of the people who adopted them was Jones, so they took on the name, Jones. They lived in the country and the Jones claimed them as theirs. When you met him he was already a man. It's probably kind of hard for him to talk about it."

"Yeah, he never wants to talk about his Daddy." Grandma Sadie Bell answered. "I appreciate you telling me this story about James; now I understand. I don't think I should cook that stew though."

"Maybe not; you may want to go over to your daughter's house and do it so James won't have a fit."

"Okay Carry, I'll make sure and do that."

"Got to go now Sadie, the sun is going down and I've got a lot of things to do."

Mrs. Carrington slowly lifted herself up and stepped off the porch. She walked across the street to her house as Grandma Sadie Bell continue to rock on the porch. Mrs. Carrington was famous for delivering babies. It was amazing the way she would enter the home and take total control of the situation. Cool and calm was her attitude, while everyone else would be nervous and excited. Mrs. Carrington was truly a work of art; she was always off into someone else's business.

CHAPTER III

THE NIGHT WITH BENNY

Down the street Sara stepped out of her little wooden house to tell the boys to come inside. She yelled their names and out of nowhere they came running, trying to startle their mother.

"Boo!" shouted the boys.

"You boys better get inside and wash up for supper."

"Okay, Momma we're going," said Cleabo.

Sara put her hands on her hips and watched the sunset. What a pretty sight she thought. There was nothing prettier to Sara than watching the golden rays of the sun; she loved it. She inhaled and exhaled deeply into the air, enjoying the nice smell of the southern atmosphere.

The smell of the south was cleaner than the industrial pollutants that existed in New York. Sara enjoyed being home again. While appreciating the night air, she thought about her day at the interview. A smile came across her face as she recalled how humorous it was. When Sara turned away from the sun to go inside, she heard a voice yelling at her. "Hey sweetie! Hey sweetie!"

It wasn't uncommon for Sara to have men yelling at her; she thought it was just another admirer. She didn't bother to look back, she kept walking. When Sara reached the top of the steps to the porch, the rude person yelled again. Only this time he yelled her name. "Hey Sara! Sara, how are you doing, Sara?"

Sara turned around to see who was calling her name. She noticed the fine new Cadillac the man was driving, then she looked harder to see who he was. Before she could identify him, he shouted again. "Sara! It's me, Benny!"

Benny jumped out of the car to properly greet Sara. Sara slowly walked down the steps.

"Hi Sara, what's going on, how long have you been back? I heard that you were home; I just got back from up the road myself."

"I've been back for almost four years now."

"Sara, you still look good. Damn, I wished we'd gotten married. How is my son doing?"

"He's fine, he's inside getting ready for supper."

"Can I come inside and see him? That is if your man don't mind?"

"I don't have a man, and don't want one either. Come on in, I would never deny you the privilege of seeing your son. After all, he's yours too."

"Thank you Sara," Benny said looking somewhat uncomfortable for a minute. Then he regained his composure and continued. "Tell me, how have you been? You know you broke my heart running off like you did. I was in love with you."

"I loved you too Benny, but it just wasn't right. My dad was whipping my ass left to right. I felt so alone and you weren't there for me, Benny."

"I know Sara, and I'm sorry," he said, once again looking somewhat disconcerted. "I feared your dad too and I knew he was going to be looking for me. You know how crazy your dad was back then; he would have killed me. After I left, I heard he came looking for me. Sara if I could turn back the hands of time, I would; so help me. Baby please forgive me." He looked and sounded sincere to Sara; she really had no bad feelings toward him.

"Benny, there's no sense in thinking about those times. That was an awful time in my life, now I'm looking forward to the future. I've got a job and two beautiful kids."

"Oh, you have two kids?"

"Yes, I do."

"Okay, good for you. I'm sure they are beautiful just like their mother!" Benny said regaining his confidence back again.

"Yes they are, come on in and see your son and stop running off at the mouth."

Benny stood at around six feet tall and about two hundred and five pounds. He was a well dressed man and quite handsome to the ladies. He had a reputation of keeping a nice car and never holding onto a job. Benny would always blame the establishment for holding him down and making him unemployable; when the true fact was he enabled himself from being employable. Like June, Benny kept a pocket full of money, fine clothes and no job.

Sara often wondered how she would always be attracted to these types of men. She basically came to the conclusion that it was because of how fine they looked. She was fascinated with dark skinned men that had a processed wave in their hair. Sara thought Benny's waves would make any woman seasick and fall in love with him. His unblemished skin was as smooth as a baby's butt. She was still attracted to Benny, but she dared not to show it. There was no way she could be easy to him, she had learned too much in the city, and her life was hard now.

"Barry, come here son, there's someone here I'd like for you to meet."

Barry came into the living room and Cleabo followed to the living room doorway. "Barry, honey, this is your father. His name is Benny."

Benny leaned down to his son's level. "Hi Barry, how are you doing? You're a handsome little fellow, and you look just like me."

"You're my dad, for real?" Barry asked, studying his father carefully.

"Yep, I'm your dad, and it's time that we get to know each other okay?"

"Okay that's fine. Momma can we eat now?"

"Yes, just wait a minute Barry."

Cleabo walked up to Benny while he was still squatting down talking to Barry. Five year old Cleabo felt that Benny was just another guy trying to come into their lives. His mother had told him about his father, so the two boys weren't ready for a man to come into their mother's life and destroy her world again; no matter how young they were.

"Hey mister, if you're my brother's father, where have you been all of this time?"

"I've been away. What's your name little fellow?"

"My name is Cleabo Jones, it means clean boy."

"Okay, and it fits you well." Benny agreed.

Sara motioned the boys to the kitchen. "Come on boys, go to the table and get ready to eat."

"Bye Mister, we'll check you later." Cleabo and Barry went into the kitchen and sat at the table patiently waiting for their food to be served to them.

"He's quite a young man that Cleabo; isn't he?"

"Yes, he most certainly is. He's just like his father, always demanding and that's one thing that doesn't work with me; you ought to know that."

"How can I forget?" Benny said with a grin, then he became serious. "Now that my son is in my life can I be a father to him? Barry is so special, I can see it, I need him in my life right about now."

Sara paused, studying him for a moment. "We need to talk about that. Let me fix the kids their food and get them to bed. You have a seat and I'll be right with you."

"Okay, I'll be waiting," he said. Benny smiled and settled himself on the sofa.

Sara went into the kitchen to fix the boys' dinner. She was a little excited and surprised by Benny's visit. However, she knew sooner or later he would have come back into her life. She was blushing all over while she was in the kitchen. Sara hadn't been with a man since she left New York. Although there were plenty of opportunities, she just didn't want to deal with another relationship after June. Sara had put up a barrier against men, it had been years since she'd had sex, and she was as ripe as a watermelon in the middle of July.

Sara knew that she shouldn't let Benny know how she was feeling. If she did, he would try to take advantage of the situation. Sara knew that at this point in her life she was vulnerable, and it wouldn't take much. Just like a spring chicken this brown skinned, perfectly shaped, brown-eyed woman was hot. All Benny had to do was to touch her and she would have melted like butter all over him. How warm Sara started to get just from thinking about Benny while she was in the kitchen. He was her first love and she was still half in love with this smooth-talking player.

Sara started thinking about how she lied to her mother when she told her how much she hated having relations with Benny. It wasn't the truth; she enjoyed it and it happened more than once. Together they were like two freaks thrown into a love nest pit. At the time, she was too scared to tell her mother the truth. How could she tell her mother she enjoyed every moment of it? She didn't try to push him away, like she had told her mother. They held each other tightly, almost squeezing the life out of one another. How romantic it was to her, she sighed as she reminisced. The kids began to eat as Sara returned to the living room and sat beside Benny.

"How have you been Benny?" she asked.

"I've been cool. Been moving here and there. I was tired of the big city life, so I came back home."

"Yeah, I know what you mean; the city life can be a rat race."

"What have you been up to, besides still looking so fine?"

"Just trying to survive in this crazy world." Sara said as she fidgeted in her seat and crossed her legs. Benny gazed lustfully at her legs, while Sara gave him the look of; 'You can look but don't even try to touch!'

"You know what Benny?" Sara said, chattering somewhat nervously. "You still know how to sweet talk a lady, but I'm afraid you've got a lot of making up to do. If you think that you're just going to come into our lives, and then do one of your disappearing acts again, you can just forget it! Barry doesn't need that from you and neither do I. We were fine before you rolled up in that fine fancy car and we will be fine when you leave."

"I understand Sara," Benny said, fixing himself straight on the sofa and speaking earnestly. "I know that I hurt you in the past, and I'm sorry. I made a big mistake not being a part of Barry's and your life; please forgive me. Sara I've changed, so help me!" He picked up one of her hands and held it with both of his in appeal. "I'm a man now, not a boy that got you pregnant and ran off. Please give me the chance to prove it to you. You still mean the world to me and I want to be a part of your world and the kids. Please Sara, you'll see how much I've changed. Let me into your heart again."

"I don't know Benny," Sara said cautiously, pulling her hand gingerly from his. "It sounds good, but I've found it hard to trust a man. I've been hurt so many times and the pain has been devastating each time; I really don't know how much I can take. Every time I get hurt, I don't want to go on. Then I look at my two kids and they make me feel better about myself; they give me the strength to go on. At this point in my life, for a man to come along and have my heart, I'm really skeptical about that."

"I understand, and I know that I hurt you badly. If we can just start all over, I'll show you how much of a man I am now. I can appreciate having a beautiful woman like you at my side. You're the mother of my child; I hope that would count for something; at least a second chance?"

"We would have to see Benny, give me some time to think on it, okay?"

"Okay, I understand." Benny said, then hardly paused as he continued, picking her hand up once more.

"That's long enough Sara, tell me you don't love me and I will leave you alone. I will only come and pick up my son on the weekends. If you can't say it then go out with me tomorrow night."

"I wouldn't mind going dancing," Sara said cautiously, knowing what she was saying was going against her better judgment. "I haven't been out since I came back home. I'd probably have to get Momma to watch the boys." "Hmm," she said finally caving into her desires. "Okay, I'll go out with you tomorrow."

"Good!" Benny exclaimed, now grinning from ear to ear. "I'm looking forward to it. I'll pick you up at seven. Let's have dinner first; you won't regret it!" Benny leaned over and hugged Sara. He tried to kiss her but she turned her head to the side making sure he kissed her on the cheek. Benny gave her a soft kiss.

"Okay Sara, I'll see you tomorrow." They stood up and she walked Benny to the door.

They said quick goodbyes, and Sara stood at the door watching as Benny strolled to his car. The truth was, she could hardly wait for tomorrow. Wondering if Benny had changed any since the last time they had their little encounter, ran chills all over her body. Stopping herself from daydreaming, Sara realized she had to get the boys to bed.

The continuous ringing sound couldn't be muffled with the pillow Sara had put over her head to reduce the sound of the alarm clock. She knew that it was time to get up. Six o'clock seemed to come so fast on the weekends. Early Saturday mornings was the only time she had to herself. After throwing the pillow at the alarm clock and knocking it over she realized she had to be quiet or the boys would wake up.

After her usual morning exercises, Sara would run for three miles every Saturday. Unlike New York, she felt comfortable leaving the boys in the house momentarily while she ran in South Carolina.

Someone was always up that time of the morning and they always watched her house. The neighbors always had each other's back. Sara walked over to her dresser to put on her tight shorts and an undershirt to jog in. She stripped down to her birthday suit, exposing all of her beautiful body, then she looked at herself standing nude in front of the mirror. Sara swaggered as she thought out loud to herself. "This can be all yours Benny, if you play your cards right. But if you piss me off, you ain't getting shit!" Quickly she dressed herself and then peeked in on the boys. Noticing that their chests were still rising was her only concern. She had to get out of there before they woke up.

The boys would normally wake up around eight o'clock on Saturdays to watch cartoons and eat some cereal. Sara was in good shape; it didn't take her long to run three miles at all. She stepped out the door deeply inhaling the morning air. While slowly rotating her neck, she began to think to herself again. "Should I give him some, or should I just tease him? He'll come running back if I just tease him, I've got it like that. I don't know, hell, I might get so horny, I might just rip his clothes off of him! Girl," she admonished herself. "Get your mind off of that man and go jogging! Besides, you might run into that cute guy that's been trying to time you coming around the track every Saturday. I hope he isn't crazy. That's all right, even if he is, he'd have to catch my ass first." She patted a place on the side of her waist. "I've got this blade at my side just in case for mother fuckers like that. Lets go body. Lets go do this, it's time to run."

Sara began her run. Staying in shape and maintaining her beauty was a priority in her life. She began to run faster as perspiration dripped from her face. After about two miles of running she came past the high school track.

Every Saturday there was a guy on the track and it seemed like he was waiting for Sara to run by. She noticed that when she ran by he would stop and glance at his watch, as if he was clocking the time she ran by. Sara would stay focused and pretend that she wasn't paying him any attention, at the same time wondering if he was some kind of lunatic or something. Whatever the case may have been, she didn't let it bother her, she just continued her run. She was almost home at this point.

Sara returned to the little wooden house, she slowed her breathing pattern down by walking up and down the street in front of her house. After saying good morning to some of the neighbors that were up doing their yard work, Sara went into the house. She noticed that the boys were waking up. "It's going to be a lovely day," she thought to herself. The most important thing to her was partying with Benny later on that night. Getting the kids ready to go over to her parents was the agenda for today.

Sara put on some music and began to fix breakfast for the kids. Music playing in the house wasn't an unusual thing for Cleabo and Barry to hear. Whenever the kids heard Sara singing they knew she was in a good mood. This time they didn't know the reason why she was so happy. The boys knew about the new job, but they didn't feel this was the reason their mother was going around the house singing like she was in a Broadway show.

Around noon, Sara took the boys with her to get her hair done. The hairdresser was on the back porch of a neighbor's house. The porch had a screen around it to keep the mosquitoes out. Barry and Cleabo were well disciplined, they didn't move the entire time; they just sat on the sofa. Sara always received compliments on how well-behaved they were.

Sara took Cleabo and Barry to her mother's house at four o'clock. Quickly they ran off to play with their friends, while Sara hurried out of the door to continue her personal body maintenance. After waving goodbye to Grandma Sadie Bell, she walked home anxiously with a scarf wrapped around her head to cover her hair rollers. Six o'clock came and she was almost ready. Her clothes were laid out on the bed as she slowly began to put her panties and bra on. Her body was now clean and smooth, smelling good from head to toe. She slipped into her stockings and glanced at her toes, admiring the paint job. "Hmm, they match my fingernails," she said to herself. "He better play his cards right so he can get some of this," she thought as she looked at herself in the full length mirror with only her bra, panties and panty hose on.

Sara finished getting dressed in order to see what her ensemble looked like. Everything was looking good; she looked like a nightclub princess. Knowing that Benny would be on time, or fifteen minutes early, she began to take her clothes off. "I've gotta make him wait; I can't look like I'm anxious. I'll wait and put my make up on once he gets here. Damn!" she said, finally admitting the truth to herself. "I can't wait to get me some! I'll know the first five minutes how tonight is going to be."

At six forty-five Benny knocked at the door with flowers in his hands. Sara opened the door with her robe on and invited him in. "I'll just be a minute; you're early. Thanks for the lovely flowers, let me put them into some water. 'Right-on-time-Benny,' that's what I used to call you. You were always on time for everything. Do you still carry those forty-five records to parties with you? The kids in school said that you had a reputation of bringing your own records to a party."

"No, I don't do that anymore." Benny answered as he stepped into the house. "Girls used to like that you know. I had my own style back then. If I wanted to hear a slow song, I knew what it was that I wanted to hear. I've gotten a little older now and things like that really don't matter." He watched as Sara walked from the kitchen into her bedroom.

"I thought that it was kind of cute. Where are we going to eat? I'm starving." Sara yelled from her bedroom as she began to get dressed.

"I made reservations at this new place called the *Chatoe*," he called to her, raising his voice some to carry on conversation. "They serve Whites and Coloreds you know. It's a new restaurant in Orangeburg. The owners are Asians or something and they don't care what color you are as long as you have that green money. Then, I thought we'd go to the *Do Drop In.*"

"Okay, I haven't been there in a long time; is that place still jumping?"

"Yeah, we'll sit close to the door. Just in case somebody starts shooting, we can make a quick get away. You know how some of these fools are in town, they might get that liquor in them and act a natural born fool."

"I know what you mean, I hope that don't happen tonight, I haven't been out dancing in a long time. When was the last time you been out dancing Benny?"

"It hasn't been that long for me. When I came back I started going, but I was seeing the same old faces from high school. It's kind of strange Sara."

"What's strange Benny?"

"A lot of the people that were most likely to succeed in high school aren't succeeding at all. They're in jail or strung out somewhere on drugs. It's a shame how the people that were so promising are just nothing." Benny said, as he shook his head. "The people you thought would be nothing are the ones that are in the nightclubs looking good, and they aren't on the streets panhandling. They don't ask you for money like the people everyone thought was going to be so popular."

"Yeah, I've seen some of those people you are talking about since I've been back, all they said to me is, 'damn girl! You weren't this fine when you was in high school!' I laugh at them, they was too busy with the other girls that they thought were so fine at the time. Now those same girls are on skid row and I'm not." Sara said as she stepped out of the bedroom fully dressed, with her purse in her hand. Benny's eyes protruded as he stared at Sara.

"Damn, Sara you look like a million bucks! You didn't let yourself go one bit!" his eyes hungrily rolled over her body. "Those guys were right, you wasn't this fine in high school. City life sure has treated you well, you look like a movie star the way you are dressed." He stepped closer as he continued. "You make my little country suit look ashamed. I just love to see a woman wear those black dresses right above their knees and yours have a split in the sides; so nice and tight it is, Sara." He added approvingly.

She laughed, enjoying the banter. "Oh, stop it Benny, this old thing?"

"It may be old to you Sara, but I may have to beat someone down for flirting with you tonight."

She laughed again, feeling good and sure about herself. "Oh Benny, you so crazy, and thanks for the compliment. But you don't have to worry, I know how to handle the dogs."

"Woof, woof," Benny barked as if he was a dog.

"Stop playing Benny and let's go."

Sara and Benny went to the car after she locked the door to her house. Although he had his left hand around her waist as they walked to the car, Sara noticed him catching a glimpse or two at her rear. She just smiled; knowing that her left foot over the right walk would entice any man she wanted to. She was pleased watching Benny drooling over her beauty.

While waiting for their food to arrive, Benny shared a story with her, about when he was up north. He sipped his wine and said, "Yeah Sara, I was a waiter in this fancy restaurant. What used to make me laugh was watching the way some of the people there ate and drank. Some of them would go through this ceremonial type of thing with their wine. They would smell the glass, swish it around in their mouth, and then drink it. I thought that it was the craziest thing I'd ever seen. I got fired from there though."

"Why, what happened?" Sara asked, encouraging him to continue.

"In the city I did a lot of partying and I'm sure you did too." He added, straying from his story for a moment. "I can tell from the way you look tonight. You look like one of those beautiful Colored girls in the city with their fancy job and plenty of money. Anyway Sara," he continued with his story. "I had a party one night and got drunk as a skunk. I didn't get up until about three the next day. Come to think of it, hell; I didn't go to bed until about twelve o'clock. *Just'a* partying like a fool, people all in the house I didn't even know. I was lucky they didn't kill my old country ass."

"I went to work about seven that night still drunk and a little irritable. The moment I served this guy some wine, he started smelling the glass and moving the wine around in his mouth. They only poured about a shot of wine into this big ass glass. I guess I just lost it. I snatched the glass out of his hands and grabbed the bottle off of the table. I said, 'Motherfucker, let me show you how to drink wine!' I filled the glass up and I gulped it down like a country boy drinking moonshine, Sara!"

Sara smiled and laughed at a respectable tone. "So tell me what happened then Benny?"

"The manager saw what happened and he fired me on the spot. Took my employee photo and put it at the front desk and said that I was never allowed to come into the restaurant again. I just told him to give me my check! He made it hard for me though," he added regretfully.

"Really Benny, and why is that?"

"Not only did he fire me, but he told other restaurant managers in the city about me. It was hard for me to take a lady out to dinner after that. If she didn't cook for us, then it was hamburgers and french-fries all the way."

Sara laughed again. "You so crazy Benny, sounds likes you had a lot of fun in Chicago."

"Yeah, I really did," Benny agreed then suddenly switched tracks. "But I missed you Sara. You are so elegant, even with two kids you still look like a young virgin. Damn, you are so fine! Any man would be a fool not to want to be with you everyday. But I know how it goes; once a fool and twice a loser, huh?"

"That all depends on you, Benny, and how far you want to take this." Sara said as she fluttered her eyelids, knowing it to be pure enticement to a man in heat.

Benny smiled as the waiter brought their food to the table, leaning close to say softly, "Sara, I would like to take this to another level if it's possible?"

Sara shifted away from him, knowing she was reeling him in. "I guess we're just going to have to take our time and see how things work out, huh Benny? You know I've changed, but I'm still a woman and I'm not about to be hurt again by any man. Do you understand where I'm coming from?"

Benny nodded his head and said, "Yeah, okay I understand."

Things in the south were changing a bit, despite segregation. Sara was pleased that in the south there was a nice restaurant a Colored woman could be taken to, other than soul food eating places. Ham hocks and collard greens were delicious to her, but when she was dressed like this she wanted steak or lobster. Dinner was lovely; they ate and had a good time.

After dinner they went to the *'Do Drop In,'* it was a local juke joint with one way in and one way out. The music was so loud it was hard for anyone to hear themselves when they spoke. *The Swing* was the popular dance, and a person had to be in good physical condition to dance to the fast music. Benny knew the earlier they arrived, the better their chances were finding a table near the door; just in case shooting occurred.

Benny discovered every time he went to the bar for something to drink, or even if he would just go to the restroom, when he returned some other guy would be at the table trying to talk to Sara. He noticed that all eyes were on her. She was hot, and all the men wanted her. He also noticed that she started getting mean stares from some of the women that were there, despite the fact that Sara wasn't in control of their male eyes.

Benny was a little jealous when he returned to the table the first time; however, he didn't want to make a scene. He knew that if he did, he would have most definitely upset Sara and that was something he didn't want to do. He remembered her telling him she knew how to handle herself, and she was right.

Sara knew how to work a nightclub. She had drinks sent to her without talking to the men. When Sara would receive a drink she would raise her glass and motion an acknowledgement to whoever had bought it for her. Benny would just sit back and watch how elegantly she handled herself. He didn't know if Sara was completely out of his league or if he still had a shot at her. Benny couldn't wait to get her out of the nightclub to make a pass at her.

Benny conducted himself like a gentleman with Sara. He knew he had to or she would have put him in check. Benny was a player and he knew the rules of the game; he had to treat a lady like a lady. For sure he had a lady with him, and he knew if he were to act a fool, she would have no problem getting a ride home with someone else.

Sara really enjoyed herself; she was dancing almost every number. Her jogging was to her advantage, as she noticed how out of shape Benny was on the dance floor. Sara wondered if they did have sex could Benny go the distance, or would he just be a waste of time? Benny knew that Sara was sizing him up each time they danced, and debating whether to take him home for mere pleasure or play hard to get. Sara was in such good shape it was becoming difficult for Benny to keep up.

Benny noticed again how the men were looking at Sara on the dance floor. They had their hand around their woman's waist, and their eyes on Sara; undressing her as she danced. The men that were on the floor were peeping over their woman's shoulders trying to look at Sara as she danced. Sara was moving her perfectly shaped rear end in the black skirt in a seductive manner, exposing every firm curve of her succulent body.

The men were mesmerized and gave her their total attention. Although, it was a long time since Sara had been in a nightclub environment, she was used to admiration. But, she wasn't interested in the small time country boys' attention. Her mind was on Benny as she recalled how he rocked her world the first time they made love.

While they danced on the dance floor Sara thought, "I wonder if he is still big like he was years ago? It couldn't have gotten smaller over the years, could it?" she smiled languidly at Benny and he smiled in returned.

Benny's desires also showed on his face as he thought about Sara, "She sure is looking good! What a work of art she turned out to be! Didn't know she had all of that going on underneath all of those long ass-dresses her parents used to make her wear! Can't wait to hit that tonight. Damn! She can drink though, all those drinks she had and she's still sober. This woman can really handle her liquor. I'd better slow down before I get drunk and can't do nothing. I remember the time I had too much liquor and it made me impotent; it took a whole week to get my nature back right again. Damn! She's hot! I'm going to rock that tonight; let me hurry up and get her out of here."

Benny smiled at Sara when the song ended, and they walked back to the table. "Whew, I haven't danced like that in ages." He said wiping his brow with a handkerchief.

Sara responded, not even breaking a sweat. "Yeah, it really feels good, I see you can still dance. You must have been a partying fool in Chicago, huh Benny?"

"No, I only party on the weekends and I didn't dance much. Most of the time I just drank."

"I'm glad you took me out Benny, I really needed it."

"Oh, I'm enjoying it myself; you make me feel proud to be with you Sara, especially with all the men looking at you. I know that I'm the luckiest man in the place tonight.

"Believe me Benny, the feeling is mutual. I saw how those women were checking you out."

"Really Sara, were they? I thought that all eyes were on you."

"Hey, you know you're looking good, don't be so shy. Those women were undressing you with their eyes."

"Okay Sara, if you say so," Benny agreed, wanting to bring the evening to its final conclusion. "Its getting kind of late, are you ready to go?"

"Yes, I'm ready to leave now." Sara told him, knowing their thoughts were mutual.

Benny and Sara stood up from the table and headed for the exit, all of the men's eyes followed Sara until she was completely out of their view. Like a gentleman, Benny opened the door of his fancy Cadillac for Sara. Sara and Benny shared small talk about how some of the people in the nightclub were dressed. They laughed as they shared views about having a good time, and how it had turned out to be such a lovely evening. Both of them really enjoyed each other's company; it reminded them of the old times.

When they arrived at her place, Sara put the key into the door and opened it. While standing in the doorway she turned around and looked at Benny and said, "Thanks for a nice time Benny, I sure did have fun. Been a long time since I partied like that."

Benny leaned toward her to within an inch of touching her. "I'm glad that you had a nice time, but why must the party end? Why don't you invite me in for a drink or something?"

"It's kind of late, and we've been drinking," she hesitated. "I'm not sure if you are going to behave yourself and act like a gentlemen. You know how you boys are." She added coyly.

"Oh, I promise to be a good boy," he answered, the suggestion clearly on how good he could be for her.

"I don't know. Tell you what, let's just make it the next time."

"Okay then, I'll just say good night to you."

Words, only words, and Benny knew it. He leaned his head forward to give Sara a goodbye kiss. Responding like a lady, Sara closed her eyes and turned her head, making her cheek available for a good night smack. Benny, however, put his hands gently on her face and softly placed his lips on hers and began to give her a passionate kiss. Sara kept her eyes closed and responded gently by putting her hands around him and slipping her tongue into his mouth as they pulled each other closer until their bodies united as one.

It was a kiss that seemed to last forever, as both of them began to feel the heat of passion. Hot and steamy they felt as their heads moved and the tips of their tongues connected together, moving in a circular motion inside of their mouths.

Sara and Benny's lips separated and they opened up their eyes feeling breathless and overwhelmed. They were warm and hot; their emotional level had escalated and they had gone too far with passion to stop now. They looked at each other in silence.

Sara's eyes had the complete expression of, "Take me Benny; I'm all yours." With that expression, Benny bent down and scooped Sara up in his arms. He carried her into the house and kicked the door shut while she laid her head on his shoulders. "Make sure it's locked," Sara whispered. Benny turned around with Sara in his arms and made sure that the door was locked, then off to the bedroom he went.

Both anxious to connect to each other, Sara began to take Benny's clothes off before he had finished sitting her on the bed. Benny was gentle with Sara's dress, pulling it over her slowly, exposing her perfectly shaped breasts and bikini panties underneath her panty hose. Sara, on the other hand, was like a wild animal; she tore Benny's shirt off, buttons popped and flew all over the place. He could easily tell it had been a long time since Sara had sex by the way she was acting. Sara was like a dog in heat and she could no longer hold back her desires.

Looking at her totally nude body, Benny was astonished and mesmerized as he took in Sara's beauty. "Damn, you're so fine Sara!" Benny shouted as he threw his body on top of hers, then gently caressed her, kissing and licking every inch of her body from head to toe. They made passionate love, taking each other into total ecstasy, exploding and releasing their hot steamy sex. Endlessly they made love for what seemed hours. Experimenting with different positions, Sara moaned and groaned as she reached her sexual peak multiple times.

After every orgasm Sara's love juice rained down on Benny's hard male organ as she was saddled up and taking him for a ride that he'd never been on before. It was sex at its best and he was enjoying every minute of it. She was like a soldier riding a horse into battle, Benny thought. He could see that she had gained a lot of experience since their last encounter.

After a few hours, the two of them were completely exhausted. They fell asleep holding each other in the middle of the wet sheets. Their fatigued bodies lay with dripping perspiration from their efforts. The sheets and their bodies filled the room with the aroma of sex as Sara and Benny went into a deep sleep.

The sun rose and the golden rays brightened up the bedroom, the sound of a rooster's crowing awakened Sara as she turned around surprised to see Benny in her bed. Then she remembered what had happened and a smile came on her face. Looking at Benny sleeping on his back, she couldn't help to notice the mountain that the covers had formed around Benny's mid section. Sara thought for a moment, 'Should I go for it again? Oh, what the hell!'

Sara woke Benny up by continuing her sexual escapade from where she had left off a few hours ago. When pleasure was achieved for both of them, she remembered that she needed to go pick up the boys. After getting dressed they said goodbye to each other. Benny said that he would give her a call and she said okay. They continued to see each other on different occasions for the next couple of months. Benny spent a lot of time with Barry and kept his word to be a part of Barry's life.

CHAPTER IV

EMBEZZLING

Sara's new job had become demanding. She was the new Administrative Assistant in charge of Accounts Receivable and Payable, it placed a tremendous amount of stress on her. The company's financial status was drastically decreasing. Customers were paying money for their monthly storage fee, however, it wasn't being applied to their account. Someone was taking the money. The customers were complaining to Sara, who had no explanation to give to them; she had only been on the job for a short period of time.

The customers were being double billed for interstate moves and were paying enormous rates for local moves. These high costs kept most of the people from being able to afford to retrieve their household goods after they completed their move. If after ninety days they couldn't get their belongings out of the warehouse, the company would auction it off. Management would go into the bins and get whatever they wanted to keep or sell. Sara knew that someone was robbing the company blind. Electricity bills and telephone bills weren't being paid. She wondered if it was Mr. Barnes stealing. Sara noticed a few times on the ledger there were transactions that were deleted, slowly she became aware of what was going on.

Everyday when she came to work everyone smiled when they said hello, arousing her suspicions even more. The home office in Houston was complaining about money being missing and that lawsuits were being filed against them. Things were really getting crazy. The company was going downhill and Sara knew it. She had the feeling that the woman before her had found out and quit. She didn't know who to trust, so Sara kept her mouth shut. She knew she wasn't going to be anybody's fall guy. Sara was a smart woman when it came to her job, but with her men that was a different story.

"Damn, I haven't had a period in two months now, I might be pregnant, shit! I'd better go to the doctor this week." Sara said to herself.

It had been about a month since she had last seen Benny. Her situation now had become more complicated; she had to deal with her job, and her morning sickness.

At work Sara began to go through all the files when she discovered what was going on. She made copies of the money paid by customers and the money applied to their account. She also made copies of unpaid commissions due to the sales representatives and the transaction that routed the money elsewhere. Sara organized all the information that would protect her from any type of allegations accusing her of embezzlement. She had an idea who was behind the scam, but it was none of her business. She knew that she had to cover herself. Mr. Barnes was receiving calls on a daily basis from a woman, but it wasn't his wife.

On one occasion the woman pranced into the company and went straight into his office. Sara could see that she was a high maintenance woman, the kind that likes expensive stuff. Sara knew Mr. Barnes couldn't afford a woman like her from what he made. Sara was in charge of the payroll; she knew what everyone was paid. The woman that walked into Mr. Barnes' office was driving a Mercedes Benz and a fox fur was wrapped around her neck. Sara thought the woman strutting into Mr. Barnes' office looked like she owned him. Sara knew the only way Mr. Barnes could have a woman like her was by buying her. "Maybe that's where the company's money was going." Sara thought to herself.

It was on a Thursday when Sara went to the doctor. She already knew she was pregnant because of the morning sickness. She just felt the need to take some of the day off from that crazy job of hers. The doctor calmly told her the results were positive and Sara kindly said thanks. She wasn't too disappointed with herself. In fact Sara took this pregnancy easier than her first two. While walking out of the doctor's office Sara felt the need for some ice cream.

Around the corner there was an ice cream parlor that recently took down their 'Whites only' sign. "I'll go get a cone from there," she thought to herself. After getting her ice cream Sara began to walk back to work, thinking how she was going to break the news to everyone about her pregnancy. The doctor's office was right around the corner from her job and the walk wasn't long at all. When she approached her office building, she saw the police carrying out files, while all the employees stood outside.

Nervously licking the drips around the ice cream cone, she walked up to the building wondering what was going on. The receptionist was talking to a policeman. Sara curiously walked up to the scene, and the receptionist pointed at her indicating to the policeman that she was Sara Jones. At that time, two policeman approached Sara and started questioning her.

"Are you Sara Jones?" one of the policeman asked.

"Yes I am." Sara answered, feeling some apprehension over the events going on.

"You need to come with us; we have some questions to ask you downtown."

"What for, what have I done? And why you can't ask the questions here?"

"Don't worry, we will ask you downtown."

Sara complied with the officer's wishes, the other employees stared at her like she committed a murder or something. Sara noticed there were about three executives on the scene from the home office in Houston. "They must have came down because of all the money that was missing. I'm not going to be the token to take the blame for something I had nothing to do with." Sara thought to herself.

The officer waved his hand towards the police cruiser, Sara gracefully walked to the cruiser and stepped in. At the station they sat her in this cold room that smelled like cigarettes and day old wet garbage; perhaps from the small garbage can that sat at the corner of the table. The interrogating detectives were mean to her, she told them she was pregnant and had just came from the doctor's office, so they didn't physically abuse her. Questions were being asked about the company's financial stability.

They insinuated that Sara was embezzling money from the company and they wanted to know what was she doing with it. Their hopes were that she would make a confession. Sara was shocked, but smart enough to know that something of this nature would happen. Sara had prepared herself for this event. At her house she had all of the important documents in a briefcase next to the dresser in her bedroom.

"Can I use the telephone to help clear my name?" she asked.

"Okay, how is it you're going to clear your name?"

"I have documents from the time I started working there that will help clear my name. Now I don't know who was stealing the money, but one thing is for sure it wasn't me, please believe me." Sara knew she could work her charm on any man. She was still a woman of power and knew how to use her appeal to get what she wanted. Sara called her mother and explained everything to her. She told her where to find the briefcase. It was helpful that her mother had a key to her house. Sara always made sure that someone had a key to her house, just in case a situation like this would ever occur. After giving her side of the story to the detectives, Sara waited for her mother to come to her rescue with the briefcase.

Sadie Bell arrived with the briefcase; the officer at the front desk inspected the briefcase to ensure that there were no contraband items inside. Sadie Bell told him that she wasn't going to let the papers inside get out of her sight until her daughter was cleared. The officer directed her to the room where Sara was being interrogated.

Sadie Bell knocked on the door and entered the room. The detectives took the briefcase away from her and started reading the documents. The detective that seemed to be in charge handed one paper at a time to the other detective. Sadie Bell went to the other side of the room and gave Sara a hug. Knowing that she would be cleared after the men read the papers, Sara stared at the detectives like a hawk. The lead detective turned to Sara and said, "We are going to have to keep these documents."

"I can make copies for you. I'm not going to give up my ace in the hole, I knew something like this was going to happen just because I'm black."

Sara used the term 'Black' loosely. When said to southerners, they displayed this surprised look on their faces. They didn't understand how someone could just call themselves black. Perhaps they thought that the word black was harsher than being called a 'nigger.' However to Sara, expressing herself as being black, instead of a nigger was the in thing to do. Folks up north were proud to be called black; it was the start of a new era in the sixties.

The detectives said, "Okay Miss Jones, you can make the copies and leave them at the front desk. We are sorry for the trouble. If we need you we know where to find you."

"Okay, thank you officer," Sara said as she gathered up her briefcase and went out the door to make the copies for the detectives.

"Sara, what the hell is going on?" Sadie Bell asked as they left the building.

"Momma, they were trying to frame me at my job for something I didn't do. I'm glad I copied those documents."

"Yeah, me too. I'm glad you turned out to be smart. You may have done some pretty dumb things coming up, but this here was really smart of you. So what are you going to do now Sara?"

"I'm going to let them fire me like I know they will. Then I'm going to sue their ass for trying to have me arrested, lying on me, discrimination and harassment. I probably can think of some more things, too."

The next morning Sara went to work as usual. Everyone was surprised to see her there. They just stared at her, wondering what had happened at the police station. Sara walked over to the water dispenser to fill her cup. The police barged into the front door and marched straight into Mr. Barnes' office. He was arrested, handcuffed and escorted to the patrol car. The executives from Houston were standing near the receptionist desk watching. After the police took Mr. Barnes away the executives called Sara into Mr. Barnes' office.

"Hello Miss Jones, we are sorry about what happened to you yesterday."

"Okay," Sara said as she waited for the next words to come out of the lead executive's mouth.

"We were called down to the police station after you were released, and we went over the documents that you provided the detectives with."

"Okay," Sara waited to see where this was going.

"Your statement about the woman that flaunted herself here was true; we confirmed it with the other employees. Now we have proof that it was Mr. Barnes stealing money from us. A search warrant was issued last night and we found him to be living beyond his salary. He had three homes and one was occupied by the woman in your statement and his bank account was enormous. The Mercedes was also in his name. So you see you were correct. However, Miss. Jones we are going to have to let you go."

Sara said to herself, 'Bingo.'

"You see Miss. Jones you violated the company's confidential policy and we can no longer trust you. Employees aren't allowed to take documents off of the property for personal use."

Sara jumped up and said "That's bullshit! If it's going to save my ass from going to jail, damn a company's policy! If it was up to you guys I'd probably be taking the fall for this shit. Let me tell you something, my life isn't up to you! Sara calls her own shots, the way she feels fit!"

"Miss Jones please calm down."

"Calm down my ass! You're a stupid bunch of motherfuckers 'cause now I own you. All you prejudiced southerners can do for me is give me my check and I'll see you in court," Sara said triumphantly. She gathered up her things and slammed the door behind her. Once the door was closed Sara smiled and said, "Yes." She marched down to payroll to get her check. After getting her pay she didn't even say goodbye to anyone, she just left the building and walked home.

"Momma, you think Mrs. Carrington's nephew can be my lawyer?" she asked as she walked in the door to her mother's house. "You know he has a degree, I need a lawyer to sue that company's ass for punitive damages."

"Yeah, but he's up north."

"I'm sure he'll come down if the money is right; can't pay him until it's over though."

"I'll let Carrie know, don't worry about a thing." Her mother told her.

A week later Mrs. Carrington's nephew came from up north to represent Sara. The moment he arrived he notified the executives of Deman's Moving and Storage, his intentions of representing Sara for punitive damages. They didn't want anymore negative publicity so they offered to settle out of court. They offered Sara eight thousand dollars, but when her lawyer countered the offer and made a proposal for ten thousand, the executives agreed. Sara's fee to the lawyer was two thousand dollars, leaving her with eight. Back then that was a lot of money. Mr. Barnes received ten years in prison.

While all of this was going on, Benny had heard that Sara was pregnant again and it was his baby. Everyone knew that Sara wasn't seeing anyone else, regardless of how fine she was. Benny was no where to be found. He had claimed that he was a man, but all of that talk was just hogwash. Benny had skipped town again and no one knew where he was. In the sixties, young black men weren't required to pay child support and Benny wasn't about to share anything in his pockets.

Society back in the sixties didn't care about black children being born with no fathers to support them financially. They just thought that it was 'Just another buck being born and let the niggers handle it.' Benny was a fool; he never realized the type of woman Sara was. Benny was intimidated by her looks and he must have felt that he couldn't keep her anyway. So, he just ran away from Sara like he did in the past.

Running was something Sara could never understand about Benny. She hated him for it and was mad at herself for ever letting him into her life again. But, at the same time she felt sorry for him. He was confused and only time and God could turn him into a real man, she thought. Unfortunately for him, Sara was finished with him. She didn't believe in three strikes and you were out. Sara had given him a second chance and this time he blew it. "Two times was too much," she would say.

The next eight months went by fast for Sara. Her family was always there and supported her during her pregnancy. They all acknowledged her feelings and understood how deeply a person could fall in love and experience so much pain simultaneously.

Love was something Sara wanted to totally forget about; it only brought her pain, sorrow, and regrets. "Time to move on. Three kids and two men, that's enough," is what Sara would say when she thought about how her life had been. She was happy most of the time and there were plenty of good and bad memories with the men she had in her life. Sara wasn't depressed at all; she was the kind of woman that could easily find the good side of every situation.

It started getting cold in the month of October of that year. Sara's belly was looking like a balloon that was ready to burst. With her swollen feet and huge belly she waddled around like a duck leaving a pond. Sara continued taking care of Barry and Cleabo up until the last minute. Sara was at Grandma Sadie Bell's house when her water burst and it was time to have the baby. Natural child birth and utilizing Mrs. Carrington for the task was the respectable thing to do. It would have been an insult for Sara to admit herself into the hospital in order to have the baby, despite the fact she had the money.

Grandma Sadie Bell counted the weeks for her the old fashioned way. Mrs. Carrington was the physician on duty. Grandma Sadie Bell instructed Sara to live with them while she was in her last week so she could keep a close eye on her. The water broke in the middle of the kitchen floor.

"Cleabo, go get Mrs. Carrington and hurry." Grandma Sadie Bell said as she grabbed Sara, assisting her to the bedroom. Cleabo ran to Mrs. Carrington house and was knocking on the door like a mad child.

"Hurry! Come quick, it's Momma! There's water on the kitchen floor and Grandma thinks she's having the baby! She told me to come get you quick!" Cleabo panted as he tried to catch his breath.

Mrs. Carrington grabbed her black bag that was filled with her medical supplies and dashed out of the door. Grandma Sadie Bell managed to keep Sara calm and helped her with her breathing. Grandpa James was home and he was pacing the floor. He then ran all the kids out of the house, including Cleabo's two aunts Louina Mae and Dora Gene. Everyone was running around like chickens with their heads cut off. They were boiling water and tearing up sheets; everyone was paranoid except Mrs. Carrington.

Grandpa James said, "Oh, no! Here comes another daggone crumb snatcher. I'm going down to the store and have me a drink. Daggone women all the time having babies."

When Frederick was born, Cleabo could hear the baby crying outside of the little wooden house. Cleabo was standing on the dirt road in front of the steps that were made of cement blocks leading up to the porch. Grandma Sadie Bell came to the porch placing her hands on her hips exhaling a sigh of relief.

"It's another boy." She told them. "You guys just had a baby brother."

"When can we see him?" shouted Cleabo.

"Not now, Mrs. Carrington is cleaning him up and your mother needs to rest."

"Grandma, does he have a big head like Barry or is he cute like me?"

Barry pushed Cleabo on the shoulders and they laughed jokingly as Cleabo pushed him back.

"Boys, stop that now!" Grandma Sadie Bell said as she walked back into the house to continue helping Mrs. Carrington.

Sara now had three boys. She was happy with her children, and Frederick made her realize how much she missed having a baby in her arms again. Frederick resembled his dad Benny; he was dark with curly black hair. Cleabo thought that he cried too much, unaware that this is what most babies do.

Frederick began to walk at an early age. Some of the older folks began to tease Sara. They teased her because in the south when a child begins to walk at six months or so, they say that the child is 'Getting out of the way.' The older folks like Mrs. Carrington were merely trying to say Frederick was making room for another child to be born. Sara would laugh and just say, 'I don't think so.' Little did they know Sara had begun taking birth control pills. In the south it wasn't unusual for a young lady to have five or six kids. Young ladies were baby-making machines and large families weren't uncommon back then.

Although Sara still had a substantial amount of money in her savings account, she knew she had to establish some sort of income, instead of just having outgoing; especially since Frederick was walking. She tried looking for a job, but she had no luck. Her name was black balled, and no one wanted to hire her because of what had happened at her previous job. She couldn't get an administrative job or any other good paying job anywhere in town. So, Sara did what any hard working black woman would do to support her children. She did what society basically felt a black woman was capable of doing, other than making babies.

Wearing a blue uniform with a white apron, she cooked and cleaned for the folks that lived in the huge plantation homes. She did what she had to do to keep food on her table for her children. Sara was a survivor and a provider, including being the mother and the father to her children.

Sara wouldn't wear make up when she went to work. She had to disguise her beauty so the women of the house wouldn't feel intimidated by her presence. If the woman of the house felt this way Sara would lose her job. She heard about some of the folks' husbands trying to use their maids as a concubine or a bed warmer. However, that wasn't for Sara; she had morals and she always let it be known at the beginning of her job to any man who indicated interest of a sexual nature. If the man of the house made his interest known, she would tell them clearly that she wasn't a whore and if he wanted sex from her, she would have to quit. That usually took care of any problems, and if it didn't, she would just quit.

The housekeeping job helped Sara financially; although, in the summertime things would get slow. The folks would take their entire family on vacation. They would go to exotic places like Europe, Italy or Spain.

Sara was always fascinated about their vacation trips. Someday she hoped to be able to do the same. Although the folks knew Sara, they wouldn't leave their house with her while they were gone. She knew they thought she would steal something while they were gone, so Sara was out of a job during the summer. They didn't stop to think, if Sara was a criminal, she already knew when they went on vacation, and if she wanted to steal something it would have been just as easy if they were there or on vacation.

Since Sara didn't have any income in the summer, Grandma Sadie Bell would insist that the entire family go pick cotton; that is, with the exception of Grandpa James. Picking cotton was a debatable issue with Sara, but she knew she needed some sort of income. It was just the idea of looking like slaves again and always riding on the back of someone's pick up truck that turned her off. They would often go to the town of Louise, South Carolina, where it was extremely hot in the cotton fields.

Cleabo couldn't pick a large amount of cotton; the sun was too hot. It was almost one hundred degrees before sunrise. His Aunt Dora Gene and Louina Mae would have to pick enough to buy their school clothes. One hundred pounds of cotton would get them four dollars, and it took a lot of picking to get a hundred pounds. After four weeks of picking cotton, his grandma would take the entire family to pick tobacco. They had to go to North Carolina in a beat-up looking, pick-up truck.

They lived on a tobacco farm. It was an old barn with rooms made into sleeping quarters. The folks that owned it lived in a white house that looked like a plantation; just like the one seen on the television show "Dallas," or the movie "Gone With the Wind." Every morning the boss or his son would arrive around five o'clock in the morning on a tractor. All of the workers would get on the trailer of the tractor and go to work. When they arrived at the fields, the driver would say, "Get out, niggers!" it would be so hot in the tobacco fields, sweat would pour down everyone faces and the taste of their own perspiration became equivalent to water.

Several times a day large green tobacco worms would crawl over Cleabo's body, but Sara would get them off of him before they could bite him. Sara tied a scarf around her head and put a hat on, his grandmother would be wearing something that looked like a Mexican sombrero. It seemed to Cleabo his grandmother would never get tired; she was a hard working lady.

At lunchtime a man would bring some lunch for them. Lunch was one of those small packs of peanut butter sandwich cookies that had six cookies in a pack; they cost a dime. He gave them honey buns or cinnamon rolls, the leftovers from feeding his hogs in the huge pig pens the day before. These items were deducted out of their pay. Sometimes water was available to wash down the molded sweets.

Mrs. Annie Louie was Sara's best friend at the farm. She was short; about five foot even. Her skin was so dark, at night you could only see her teeth and eyes, but she was the sweetest person you'd ever want to meet. At the end of the day Mrs. Annie Louie and Sara would purchase some liquor and sit around and rag on the men folks like they were dogs. It was said that Mrs. Annie Louie could out run a bobcat. In fact, the word was that she did outrun one coming home from town one night.

On Friday and Saturday the adults would go to town and party. Dora Gene and Debra would keep the kids. Debra was Mrs. Annie Louie's daughter, she was about twelve years old. Cleabo liked for her to baby sit him. At the age of seven Debra taught him about sex. His Aunt Dora Gene, who was thirteen at the time, caught Debra and Cleabo screwing and told her to stop it. He didn't like that; Cleabo thought having sex with an older girl was great. It was really fascinating to Cleabo to find out about sex at such a young age and Debra was knowledgeable on the subject. She treated Cleabo like he was a grown man during their sexual episodes.

71

One night his mother took them to town with her. It was an adventure looking for shoes all day, but, Sara started drinking and they ended up staying longer than they should. It was dark; there were no streetlights on the small country dirt roads. The walk back was about seven miles long. Mrs. Annie Louie led the way and it seemed like it took them forever. It was around twelve o'clock by the time they arrived at the farm. Later that night, after everyone had fallen asleep, Debra woke Cleabo up and said.

"Cleabo, let's do it." That's what she called her sexual episodes with him, "Doing it." So they went outside and she did it to him like she'd been doing it for years. That was the best thing to picking cotton or cropping tobacco. Although Cleabo was young it was nice to learn how ecstasy felt, he thought.

Summer was almost over and it was time to leave the tobacco farm. It was a long ride on the back of the truck, the wind kept blowing his face on the back of the pick-up truck, Cleabo somehow realized and hoped that there must be a better life.

There was a loud noise, it sounded like someone had fired a shotgun and then the pick-up truck began to swerve, and fish-tailing across the road. Luckily there was no on-coming traffic. The tire had burst and the men folks had to fix the flat. They stood on the side of the road watching the cars pass by, they received some of the strangest looks from people, especially the ones that looked like they were traveling to a vacation place.

Cleabo and his family were the poor-looking people on the side of the road looking stupid and dressed badly, but they were happy, most of the time. As the cars passed them by, no one stopped to offer help. Cleabo noticed the kids in the back seat sticking out their tongues and shooting the bird at them. Cleabo grabbed his crotch and told them what to do with it. He read the kids lips as they said, "Look at those crazy niggers!" it wasn't uncommon for the kids to use the word "nigger," as ignorance was abundant during this period of time.

They made it back home, and grandpa was chilling. Cleabo thought that his grandpa was fooling around while they were gone. Grandma didn't seem to care. Her main concern was keeping the family together. She had already lost her two sons; one to the military and the other son, Jack had married at an early age and moved to New York.

Times were hard; Jack had no choice but to go to New York. Jack was the spitting image of his father James and like James, he too had a gambling problem. Jack went to Brooklyn and stayed with his cousin. His cousin's name was Blue. Blue was a settled woman with four kids. They stayed in the projects and back then the projects were considered to be a fancy place to live.

Brooklyn was huge, with a lot of people and tremendous excitement. Jack found a job and he adjusted to city life quickly. He moved from his cousin, Blue's apartment and started working in the Bronx. Working in the Bronx was incredibly interesting to him. He was making good money, more than he knew what to do with. The only thing that he had ever owned was a nineteen fifty-seven Pontiac that Grandpa James had given him.

Within a few months, Jack came back to get his family from South Carolina. He had a shiny new car and was nicely dressed, spending his money everywhere. His wife and their two children packed and went to New York with Jack. He told Sara that he would send for her as soon as he found a bigger place. While waiting for Uncle Jack to send for them, occasionally Sara and the kids would visit her parents.

After a few drinks the grown-ups used the kids as a form of entertainment. Sometimes it would be dancing or imitating how famous people dance; doing the split was Cleabo's favorite. But tonight it was fighting. The grown ups wanted to see who could beat who. So, they had the kids fighting as they gathered around and placed their bets.

Barry and Cleabo were wrestling and Barry threw Cleabo against the stove. Cleabo was lying on the floor and his grandpa said, "Boy, get up! Boy, I said get up!" he then reached into his pocket for a dollar bill and showed it to him, however, Cleabo couldn't move. "Something is wrong with the boy!" his grandpa shouted, "Take him to the hospital quick!"

The hospital bill was expensive, Sara had to dig into her savings to pay the bill. It was worth it though, because his leg was broken. Cleabo went to school with a cast on his leg for three months. After a while he started walking without the crutches and even running with the cast on his leg. At that time Sara decided that it was time for the cast to come off. Mrs. Carrington found it senseless to go to the doctor to have a cast removed, so they became his doctor. Mrs. Carrington and Sara used a hacksaw and they sawed the cast off. The grownups pasttime of getting drunk and watching the kids fight stopped after Barry broke Cleabo's leg.

CHAPTER V

IN THE CITY AGAIN

Uncle Jack finally sent for his mother, and Sara purchased the tickets for the bus fare. The clothes that they had on their backs were tacky and people gave them strange looks on the bus. They were amazed by the different cities and the tall buildings. Cleabo nor his brothers knew their mother was afraid of the trip. She was making the biggest move of her life and even though she was leaving nothing and going to nothing, it could've been a terrible mistake again.

Port Authority Bus Terminal, downtown New York City, was the final stop for the bus and it was more different than anything Cleabo could've imagined. Tall buildings were exciting to him; somehow he knew that they wouldn't be staying in some old shack this time.

Sara and the kids hailed a taxi to get to Uncle Jack's place. The taxicab driver looked at them strangely, like they stunk. Sara told him where to go, but he knew by the way they were dressed, they weren't from New York. Cleabo's mother had lived in New York before and was aware of the games that cab drivers played. She knew he would drive the long way for a large fare and she felt as though she was being taken for a ride.

When the cab arrived at Jack's apartment his mother told the cab driver she knew the game he had played and it was a shame that he would try to take advantage of a woman with three kids.

"You can call the cops." She told him. "I'll tell them you drove me all around New York." She then gave the cab driver the fare minus ten dollars and they exited the cab. Jack stayed in an apartment house in the Bronx. At first, the area was nice, but later on it started going downhill. By the time they arrived at his apartment, Jack had his third child. They lived on a street named Lafontane, right down the street from East Tremount Avenue. Crotona Park was right around the corner.

The building was three stories high and some people were hanging out on the steps, drinking and playing with what looked like little white blocks with black holes in them. At the time, Cleabo didn't know what dice were and he asked his mother what they were playing.

"Oh, it's just a game," Sara replied evasively.

The hallway inside the building was small, narrow and dark. He could see writing all over the walls and the banister was made of old oak wood. They had to step over a man on the steps, he was wearing a long raincoat with a brown paper bag in his hand. Sara knocked on the door and Jack welcomed them in. Jack's apartment wasn't big at all; in fact, Cleabo and his brothers slept on the floor on a pallet, while his mother made use of the sofa. The sleeping arrangements were no problem. Just to have a place to lay their tired bodies after the long bus ride, was contentment to them. Things were pretty hectic in the little apartment, there wasn't much room and Jack stayed gone most of the time.

In nineteen sixty-five, Cleabo and his family experienced an emotionally, significant event. Grandpa died. His death was a shock to the entire Jones family. Grandma Sadie Bell had called and told Sara that Grandpa James was on the side of the house throwing up blood and they had to rush him to the hospital. No one had expected him to die and it was hard to believe. Cleabo thought his grandpa would always be around, but now he was dead; it was devastating to him.

Sara made arrangements to go back down South, the death of her father hit her kind of hard. Jack too, was a bit distressed as he drove the family down South in a rental van. When they arrived everyone was happy to see them even though Grandma Sadie Bell was still in a state of shock over Grandpa's death. Everyone in the house was crying and when things quieted down, Grandma Sadie Bell sat in the rocking chair on the porch and began to sing. She was always a good singer in church. She would sing her heart out and make you want to cry.

"Swing low, sweet chariot. Coming to carry me home…" That was her favorite song. The entire house would stop and listen to this woman sing as she rocked in the chair. Grandma Sadie Bell started talking to herself. "Oh, James! Why you had to leave me? You know I've got to raise these chillen and these grand's yahn."

His grandmother was in a good state of mind prior to the death of Grandpa James, however, after the funeral she was still talking to him. Grandma Sadie Bell was having conversations with him, like he was in the room. One evening after the funeral, Cleabo was sitting in the living room with Grandma Sadie Bell. While they were talking Cleabo heard a squeaking sound, then he watched as the door to the to the liquor cabinet swung opened. Then Cleabo was sure he could hear the gurgling sound of a drink being poured. His eyes went round with fear as he looked at his grandmother.

"Oh, that ain't nobody but James." His grandmother told him.

Cleabo didn't care who it was, it scared him so bad, he could feel the hairs prickling on the back of his neck.

The idea of his grandfather actually coming back into the house as a ghost, scared him to death. He could hear Grandpa James coming in late at night stumbling around like he'd normally do when he had too much to drink. Cleabo would jump up in the middle of the bed and start to shake, too scared to move. He would pull the covers over his head and hope not to hear anymore. He was so happy when it came time to go back to New York, he even helped his mother pack up their belongings. Grandma Sadie Bell didn't want to go but the family convinced her, saying it would be best for her.

Back in New York, things really were crowded in that small apartment. The neighbors wondered how all of them fit in there. Sara found a job working for a law firm, so she decided to move into her own place.

They moved to a Puerto Rican neighborhood, where some of the folks were friendly and some weren't. Cleabo and his family were better off having their own place, rather than being bunched up at Uncle Jack's apartment. Of course, the apartment wasn't great, it was like those you see at the movies; the Hollywood version of the ghetto.

An Italian family lived across the hall. The mother's name was Mrs. Doria, she was a loud, but sweet, middle aged woman with a large nose and gray hair. She didn't have a prejudiced bone in her body, or at least she didn't display one. When she wanted one of her sons, she would come to the door and scream her head off. This was irritating to Cleabo. Mrs. Doria's sons were the most devious, criminal minded kids he had ever seen.

Mrs. Doria's oldest son Richie, was strung out on heroin. There would be times he would almost overdose and the sound of Mrs.

Doria coming to the hallway, yelling at the top of her lungs, probably could have been heard miles away.

"Sara, Sara! Come and help me with Richie, quick!"

Then Cleabo and Barry would have the task of trying to keep him conscious. Cleabo and Barry were only kids, yet they would put Richie's arms around their shoulders and walk him as his legs dragged the ground while they periodically slapped his face. They would also throw him into the stream of water from the fire hydrant in order to keep him alive.

Being young, he didn't understand what was going on, but he would help walk Richie up and down the streets. Richie had blonde hair and blue eyes and his skin was always pale, especially when he had too much heroin. It became a normal routine walking Richie. Sara didn't mind her boys helping Richie out since he was always doing things for her whenever he was straight. Richie would steal from the public schools and give Sara a lot of food. One time before Thanksgiving, he knocked on the door and said. "Here, Mrs. Sara! This is for you, Happy Thanksgiving."

It was a large ham and they were able to eat off of it for days. He also gave Sara some cold cuts, and the canned goods had "Board of Education" written on the side of them. Although Sara didn't approve of the stealing, she could hardly say anything, since what she received was badly needed.

City life didn't agree with Cleabo's Aunt Louina Mae. She had been writing home to her boyfriend who had joined the Air Force. Eventually they were married and she moved to North Carolina with him.

Dora Gene, his other aunt, was still hanging tough and Grandma Sadie Bell started receiving her social security checks, so they were ready to move. Sara was tired of all of them living together and she decided that they needed two apartments, but near each other. They found two apartments in the same building on Dawson Street, right off of Interval Avenue in the South Bronx. Cleabo lived on the first floor and his grandmother and Dora Gene lived upstairs on the second floor for a couple of years, eventually his grandmother and Dora Gene moved back south into their boarded up wooden house once Grandma Sadie Bell became stable again.

Dawson Street is where Cleabo spent the remainder of his adolescent years, until he was sixteen. Cleabo lived at 876 Dawson Street apartment 1-B. The hallway was cleaner than the building at his uncle's. He attended Public School 63, which was directly across the street. The school yard had basketball courts and a little area for small kids to play in. Most of the muggings, killings, and robberies took place on Rogers Place; it was the street in between the schoolyard and Dawson Street.

On Dawson Street there was a pool hall and Cleabo learned how to rack balls for fifty cents a rack there. The cross street at the top of the hill was Longwood Avenue, where a lot of prostitution went on. Cleabo learned street terminology and the sense of dog-eat-dog quickly. In the Bronx only the strong survived. If you were outspoken you were *kilt*; not killed, but *kilt*.

Someone getting killed in real life, or on television, is a normal killing. However, when someone gets *kilt* it's an entirely different story. It's one of those nasty, brutal killings. For instance, in a normal stabbing a person would merely be stabbed with a knife once or twice. To be *kilt*, however, is the kind of stabbing where a person could have a tic-tac toe or other design carved into the chest or other places.

Cleabo's block was mainly filled with drug pushers. They hung around in packs like wolves, shot pool and played basketball. Cleabo always admired the way they dressed. With their name brand clothing, they wore at least three millionaire's names on their garments. The fact that he would have to work or hustle real hard to dress the same way as the drug dealers didn't phase him. At the age of eight or nine he was more mature than his other two brothers were and much wiser. Cleabo and his brothers didn't hang out together but when one found himself into trouble all three of them would be into the battle. Sometimes he fought and didn't know what he was fighting for.

Sara had a nine o'clock curfew on him, but he was always late and he would get a whipping for it. Cleabo really didn't care about the whippings. He was finally learning how to enjoy life. He went from racking balls at the pool hall, to cleaning up the pool hall after school. He didn't say much to anyone in the pool hall and the people there liked him because he was quiet.

At the pool hall he received his first task, a sort of welcome to New York kind of deal. A guy by the name of 'Speed' asked him to do something for him. Speed was about twenty eight to thirty years old and was one of the regulars. It was easy to see how Speed observed everyone in the pool hall and Cleabo knew that this man was reading him for something.

Finally, one day Speed was shooting nine balls with a cigar in the corner of his mouth, he said in a low tone of voice. "Hey kid! You don't say much, do you?"

Speed had on some high-top suede Playboy's shoes. They were in fashion in the sixties. The shoes were complimented with the Florsheim cap that was tilted to the side of his head. He was an impressive dresser.

"No sir, I don't say much."

"Another thing kid. When you are out here in the streets, it's not sir or ma'am. I know your mother taught you well, but here in the streets, you don't give respect. Respect is something hard to come by. So, you take it after you earn success."

"Yes sir."

"Boy, what did I just tell you?"

"Okay man."

At that moment, Cleabo knew Speed was going to ask a favor of him.

"You see that bag on that bench over there?" Cleabo turned around and looked at the bag.

"I'll give you twenty dollars to take it to 758 Kelly Street, apartment 2A."

Cleabo thought about it then said, "Okay."

"Hey kid, only give the package to Annie; no one else." Cleabo started thinking about what his mother told him about never trusting a stranger, but right now he could only see that dollar sign. Cleabo grabbed the bag and left.

When Cleabo left the pool hall, he noticed Speed standing by the door with a cue stick in his hand and his cigar hanging out of the corner of his mouth. Speed had a grin on his face that made Cleabo paranoid.

When he arrived at Annie's house she greeted him with a smile; she could easily see that he was nervous. Annie's apartment looked exceedingly clean considering the neighborhood. Annie was wearing a long dashiki and she was a nice looking red bone with a well groomed Afro. He told her Speed said the package was for her. She smiled and said, "Thank you," then closed the door. Cleabo hastily walked back to the pool hall but it seemed like the journey took forever. He never told Speed how he felt about the trip or how fine he thought Annie was. Sweat was pouring down his face when he returned to the pool hall.

"What's up young blood?"

"Nothing much."

"Did you deliver the package?"

"Yeah, I took it to her."

"What did she say?"

"She didn't say anything! What was in it anyway?"

"There was nothing in it but a carton of cigarettes, but let me tell you young blood, never carry anything and not know what the hell you are carrying, understand kid?"

"I understand," Cleabo answered, figuring the "Cigarettes," were of the "Mary Jane" type.

"Here's the twenty dollars for doing that for me," Speed told him approvingly. "I like the way you handle yourself. Now tell me, if I need anything else can I depend on you?"

"Yeah!" he answered quickly, "You can depend on me." Twenty bucks seemed liked a million to Cleabo and he wanted the opportunity for more.

Cleabo already knew the next task would be more difficult and more than likely illegal. Cleaning the floors at the pool hall was much easier that night for Cleabo, probably because of the twenty dollars in his back pocket. By the time the pool hall closed all he could think about was ways to make more money. This first twenty was the most money he had ever had on him at one time.

That night when he left the pool hall Cleabo met a girl named Lee Ann. She was the prettiest thing Cleabo had ever seen. Lee Ann was his friend Danny's sister and it was love at first sight. Since Cleabo started working at the pool hall he had picked up some pointers from Speed on how to get next to a woman. Speed would totally ignore most of the females he dealt with. He would never let them know that he wanted them just as bad as they wanted him. He had this theory about controlling pressure and remaining cool, but Cleabo had to let Lee Ann know that he existed.

He looked down at the clothes he was wearing and he realized how tacky he was dressed. How would he ever make a good impression on this young lady? Cleabo finally built up enough nerve to walk over to her, tucking in his shirt and then stopping by the park bench where Lee Ann was playing a game called Ring O Leavey O. It was a game similar to Tag. He walked up to Lee Ann, and said, "Hi."

She looked at him, smiled and said hi, then she ran away. He could see her checking out his gear but he wasn't dressed to impress. Lee Ann dressed neatly and her brother Danny always bragged about how they were distant cousins of a famous basketball player.

Lee Ann's family wore expensive name brand sneakers which gave everyone the impression that they had a lot of money. Cleabo knew he had to get her attention; but he didn't want to play with her like Speed played his women. The thought of playing the "Girl you ain't nothing role," was pretty stupid and it wouldn't be the right thing for him to do in order to obtain a beautiful creature like Lee Ann.

Later on that night Cleabo couldn't sleep, his mind was thinking of different ways to get to know Lee Ann. He figured the idea of having money in his pocket and wearing better clothes would increase his chances. Lee Ann was all over his mind, she was '2' fine. Once he fell asleep, he dreamed about her.

The sun came shining in through his window, he could smell the bacon his mother cooked every Saturday morning. Making money and buying new clothes was on the agenda today, he thought. This was one time he would've liked to miss breakfast, but he knew that his mother wouldn't go for it, so he threw down a few bites before dashing down to the pool hall. He told Mr. Johnson that he needed to get off early; around three o'clock.

"What's the matter boy, you got a hole in your pocket?"

"Yeah, I need to get me some gear, so I can look sharp, like you."

"I heard you say you want to get some clothes. I'm going to tell you kid, you're doing the right thing. Look good, act good and you will feel good," said Speed. "Another thing, kid. Always know what you are carrying, so that you know how to react to different situations, understand?"

"Yeah, Okay."

"Also kid, remember pressure will burst a pipe, so don't let it mess with you."

"Yeah, I know what you mean. Hey, Speed?"

"Yeah, kid?"

"What makes a young girl my age get turned on?"

"You got one in mind?"

"Yeah."

"The worst thing to do is to let her know you want her more than she wants you."

Cleabo then realized that he did know some of Speed's techniques when it came to women.

"You see, kid," Speed told him, waxing on his philosophy regarding women. "A woman is one of the most beautiful, yet lowest things on earth. They like to feel like the underdog and they will want to rise up on you at the right occasion. Some women have class and some don't. The ones with class you still make them feel low and they will come around. The ones without class you treat them like dirt. Tell them what you want, when you want it and be hard on them, but do it on a one-on-one basis and never tell me or anyone else who you slept with, understand kid?"

"Yeah, Speed, I understand."

Cleabo wanted to ask Speed how to make more money, but he knew in order for Speed to truly trust him to make some illegal money, he had to gain his confidence. Cleabo knew Speed would be asking him to do important things rather than delivering packages. Time was a major factor and Cleabo had to mold this gangster of a man into believing in him. Everyday was a challenge for Cleabo, he was fully aware of Speed's technique of sizing him up for a bigger and more important job.

At three o'clock he put down his broom and headed for the train. Cleabo took the number two train to Third Avenue to find some new gear. Whenever he traveled alone, he would put his money in his socks underneath his foot. If anyone would try to rip him off they wouldn't get much.

Whenever a gang of guys would try to take his money, he would tell them he hopped the train and only had forty-five cents or something like that. He had seen some people get their new sneakers and even their socks ripped off, but that was on rare occasions. At

Third Avenue, Cleabo shopped at almost all of the stores on the streets like Florsheim and Alexandra. He bought a nice tan Applejack and some high-top suede, Playboy's shoes. Playboys were the 'whip' back then. At Alexandra he bought some shadow striped pants; they went well with the black nylon T-shirt.

After shopping on Third Avenue he knew that once he wore his new gear it would be impressive but it couldn't last long; soon he would have to resort back to his old gear. He remembered what his mother always said, 'It's not what you have, it's how you take care of your clothes.'

On the subways in New York people with bags normally represented money spent or money in their pockets. Cleabo received a lot of close looks, but he made it look as though the bags were all he had ever owned in his life and if confronted, he would die for them. His train arrived at Prospect and 163rd Street, which was right around the corner from Kelly Street. On Kelly Street, he picked up a delicious slice of pizza and folded it, the cheese was dripping from the sides while he walked the block or two.

Cleabo finally made it home, tearing off his clothes and putting on his new gear. His mother looked at him like he was crazy. After he changed, he went racing down to the park to show off his new gear to Lee Ann. All of his peers were impressed with the gear he had on, they thought his clothes were 'Chilled' and didn't 'Front' him. This was typical street terminology for cool clothes and not teasing him in the company of others about his new garments. Lee Ann was playing tag but she stopped when she saw him and said. "Where have you been?"

He was tempted to *'Igg'* her, but she was too fine to ignore. He thought that by saying something smart like Speed, might get her attention, so he played it cool and said, "It takes more than a few words to get to know me, let alone be my keeper."

"Let me be the judge of that." She responded swiftly.

"If it were meant for a woman to judge a man, then baby, you wouldn't need me!"

"I know that's right! I don't need you!" Lee Ann said and then ran away, continuing her game of tag.

It took a few days for Cleabo to build up enough courage to ask her to be his girlfriend. Finally, he did and Lee Ann said yes. She really inspired him and made him feel good about himself. He tried his best to school her on the facts of life after they shared time together, but working at the pool hall took up most of his time.

The Bronx had a lot of crime and he was right in the middle of it. While growing up his family didn't have much money, other than savings, but they made the best of what they had. Speed helped Cleabo in realizing what reality was all about. When Cleabo wasn't working at the pool hall he attended school. Cleabo had a Puerto Rican friend named Julio; they were both in the fifth grade. One morning he came to school and Julio was nodding off something serious, the teacher said, "Hey Julio! Wake up!"

Cleabo responded, "Yo teach! Leave him alone! We hung out all night, and he's tired."

Then he leaned over the desk and asked Julio if he was all right. With half-opened eyes and upside-down horseshoe lips, Julio said. "Yeah man, I'm all right; just a little tired from last night."

The next day Julio was on the second page of the New York Times for OD'ing at the age of ten. It's hard as hell to make the front page in New York. You have to do something like attempt to kill the president or something of that nature. For a kid to have an overdose of heroin at the age of ten was some serious news. Cleabo had to make the adjustment of living in the fast lane.

After Julio's overdose, Speed had a long talk with Cleabo. He told him there were a lot of things he could never change and that a person is always going to be just who they are. They will lose respect in the streets if they're drug addicts. Never respect an addict, just watch them. Never let them know you are watching their moves and always be on your p's and q's around them.

Speed finally introduced Cleabo to running numbers and selling marijuana. Some of the people he dealt with were really crazy. Sometimes they wouldn't have the money and he would give them credit for the reefer or the numbers. For a youngster, when it came to running numbers or selling marijuana, his game plan was smooth. Reefer and cocaine were the items to move, though Speed didn't let him get involved with the cocaine; it was out of his league at the time.

With the money he made, Cleabo started changing and he dressed well now. Lee Ann perceived the difference, she never asked him what kind of work he was doing, now that he looked good. She just assumed that he was still cleaning up the pool hall and wasn't trying to be one of the big shots that hung out there. Later on, the word did leak out about what Cleabo was doing. His popularity within the neighborhood increased and it was hard to keep it a secret. Whenever Cleabo ran numbers, he always had to watch his back. There were always people wanting to take his money; most of the time it was people from other neighborhoods.

One day he was coming out of a building on Kelly Street after collecting some money when he heard a voice. "Hey, you. Come here!"

Cleabo didn't look back, he just ran. After being chased three blocks, he finally managed to get away. Cleabo was a fast runner and he held on to the money he had collected. He made his way to the gambling house to deliver the money to Speed. The gambling house was an apartment filled with smoke and men, and there were a few ladies too. The apartment building where they gambled was dark and filled with a wet odor. It smelled like dead rats that had been removed out of those jumbo rattraps. He knocked on the door and someone looked out of the peephole.

"Hey Speed, its young blood!" the man said after recognizing Cleabo. "Come on in."

No one there was his age but they knew that he was Speed's runner. When Cleabo entered the apartment, reefer and cigarette smoke hit him in the face. He saw a few people tooting while he was in the hall, then he walked into the area where they were playing cards. Speed and Cleabo exchanged greetings.

"Hey Speed, can we talk?"

"Sure kid, just a minute. Let me finish this hand." Speed continued, "I'm killing these suckers."

Another voice said, "You ain't doing jack, I've got big money."

"Tunk out!" shouted Speed, then he collected his winnings and stepped from the table to talk to Cleabo privately. "What's up young blood?"

"Speed, here is your money man." Cleabo said handing him the cash.

Speed took the money and slipped it into his pocket.

"Nice going young blood."

"Thanks, I had to shake a few fools off of me." Cleabo said then continued, "Speed, it's getting hard to make a buck these days; you know what I mean?"

"I hear you talking little brother, so what you want to do? You're only ten years old, that's a little too young to sport a piece." Speed ruminated on the problem for a moment.

"How about a blade?"

"No, Speed," Cleabo declined. "A blade will let them suckers get too close to me. Let me sleep on it. I'll come by your place early in the morning." Cleabo and Speed walked back into the room. Cleabo only stayed for a few minutes watching the game, then he told Speed that he was leaving.

"C J, I'll see you tomorrow?" Speed said.

"You bet."

At that time a woman's voice called out, "CJ, does that stand for cunt juice?" The entire room started laughing. Cleabo realized at that moment he wanted to pack a piece. The woman was trying to crack jokes on him and it upset him. Cleabo wanted to put a bullet right down her throat.

"Hey, back off of the kid, he's my runner." Speed told her.

"Oh, I didn't mean any harm, besides he's kind of cute Speed, and he dresses so well, maybe I can show him a thing or two," the woman said as she rubbed Cleabo's chin.

"Slut, get your hands off of that boy; you are lower than a broken down dog with the mange. That boy wouldn't sleep with you and your old ugly ass!"

The entire room started laughing as Cleabo said good-bye to everyone. For the time he ran reefer, he didn't smoke it, until he was almost eleven. Cleabo went home that evening and every step he took was like being in a spy movie. Wondering if he was going to be followed or chased, he was nervous and constantly watching his back.

He passed the schoolyard and all of his friends were playing basketball, stickball, and chug-a-lug. Chug-a-lug is a game that is played on a piece of cardboard. With a black marker, six boxes are made. Each of the boxes has a number in the center, in consecutive order from one through six. Three dice in a cup are shook, revealing the numbers. Money was placed on each block and if your number appeared you were paid whatever you bet. If your number appeared twice you were paid double. If it appeared three times you were paid triple the amount you had on the board.

It was a fast hustle for a kid. Cleabo used to have his own board and would sometimes use this hustle in the summer. The only thing he didn't like about this hustle was that he had to have a back up partner in the crowd of people with a weapon watching his back to make sure no one would try to take his money. On a good day, he would make fifty to seventy five dollars. A portion of it had to go to the back up guy though.

Cleabo wanted to play basketball with the other kids, but he knew he didn't have the time because he had to make money. It had gotten to a point he couldn't stand having only twenty or thirty dollars in his pockets. Money meant more to him than playing street games. Cleabo didn't realize that he had missed a big part of his life, playing with the kids his age could've helped him regain his youth. Lee Ann moved away and it was one of the saddest occasions in his life. He never knew where she moved to, he only knew that it was far and he wasn't going to be able to see her.

Cleabo started seeing his body structure begin to change and his mental attitude about life, also. With all of the number running and selling dope for Speed, the Puerto Rican gangs began to be a problem. There were a lot of them and they were everywhere. They wouldn't confront someone if they knew who they were, or if they were from their block. There was a gang named the Savage Skulls and they tried to be vicious. The Roman Kings were also around, but they never fought each other.

Then there were the Black Spades and the Black Pearls. The Black Pearls were all brothers. They wore black turtleneck sweaters with a pearl earring in their left ear and they studied martial arts. No other gang would challenge them. They didn't do any crime like the other three gangs, they were into the preservation of the neighborhood, and they knew how to protect themselves from anyone who would try to confront them. The Black Spades were a mixture of all races, full of thieves and dopeheads. Cleabo didn't want to join any gang; his family made it clear how much they opposed gang violence. If his mother really knew what he was doing, his ass would've been in so much trouble!

One day while he was running his reefer, he was approached by three Savage Skulls, after leaving a building on Kelly Street. One was black and the other two were Puerto Rican. They said, "Hey kid. What are you doing?"

Cleabo didn't answer.

"Hey kid," one of them called again. "We've been watching you, and we know for a fact that you are doing something, running from building to building, like you are some damn insurance man. I said, what are you doing?" he repeated.

"I'm looking for my brother," Cleabo answered sarcastically, "My mother sent me for him."

One of the skulls started coming at him. It was Blackie, their leader. People said that he was the meanest. All three of them were dressed poorly and they stunk. Blackie approached Cleabo, and Cleabo fell to his knees, scooted between Blackie's legs then jumped up and started running. It was a long run for him and everyone on the streets watched, while the three guys tried to catch him. He ran up to the roof of one building and began to jump rooftops, but they were still behind him. He went charging down the stairs and out onto the streets again, but they finally caught him at the end of the street. They grabbed him and threw him down. Blackie put his revolting body into Cleabo's face. "Give up the money, kid!" Money fell everywhere as the three skulls ripped his pockets open; he had sixty dollars of Speed's money on him. One of them had a knife, he swung it at Cleabo trying to mark his face for life. Cleabo held up his forearm and the blade of the knife went piercing down the side of his elbow grazing the bone. He cried out in agony. His elbow began to swell while he bled copiously. When the Skull tried to cut him again with the knife, a hand came from out of nowhere grabbing the guy's wrist. Then a stranger stepped in with a sweeping karate motion and knocked the guy to the ground. The man said, "Leave this kid alone," then he helped Cleabo up and asked, "Are you all right?"

"Yeah," Cleabo answered as he held his injured arm. "But who the hell are you?"

"I'm Cedric, warlord of the Black Pearls, and those two are my councilmen, and, if you look around you, you'll see some of our Noble Knights."

At that time, it seemed like all of them made a karate sound, that 'kee-yaa' type of sound. Blackie then said. "Who you guys think you are? We've got a peace treaty with you guys."

Cedric then said, "Yeah, but that don't give you the right to mistreat our people like this."

More Savage Skulls suddenly made an appearance and the block was filled with Skulls and Pearls and Cleabo was in the middle of all of them. There was a shot fired, then chains and bottles were thrown all over the place. Cleabo heard a voice say to him, "Run little brother," and a hand pushed him aside.

The two gangs were furiously fighting with baseball bats, brass knuckles, and chains. The Skulls were unable to defeat the Pearls. Cleabo stood from a distance and watched them, some of that karate stuff really helped the Pearls. The brothers were doing flips and kicking butt. From that point on he idolized the Pearls.

In the distance and gaining were the sound of police sirens. The police arrived and everyone scattered, making threats of, "We'll see you tonight!" Neither the Savage Skulls, Black Spades nor the Roman Kings wanted to deal with the Black Pearls. Cleabo went home bleeding, and trying to hide from his mother; knowing the sight of blood would get her upset. In the bathroom, he managed to control the bleeding and apply a patch on his elbow, so that he could dash out the door to Speed's house.

The night air was hot and humid, some people in the park were playing the bongos and singing while they drank Wild Irish Rose wine. They were just chillin' in the night air. The park was right across the street from his house, it was easy to see some young ladies talking and listening to a boom box while playing spin the bottle or some other juvenile game.

When he arrived to Speed's house, Speed looked at him and said, "Yeah, young blood I heard about that rumble over on Kelly Street today; they said it had something to do with a kid being cut. Boy, them gangbangers sure is crazy, cutting a kid. They must have been at least seventeen or eighteen years old. You let one of those fools mess with me and his ass is six feet under. I wouldn't give a damn if he's my brother's son." Speed glanced down at Cleabo's arm, after noticing how he was holding it in a discomfortable manner. "Holy shit! Was it you young blood?"

"Yo! Hold up, Speed." Cleabo jumped in with the life threatening situation still on his mind. "I need to rap to you. Hey man, like I'm only eleven and man things are really happening too fast. I mean, you know like," Cleabo scrambled for the right words. "I just want to be able to sit back and relax when I'm your age and at the rate things are going now, I don't even know if I will ever see your age!" He looked Speed in the eyes and said seriously, "I dig the green and I like the clothes, but I'm starting to get real scared. Things aren't like they were when you were growing up, Speed. They have changed. Man, it's a jungle out there! A jungle!" he repeated.

"Yeah, you're right but there are kids out there that would give anything to gain the knowledge and wisdom I've given you. I taught you every damn thing you know. You name it and I gave it to you, you're more or less like a son to me."

"Yeah, but you didn't teach me that one thing, Speed," Cleabo said emphasizing the one word.

"What's that, young blood?"

"You didn't teach me how to relax like you. Maybe I'm young, but I put myself on the line for you Speed. I'm only eleven and I'm already tired of having my life on the line for you or anyone else."

"Maybe you just need a break young blood. Ask your mother to let you go back down south for the summer or something."

"You know Speed, maybe you're right." Cleabo said starting to think about that. "Who knows? When I'm fifteen years old maybe I'll be the youngest pimp in New York or something. But right now I need a break from what's happening. I'm just not down anymore; can you dig it?"

"Yeah, I can dig it." Speed answered agreeably. "Tell you what, little bro. When you are ready for something big, you let me know. I'm moving up in life now and I'm starting to enter the big league. I just might need someone like you again, someone I can trust. So keep in touch," replied Speed.

"I sure will." Cleabo said, as he turned to leave.

When Cleabo stepped out of Speed's building, a guy sitting on top of one of the garbage cans said, "Hey kid, Lucky wants to see you."

Cleabo stopped and looked closely at the guy. "I don't know anyone named Lucky." Then, he looked and noticed that this guy was wearing a black turtle neck sweater and a pearl earring. He realized

91

that the guy was a Black Pearl and he felt that he owed them for saving him earlier in the day. "Okay, let's go." Cleabo said.

They started walking and didn't say two words to each other. Later he learned that one of the dudes name was EJ. EJ was their best man in Kung-Fu. They walked down to the Trenton Projects and there everyone was doing karate in the basement, or just relaxing. Lucky sat on a throne type of seat. He had on a dashiki and sunglasses, and had two females at his side. He said in a loud, scary type of voice. "Who are you?"

"I'm Cleabo Jones."

Lucky started laughing, "And who the hell is Cleabo Jones? A savior of thugs delivering that almighty white powder and hauling numbers? A boy who destroys our neighborhoods and our people?"

"No!" Cleabo shouted. "Cleabo is someone who is just trying to make it in this messed up world, the only way he knows how."

"Don't you know you are making it more screwed up with your illegal drugs? There is someone behind you who is just sitting back, sending you out to corrupt our people. We've been watching him, too. That's how we knew where to find you."

"I'm not down with his shit or no one else's anymore. I've got to survive on my own now and if all I have on my side is luck, then that's what I'll live with."

"You sure do talk a good game for such a little pip-squeak," Lucky said, leaning back in his throne. "Just remember that a lot of big people got started here in the city. People like Rap Brown, Stokely Carmichael. Do you want to be a part of the elite?"

"What's so grand about your operation anyway? Will I make any money?" Cleabo asked warily.

"No, but you can survive and watch others survive and have power." Lucky told him, as he raised his hand to illustrate his powers while his people conducted their martial arts. "Don't you know I can have you killed at a snap of my fingers? Now that's power."

"Yeah." Cleabo admitted. "That's why I came here. I needed to talk to whoever I have to talk to before I die. I'm not afraid of dying; it's the living part that scares the crap out of me."

Cleabo started walking out of the door, and Lucky said, "At six o'clock tomorrow morning there will be two knights across from your building. Go with them." Cleabo thought this request of Lucky's sounded more like an order, but he said, "Okay."

That night, all he could think about was what Lucky had said to him. He set the alarm clock for five o'clock in order to get an early start. Morning came and he didn't know what to expect, but he knew that they would be outside waiting for him. Just like clockwork, they were looking and waiting. The knights took him back to see Lucky.

"Good morning little brother," Lucky greeted him. "I'm going to teach you the essence of life. Then, I will let you make a decision of choosing right from wrong, and after that I will let you go. First I will be your tutor for everything you will need to know that is good. I will teach you how to control your temper that gets you into petty fights. Then I'll show you how to handle bullies with your mind and your strength. I hope you're willing to learn." From that point on, Lucky was his mentor.

Cleabo pierced his ear and wore a pearl earring. Lucky began to teach Cleabo Tae Kwon Do along with Kung Fu. Cleabo became skillful at the martial arts and he was like the mascot of the Pearls. They enjoyed watching him work out and doing different forms. His kicks and blows were flawless, including his rope climbing and swinging from one rope to another, then he'd somersault to the floor for a perfect landing. Having a private tutor was the best thing that could've happened to him, he thought. The Pearls helped him develop self-pride, to be strong and never take any static from anyone.

Summer was over and it was time to go back to school again. His school clothes were already bought and his mother didn't understand why he carried himself differently. Cleabo acted mature now.

On his block there was a bully named Dorey. Cleabo always sensed that Dorey wanted to fight him, but as long as he was working for Speed, Dorey dared not challenge him. Dorey feared what would happen to him if he tried to bully Cleabo while he was a member of Speed's organization. Unfortunately, the word had seeped out to the streets that Cleabo was no longer with Speed, and this gave Dorey the green light on Cleabo. Dorey was unaware that Cleabo was studying martial arts with the Pearls. Perhaps he should have done his homework a little more carefully. Like most bullies are in comparison to their victims, Dorey was much larger in size than Cleabo. One morning Cleabo was coming out of his building, Dorey was waiting for him.

"Where the hell you going, Peanut Head?" Dorey yelled.

"None of your business." Cleabo answered unafraid.

After they exchanged a few words Dorey and Cleabo began fighting. Dorey was using his weight against Cleabo, resulting in the need for an equalizer. Cleabo picked up a stick that was sitting off to the side of the building. He twirled it and tucked it underneath his armpit, extending his other forearm outward, as though he was doing a routine for Lucky. Quickly and forcefully he snapped the stick from his armpit hitting Dorey in the face. Stunned, Dorey staggered around trying to regain his balance. Cleabo then used the stick like it was a staff and he swept Dorey's feet and the boy fell to the ground. Cleabo jumped on top of him and continuously punched him in the face until someone pulled him off. Dorey never challenged Cleabo again.

One morning while walking to school something happened to Cleabo that affected him for the rest of his life. It was around October, when a fast moving truck struck Cleabo while he was walking to school. It happened under the subway el at the crossing of Interval Avenue. Cleabo had looked both ways for cars, but unfortunately as he started to cross the street, he heard a big boom and a pow! His body was sent flying in the air, he remembered hitting the ground with his body and rolling for what seemed about a block on the cobblestone.

After he stopped rolling, he noticed the rain was pouring down on his face and that his left leg was swollen. His entire body was wet with blood and rain. Cleabo tried to sit up, but couldn't. He couldn't move any parts of his body on his left side. He remembered seeing his brother Barry, getting off of the truck that apparently hit both of them, although he suffered the majority of the impact. Perhaps Barry tried to jump out of the way of the truck and landed on the hood, he thought. He watched Barry picking up his hat off of the street.

"Cleabo!" Barry shouted as he ran over. "Cleabo, get up!"

"Yo, man," Cleabo managed to moan out the words. He knew he was hurt bad. "I can't move! Go get Momma," he finished weakly.

Barry went to get their mother. When Sara arrived at the scene there was a crowd of people and paramedics standing over him.

"Oh God!" Sara screamed when she saw him. She threw herself on the ground beside him. "Oh, look at my baby! Cleabo are you all right?" she cried. She looked him over carefully, trying not to move him.

"Don't let him go to sleep! He might not wake up!" shouted one of the paramedics, as he hurried to get Cleabo on the stretcher.

While strapping Cleabo down, one of the paramedics looked up at Sara and recognized her from years ago. Sara recognized him too, but there was no time for small talk, her son's life was at stake. The paramedic was Jonah Walker, the orderly from the hospital in Rochester that Sara had met when Cleabo was born. He had moved to the Bronx and had become a licensed paramedic.

Cleabo was put into the ambulance, which was a painful process. During the time they were in the back of the ambulance, his mother didn't have time to talk to Jonah; they were all busy trying to keep Cleabo awake. Cleabo couldn't stay awake though. He heard them telling him to stay awake; he felt the slaps on his face, then he just drifted away, he felt so tired. The sensation was that he was floating. It felt like he was floating down a long dark hallway, and at the end of the hallway, he knew it was so warm there. He knew he wanted to be in that warm, peaceful place.

By then everyone in the emergency room was moving extremely fast. The word was, they thought that he had died. The doctor told his mother he needed a blood transfusion right away, so he was taken to the operating room. The operation was successful, and he was revived. Having AB negative blood made it difficult for the transfusion, everyone in his family wanted to donate but couldn't; they were scared that he wasn't going to live. With the help of God, he did. The nurses at Lincoln Hospital were sweet and they thought Cleabo was cute, but in the back of their minds they were thinking how lucky he was to be alive.

When Cleabo woke up in his hospital room he discovered that on his left side he had a broken leg, all of his ribs were broken, and his left arm was broken in two places. Jonah visited him everyday. They became friends and Cleabo thought that he was a good man. Sara talked to Jonah every day during the time that Cleabo was in the hospital and Cleabo knew they went out a few times. Cleabo only wished that his mother had fun; he knew she needed it.

Cleabo stayed in the hospital for three months. He was glad to get out of there, it had started to feel like prison. Right around the time he was almost out of the hospital, his mother gave him some startling news. She said that Jonah would be living with them now; he had already moved in. Cleabo was shocked and at the same time he was happy. Knowing his mother and her history with men, he knew that she would never bring a man into her home, unless he was her soul mate. Jonah was nice to him and if a man's presence in the house was what his mother wanted, he was pleased that it was Jonah. Cleabo was content to be at home again. He had to use crutches until his broken leg healed, then after his cast was removed, he was in therapy to learn how to walk again. His ribs took the longest to heal.

After the accident, he couldn't run as fast as he used to. He started playing basketball to build his stamina and he found he played much better now. The recuperation period helped him to concentrate more on his game. Going back to school was a change. He began to get into his work, and hanging out with different people other than Speed or Lucky.

For a while Cleabo started dating Cookie; she was Puerto Rican and fantastically sexy. Her father was his apartment manager. He would go down to her house in the basement and have dinner with her family. It was the first time he had ever eaten octopus. Cleabo didn't stay with Cookie long, her father started being overly protective and acting differently toward Cleabo. Her father stopped letting her go to the movies with Cleabo or doing anything with him. He knew how little boys were, being that he was once a little boy himself. Cleabo never had sex with Cookie; the closest they ever had gotten was rubbing on her jeans on her vaginal area at the movies. She was so hot and squirming in her seat. He knew she was ready, but nothing ever happened with her, the same as with Lee Ann.

Life became more relaxed for him. He had already made a name for himself and he kept some money by doing odd jobs. He learned how to shoot pool exceptionally well, good enough to beat Speed one day at the pool hall. Speed kept hinting around how much he wanted him to come back and work for him, but Cleabo always did his best to show Speed that he could stand on his own two feet. He didn't want Speed's help anymore.

Although Cleabo's life started to take a turn for the better, he started getting bored and being bored was something hard for him to deal with. Next door to Cleabo's apartment building was a furniture store with trucks parked in the parking lot. One night Cleabo tied a rope to his balcony and swung into the truck lot from his apartment, like Tarzan. He opened up the furniture store and a neighbor that was passing by saw him. The neighbor yelled to some other people that were on the streets and everyone in the neighborhood came looting. The loud alarm was going off as they were stealing lamps, tables, and whatever they could carry.

Finally a police car arrived. The car was parked on the side of the building. Two policemen exited their cruiser and opened the trunk. The police were also stealing since they were the first patrol car to arrive on the scene. Cleabo bumped into one of them carrying out a table. When their cruiser were filled, the two officers drove off.

More police officers arrived and the crowd of neighborhood thieves commenced to disperse. Guy, a friend of Cleabo's had a hearing problem; however, he was great in the martial arts. A cop grabbed him and told him to stand against the wall. Guy couldn't hear the officer's command to get against the wall because of his hearing impairment.

Cleabo yelled to the officer, "He can't hear you!"

"Let's see if he can feel this damn club," the police officer said as he struck Guy in the back with his night stick. That was a mistake. Guy did a spinning heel kick on the police officer and knocked him down. The officer fell to the ground and Guy attempted to throw a roundhouse kick at the other cop. The other officer managed to catch his foot and threw Guy to the ground then both of the police officers started working him over with their clubs. They beat him up so badly that they almost broke his leg.

Living in New York was totally different than South Carolina. There were so many different and unusual lifestyles. In the summertime the policemen would barricade the block and there would be block parties. Local bands would come to perform, as they tried to reach stardom. The block parties would last all night; it was something like a large fiesta. At midnight when everything quieted down, the transients would lay on the ground with their bottle of wine and fall asleep. Cleabo liked it because everyone he knew was so drunk during the festivities, and his mother never knew what time he came in.

Cleabo's other Uncle Tyrone was in the military and he was stationed in Thailand, where leather was inexpensive. Cleabo's mother received a package from him and it was three leather jackets for him and his brothers. A lot of kids envied them for having such nice genuine leather at such an early age.

One day Cleabo was walking to school with his friends, David and Daryl. They were walking when some guys were looking them over. They stopped David but, Cleabo and Daryl kept walking. Cleabo didn't want to leave David alone, so he said to Daryl, "Let's go back and find out what's going on."

Daryl said he wasn't going to get involved. Cleabo thought that Daryl was scared, so he walked to where the three guys surrounded David. Cleabo said, "What's up?"

One guy said, "What's happening? That's a nice jacket!"

"Yeah, I know," he answered then asked David. "David, are you ready to go to school?"

Another guy said, "Don't worry about David! Let me try your jacket on!"

"Hell, no!" Cleabo said.

"Yo, let me try your jacket on!" the guy insisted, stating his words slowly and menacingly.

"No!" Cleabo said just as menacingly.

The guy started coming at him and Cleabo stood in a three-point kung-fu fighting stance, prepared to fight. Cleabo and one of the guys were about to fight when Cleabo noticed another guy coming from behind. Cleabo turned around to fight the other guy; however, he was a little too slow. All he could see was a fist coming at him. It was a solid blow to his eye.

The blow almost blinded him. He fell to the ground and all he could hear were bells as they stripped him of his coat. He was taken to the hospital and his mother met him there. After he told her what had happened, she took him down to the precinct and the police went through the mug shot book with him to identify the individual that punched him. All three of the guys he identified were on probation.

"Damn, beating up on a little kid. They are eighteen or nineteen years old!" his mother Sara said.

It was kind of embarrassing going to school with a patch on his eye, but all the kids knew that Cleabo had gone back to help David out. Cleabo's friends admired his courage and Daryl created a cowardly reputation for himself. Although he was a coward back then, at least he did live to see another day without any injuries.

The next week Cleabo was in the house helping out his mother in the kitchen and there was a knock at the door.

"Cleabo, get the door," Sara said.

"Who is it?" he called through the door without opening it.

"David," a voice said. "Let me talk to you Cleabo."

David came into the house out of breath, like he had been running a long way. He said, "Cleabo, those guys that hit you and took your coat and my money, they are up on the corner of Longwood right now."

Jonah was sitting in the living room and heard David. Jonah pulled out his thirty-eight and went walking out of the door. Cleabo heard his mother saying, "Oh, shit!" While Jonah was walking up to the corner, it seemed like the entire neighborhood followed. Before they arrived at the corner they were in viewing distance and Jonah asked Cleabo which one of the guys had hit him.

"The one with the white Godfather hat on." Cleabo told him.

Jonah tapped the guy on the shoulder and started whipping the living daylights out of him. The guy fell to the ground; he didn't have a chance. Jonah almost killed him! Then he took Cleabo's jacket off the guy and just looked at it. He threw it in the guy's face and said, "It's dirt now, just like you are!"

A police officer came, but he was from the neighborhood and he knew Jonah. They shot pool together; his name was Joe. Jonah looked at Joe and said, "Do I have to file a report or something?"

"No, that won't be necessary. I'll take care of this one," Joe said as he picked the guy off of the floor to take him to the precinct.

The next day Cleabo and his mother went grocery shopping. When they returned, as she opened the door to the apartment, she saw two junkies inside of their apartment. One was in the kitchen and the other was in the living room. She started screaming. The one in the kitchen ran past Cleabo almost knocking him down and the other one grabbed the portable television set and ran down the stairs.

One ran to the roof and jumped from one roof to another. He finally came down the stairs two buildings away and escaped. Cleabo grabbed a knife and started chasing the junkie with the television set down the stairs. Jonah was getting off work at the time that all of this was going on. He saw Cleabo running after this guy, so he started chasing him too. The junkie couldn't run fast with the television, so he threw it into the bushes. Jonah couldn't catch him, but later he found out who he was. A few days later Cleabo heard that Jonah had taken care of him in the pool hall real good.

CHAPTER VI

THE HEIST

At the age of fifteen, Cleabo started hanging hard. Sometimes he wouldn't come in until five in the morning. He started going back to the poolhall. Speed had asked him to do a few jobs for him and he started making money again. One day he was shooting pool and Speed came over to him.

"Hey, kid! I need to talk to you tonight at my place."

"What is it about?"

"Just be there kid, around seven o'clock."

When Speed left, Cleabo said to himself, "Oh, shit! What am I about to get into now?"

It was almost pitch dark going over to Speed's house. While walking down the alley a big headed alley cat jumped on Cleabo's back and he had to fight him off. He arrived at Speed's house at seven sharp. There were three other guys there, Cleabo had seen them before and knew that they pushed a lot of drugs for Speed. One of the guys was Tony; Tony was Cleabo's friend Ronald's older brother. PeeWee and Larry were there, and Slim came in a few minutes later. Speed started talking and when he talked it was like magic. Speed could talk a French whore out of her drawers and make her pay for the sex.

"I guess you guys are wondering why you're here." Speed began.

"Yeah, the thought did occur," said Tony.

"Let me tell you dudes something. I have you here because at one point in time, you used to or still do work for me." Everyone nodded their heads in agreement. "Not only that, but I feel that I can trust you." He continued.

"Yeah, you know you can trust me, Speed," said PeeWee.

PeeWee was kissing Speed's ass. Speed really didn't like anyone that brown-nosed or kissed ass. Speed looked at PeeWee like he really didn't trust him. He admired men that had discipline and pride in whatever they did, right or wrong.

"You see gentlemen, I have a proposition that I would like to make with you," he stopped and looked slowly around at everyone before saying clearly, "Don't stop me until I'm through." He paused again for emphasis before continuing. "It has been brought to my attention that we aren't making any money down here in the Bronx and I need to expand my horizons. I have an inside tip on how to get some money, but I need your help. Everything I want to do involves time and timing. The job that I want to pull off is heavy," he paused again. "It's a life or death situation."

"Hey, Speed. What type of artillery might we be going up against?" Slim asked.

"An Uzi or two and maybe some .45s." replied Speed.

"Hey, man! That's some heavy artillery!" Tony said, he sounded happy over the strong arms.

Speed turned around and looked at Tony, "Yeah, and we have to be ready for them. I have two weeks to map everything out before the deal happens. I want you all to keep your mouths shut and your eyes open. You probably won't be seeing me around because I have to filter my way in, but be ready when I get back because all hell will break loose."

"Speed, can you tell us a little bit more about this job?" Larry asked.

"No, but I can tell you that it's dangerous and can change the course of your life. Cleabo, I want you to practice the rope routine you're always telling me that you are so good at," Speed continued.

Larry was next, "Larry, I want you to stop playing around with those silly light bulb gasoline bombs and get into something more serious, because I'm going to need a distraction, outside and inside the place. You guys know I'm getting old and I can't run fast, so we are going to have to do it and do it quick." He stopped and perused them all, trying to catch their thoughts.

"I want you boys to go home and get a good night's sleep. Sleep is important now. You must get all the rest you can. Two weeks will come quicker than you think." Everyone told Speed, okay, and they would see him later. While walking out of the door, Cleabo told Speed that he was ready for whatever he wanted him to do.

Speed placed a hand on Cleabo shoulder and said. "Good Cleabo," Speed slapped him kindly on the back and said, "I may be needing you to do me a favor before the job, I'll let you know. You see, in order to get inside, I might need some help from you. Just a little odd job; nothing dangerous," he added.

The next day Cleabo went to school and he couldn't get into anything they were doing. It seemed like he couldn't concentrate at all. He pretended like he was going to use the bathroom but he went outside. The clouds were moving in an unusual pattern and it looked like it was about to rain. The wind was blowing the bushes and making a sweeping noise. He said to himself, "There's going to be a storm." Too tired to go back inside, he sat on the bleachers at the track field, and began to smoke a joint.

Cleabo really started to relax now; he was ready for the world. He remembered Speed telling him to practice his rope routine, so he left the schoolyard to go home and try to find his old rope. He looked in all his closets but there was no rope. He knew it was time to get another one anyway. While walking down the street trying to find a rope, he noticed some guys painting on a building. They had a long piece of rope hanging down the side of the building. He tied one end off so that they couldn't come down, and he cut the other end off. One of them saw him and said, "Hey, kid! What the hell you doing?" Cleabo ran with the rope in his hands. With the heavy rope he made some knots and practiced repelling, mountain climbing, and a few other tricks. He tied the rope on top of his building's roof and with another rope on his body he was able to get off the roof in a matter of seconds.

He would practice everyday after school, waiting on the moment of truth. A week went by before he received a call from Speed. Speed told him to meet him at Grand Concourse at six thirty p.m. He went down to Interval Avenue to catch the number two train. When Cleabo arrived at Grand Concourse he didn't see Speed. Instead, he felt something stick him in his back and someone said, "Give me your money or your life."

"I don't have enough money to die for, but then again I'm tired of living. Just the other day I was trying to figure it out; should I jump off the roof I was standing on?"

Cleabo quickly dropped to his knees and with a sweeping motion he grabbed the gun and looked up to see that it was Speed.

"Hold up! Hold up, kid! It's me, Speed! Not a bad move, not bad, but it was a little slow. Moves like that may work on those street thugs, but not on these professional hoods that we're going up against."

"Speed, I'm ready for them," Cleabo insisted. "I knew who you were. If I didn't, I would have been a fool for making a move like that. Just because you are dressed up like an old man doesn't mean that I didn't recognize you. So what's up, man?"

"I've been working in Manhattan as a janitor, my cousin gave me an inside tip on a deal that is going down. I have to get rid of the janitor that works in the building where we are going. I have to take his place and I need you to do something for me."

"Sure, Speed what is it?"

"I want you to get some thin metal piano key wire, the thinnest kind they have. I forgot the name of the wire, but you know what I'm talking about."

"Yeah, Speed." Cleabo said nodding his head affirmatively. "I know what you are talking about."

"Then, Cleabo," Speed told him, handing him a small slip of paper. "I want you to go to this address in Manhattan and set up a car bomb on a white and red Pontiac. You'll see it; it's parked on the street. This has to be done between twelve and one o'clock tonight. Let me know when it's done. I have to filter my way in tomorrow but I need the person who drives that car out of my way."

"Hey, Speed, what time does this person go to work?" Cleabo asked as he tucked the piece of paper in a pocket.

"Around seven thirty in the morning."

"I'll come back then to make sure that it's done."

"No, you don't have to. I've got to make sure that it's done before I can go inside, so I'll look out and make sure. You just get the job done! Okay?"

"Okay, Speed. I'll take care of it." Cleabo told him, sounding more confident than he actually felt. Speed went off to take care of more business, and Cleabo went to the subway station and caught the train back home.

On the train Cleabo felt like he was getting into some real heavy Mafia business. He kept his eyes open, assuming trouble might come his way. He always felt uncomfortable riding on a train that didn't have any trash or at least a newspaper thrown on the floor, or some graffiti on the walls.

Cleabo went to the music store and obtained the metal piano key wire, then he went home and thought about what he had to do. He knew he had to find a place to hide out and then scope the area out. That meant he had to leave early. By nine thirty everyone was in bed at his house, so he crept out of the house and caught the train. He exited the train at 125th street; downtown Harlem. There were a lot of people out on the streets and some of them were hookers. It was kind of hard finding the house, but sure enough, the car was sitting in front of the house just like Speed had said.

Cleabo had become so cold-hearted, he really didn't care about innocent people being hurt after the explosion; but, there were too many people on the streets to make the connection without being seen. He couldn't do the job right then, he had to wait. While he was trying to figure out where to wait, it dawned on him. Perhaps a poolhall, he thought. Across the street and down from his mission, was a small poolhall. He went across the street and walked into this low life poolhall.

Everyone there looked at him like he was a kid. Cleabo grabbed a stick and said, "Who's next?"

One gentleman said, "It sure ain't you, sonny! It's past your bedtime, isn't it?"

"Sir, I don't have no bedtime. All I know is this wooden stick. This is how I make my living, and all the education I have is in my hands. Would you like to get educated?" When Cleabo said that some people at the bar said, "Whoooooooo!"

"Sonny, you know who you're talking to? That's Rodney, one of the best pool players in Harlem," the lady at the bar said.

"Lady, my name is Cleabo Jones and I'm the best in the Bronx. I'm just here visiting my cousins, they go to bed too early for me. I've been racking balls since I been eight years old, and I know that I can make this cue ball dance when I want it to. Mr. Rodney you come down here and get you some of this." Cleabo put twenty dollars on the table.

Rodney stepped down off the barstool and sauntered to the table. "Give me two beers and bring them to the table. This boy here is trying to wear men's shoes." Rodney said.

He was a man about to burst with self-confidence and pride. He could hardly believe the audacity that Cleabo demonstrated and he liked it, but wasn't going to let it stop him from taking the boys money.

"Boy," he said to Cleabo, "I have wrestled alligators and trained snakes and I'm just going to have to take your little bit of money. Rack those balls and rack them well; I'm going to send you back to the Bronx with a story to tell. You came in this joint with your lips running out of socket, now I want you to watch this damn 8-ball go in the side pocket!"

Everyone in the joint started laughing and somehow Cleabo knew that he had to retaliate, so Cleabo looked at the crowd and responded in kind.

"It's nice to see you're a shithouse poet, but I'm going to put an ass whipping on you so bad that the whole world will know it."

The lady at the bar said, "Ohoooo, I heard that, young blood! Let's see it." Rodney and Cleabo shot for about an hour but they could only break even and talk noise to one another.

Time was running out and Cleabo knew he had to make his move on the car.

Rodney said, "Hey, kid! You're different, aren't you? I mean you're not the average kid, are you?"

Cleabo said, "No, and I have a mission so I have to go. It's been nice."

Rodney made a point of shaking Cleabo's hand.

"All right. You be easy, little brother." Rodney told him.

Cleabo went back across the street and checked out everything. It was getting close to the time to set the car up for the explosion. He knew that he had to do it quickly and there wasn't that much light except for the street lights. He slowly walked over to the car, then looked both ways to see if anyone was watching. A lady came by walking her dog.

"What the hell is she doing walking a dog this time of the night?" Cleabo mumbled to himself; as he waited impatiently for her to pass by. After she was gone from sight, he crawled underneath the car and began to sabotage it. He connected the thin metal piano key wire to the starter, and the other end to the fuel tank, knowing that when someone started the car it would blow up instantly.

Everything went well. He made a solid connection and it was now time for him to get the hell out of there. The connections were important. If they weren't properly connected the car wouldn't blow up. Cleabo was back on the subway and headed home. He arrived there around three o'clock a.m. Speed had told him that he would make sure it was done, so Cleabo went on to school that next morning. All day long he thought about someone getting into the car and it just blowing up. After school he heard over the radio about a car blowing up in Manhattan hospitalizing a man and killing a dog that was walking by. The dog's owner received minor injuries. Cleabo felt bad about what he had done. He knew he had to do it though, if he didn't Speed would have probably had him killed. He was pleased the man didn't die.

A week went by and Cleabo heard through the grapevine that Speed was back and wanted to see everyone at seven thirty that evening. He went home that night and ate his super fast, and told his mother that he would be right back.

"Whoa son," Sara stopped him, "Where are you going?" she asked.

He was shocked, but answered in a steady voice, "Mom, are you really asking me where I'm going?"

She said, "Yes. I know it's a trip, but I'd like to know."

"Momma," Cleabo hedged, "It's like this. Ugh..." words failed him and he just stood there staring at her.

"That's all right," Sara said, deciding she didn't really want to know after all, "Just get on out of here and don't hang out too late."

"Yes ma'am." Cleabo answered, grateful to escape.

It was a short walk to Speed's house, everyone else was already there when he arrived. "Come on in, young blood," Speed welcomed him in. "That was a nice job you did, worth it's weight in gold."

"Yeah, Cleabo. It was real professional," added Tony.

Cleabo didn't know how Tony knew about the deal, he thought that only Speed knew. Speed had a chalkboard and he was mapping out what everyone would be doing.

"Hey, you guys. Listen up! By now I hope that all of you are ready. The deal will go down tomorrow night. We're going to have to use precision timing." Speed continued.

"PeeWee," he began giving the orders like a general planning a war. "I want you to steal a car, one that is dependable, and meet us at the corner of 138th and Lenox at six o'clock. Larry; I want you to have two hand grenades and make sure they work. Cleabo; I want you to carry two ropes and bring two walkie-talkies with you. Come to think of it," he added, swinging his eyes around to include them all, "Everybody bring two walkie-talkies. I'll set them all on the same frequencies." While Speed talked, he walked up and down the room on the hard wood floor. He paced so much Cleabo wondered why he hadn't dug a hole in it.

Speed continued, "Everyone will take a different train and meet at the corner of 138th and Lenox by the Bathhouse. Bring .45s. Cleabo, I want you to have a sawed off, twelve gauge with you. Dress in black and bring a ski mask. Wear sneakers and bring everything you think you might need. We are going to go to this place where a major drug deal will be taking place. Some of the people there are from out of town and some are from Queens, Brooklyn, and even the Bronx," Speed said as he continued with his briefing and his pacing.

"At six thirty we should be at their doorstep. There will be a guard at the front door. Larry, you will cause a distraction to bring him to the glass door." He paused for a moment as he thought. "Make it a fire or something, but nothing loud. I guess you guys are wondering how I know where everyone will be. I'll tell you. Cleabo, that car that you set up was the janitor's who works there. They were paying him off to keep his mouth shut. I took his place as the janitor, and in a week's time I found out where everything is. Those guys don't trust me, but I'm not going to help them mothers out one single bit. I need to get mines just like they're getting theirs."

"After the distraction, when the guard comes to the door, Larry, I want you to take one shot and one shot only. If you miss, the deal may be off; we'll have to see. Once we are inside, then we can go for broke; but if you miss there is going to be a whole lot of shooting that we really don't need. Got it?"

Larry nodded to show he understood and Speed continued his military dialogue.

"Larry, I want your shot to be silenced. I'm going to get some silencers, but in the event that I can't, you can use a potato, so bring some with you. Once Larry has taken the first guard out, he will take the first position to the right behind the wall. Slim you will take the left side and I will come in with my back turned toward the door, so cover my back."

"Down the hall there will be a door. Tony, you run and open it; I'll leave it unlocked. The guard down the steps will hear you open it and hopefully he'll come up to check it out. If he don't, I'll throw something down the hall to get his attention. By that time, I want you to cross the hall and go into the room directly across from the one you opened and the first voice you hear, that's when I want you to take the guard out."

"You see, the second guard is going to come up when he hears the door open, but in the event that he doesn't, then we will have two guards to take out on those steps. Tony, when you hear me say something, that means that the guard is at the door. If he doesn't come up, Larry you better be one hell of a knife thrower, because you are going to have to take both of them out. Larry, you'll have to kill the guy at the bottom of the stairs and the guard at the door. But don't worry, I will be there with you to shoot one of them. I just don't want any noise. I want to get in and get out." Speed continued.

"When the guard is at the door, Tony, you should take him out with one shot. From that point on, we only have one guard to deal with. Larry and I should be close beside you. Take the lead and Slim, you cover the rear the entire time. When you are in front of the steps, the guard will see you and will probably be reaching for his piece. Larry you have got to throw a knife into or close to his heart."

"At that time, I will run down the steps along with Tony and Slim; Larry you follow. At the bottom of the steps, Cleabo, I will tell you by walkie-talkie when to hit it. Cleabo, I want you to swing from the other side of the building and come through the glass and fire your shotgun at the first person that moves. When I hear the glass break, we'll be coming in at the same time. I will not call you unless we are ready to come in. Trust me." Cleabo nodded, he was in all the way.

"When we go in we will be facing a round table. Some of the people, or should I say most of the people, will be armed. Tony, I want you to take the left side, and Larry you take the right. I'll be in the center, and Cleabo wherever you land you be ready to make some noise. PeeWee, you be cool and the first shot you hear you pull in the alley where Cleabo is going to swing from. I will put both of you into position."

"If everything goes as planned, we will be in and out of there in eight minutes. If something goes wrong we will have to react on instinct. I want this to go smoothly. We will drop the car off at Flushing Meadows in Queens. Each of us will travel separately back to the Bronx. Come directly to my house. Tony, you and Cleabo stay close to each other, but pretend you don't know one another. Cleabo, you will have all the money or dope, whichever it may be. All of it's money to me. Now, do anyone have any questions?"

"Yeah, Speed, what the hell is up with you?" PeeWee said. "What if there are more guards or people there? Or if something goes wrong, what are we supposed to do then?" PeeWee asked, sure they would all be killed.

"Baby, life is a chance!" Speed answered quickly. "What I'm offering you guys is success!"

Slim was in. "All right, let's do it!" he said enthusiastically.

Tony asked, "Are you in, PeeWee? You don't sound certain."

PeeWee said reluctantly, "Yeah, I guess so, just put a joint in my mouth when you bury me."

That night, after hearing the whole deal, Cleabo really started to concentrate on what he wanted out of life. He knew it was too late for him to back out of the deal now. He knew that if he tried, Speed would have him killed for knowing too much. He knew for a fact that if he didn't show up they wouldn't go through with the plan. They couldn't; he was a key player.

Cleabo couldn't sleep at all that night. He had dreams about busting through the window and all of those guys had their guns pointed at him, waiting for him to enter. All kinds of crazy thoughts were running through his mind. He started thinking about his grandfather. He knew his grandfather wouldn't want him doing this thing. Putting his life on the line made him realize what life was really about. But, Cleabo knew he had to go through with it. He couldn't let anyone see that he was scared, it wasn't good for his image. He was one of the toughest kids on the block and he couldn't back down from the deal of the century.

Daylight hit him smack in the face and somehow he hoped God would be with him, even though he knew God wasn't going to be with him, especially when he would be doing something wrong. He would probably have to take someone's life, so he knew that God couldn't be with him. Cleabo thought to himself, "So this is what you get when you are trying to be tough." At this point he didn't want to be tough. He just wanted to live a normal life like any kid his age, but it was too late now. Like the old people would say, you made your bed, now it's time for you to lie in it.

Later that afternoon Cleabo began to get all of his gear together to meet Speed and the crew. He had on a backpack and a twelve-gauge shotgun at his side, covered by his long coat.

For the first time in his life he felt comfortable getting on the train. He didn't care if anyone tried to rob him. He would've just blown them away with the twelve gauge shot gun. While he was on the train he felt like he was going up against a firing squad, the kind where you have your last cigarette before hand.

Cleabo started thinking about the girls in his past when some girls entered the train, one of them was as fine as hell. He wanted to rap to her, but he didn't have the time. She just smiled at him and he returned the gesture.

When he exited the train he had about two blocks to walk. Speed and the boys were sitting on the corner talking. He noticed the car that PeeWee had stolen, and Speed told him to get in; the other fellows followed. Speed briefed everyone of their duties again inside the car while Pee Wee stood outside on watch. He showed Cleabo his position and pointed at the window he wanted him to enter.

Speed, Larry, Tony and Slim walked to the back of the car, then Speed turned around and said. "Now you be careful, Cleabo, and wait for my signal. Don't worry. I think that everything will go pretty smooth."

Cleabo said "Okay," but he was scared.

"Are you scared, Cleabo?" PeeWee asked him, looking at him closely.

"PeeWee, right now I feel like I'm about to have a fight. My stomach is turning and my toes are twitching, but I know that I've got to do good because if I don't someone will get killed." Cleabo said at a low tone. Cleabo was nervous, he asked PeeWee for one of his cigarettes to calm his nerves. After a few puffs he threw it on the ground.

"Let me get to my point."

"Okay, I'll be here in the car on the look out and waiting for you guys, be cool." Pee Wee said, as he looked around the alley impatiently.

From the roof of the adjacent building he tied one end of the rope, then a spare rope in case his swing rope broke. With the spear gun from his back pack he shot the spear and a rope to the other roof top. After pulling on the rope, he ensured himself there was a good connection. He put on his body harness that had a reel of rope, then he made the necessary adjustment to enter the target window, by reeling into it. His reel was at his mid-section, and the roller was connected to the horizontal rope, stretching from one building to another. Cleabo had to swiftly reel from the building across from where the heist was to take place. His walkie-talkie was at his side along with the twelve gauge shot gun. He stood on the windowsill impatiently, waiting on Speed to call. Then, before he knew it, it was happening. He heard Speed say, "Now! Hit it!"

Cleabo reeled through the air, broke the glass, and landed behind the round table, firing one round from the shotgun, and splattering the glass table that was in the small break area. Simultaneously, Speed, Larry, and Tony came in, while Slim walked in backwards with his weapon, protecting the rear. The only thing that didn't go as planned was the man standing over at the coffeepot at the other side of the room; the rest of them were sitting down. When Cleabo came crashing in the man reached for his gun to blow Cleabo away. But Speed saw it and shot the man. Speed turned around and said, "Don't move!" he looked at Larry and said, "Get his gun! Keep your hands up and walk to the center of the floor. Lay face down on the floor; spread your arms and legs out," demanded Speed. "Time?"

Slim was at the door and he said. "Four minutes." Speed directed Tony to get their wallets and he told Cleabo to pick up all of the coke, heroin and the money that was on the table.

"You'll never get away with this," a man on the floor said.

Speed said, "We sure as hell going to try, now shut the hell up! Time?"

Slim said, "Six minutes."

"Let's go!" shouted Speed.

Cleabo had never seen Speed so nervous in his life; he made Cleabo look cool. When Tony collected their wallets he also disarmed them and put all of their pieces into his backpack. Cleabo connected the rope with the knots in it to come down from the second floor landing. Slim was the first out of the window. Larry quickly wired up a grenade to the door so that if anybody tried to open the door it would blow up. Once the grenade was put into place the slightest touch would set it off. Tony went out of the window next. Cleabo was still holding the shotgun.

Larry shouted at the men on the floor, "If any of you try to open this door the whole room will be blown away and don't come to the window until you are sure that we are gone, because I will be shooting at the first person I see." Larry climbed out the window, then Tony and finally Cleabo with Speed right behind them. When they made it to the car, a man looked out of the window and Speed shot at him using a silencer and the man went back inside.

"They know what kind of car we have;" Speed said, "We have got to ditch it. PeeWee be careful!" he shouted as PeeWee swerved too fast around a corner. They all had to change clothes in the car, Cleabo felt relieved after taking off his ski mask.

"PeeWee, I want you to drop Larry, Slim, and myself off at the bus stop. The bus will be coming in about two minutes, if it's on schedule. Slim and Larry, from this point on we travel like we don't even know each other, understand?" Speed directed his men again.

"PeeWee, I want you to take Tony and Cleabo to the subway station around the corner after you drop us off. The number two train will be coming in five minutes. Make that train. We will rendezvous at my house. I have a key and there is one under the mat, then take the car to Flushing Meadows. Get yourself a bottle of wine and go to my house, knock twice at the door when you get there."

"Okay Speed. Damn! We did it!" PeeWee said excitedly.

"It's not over yet, not until the fat lady sings." Speed said.

Slim said, "Well I can hear the bitch humming now."

Tony and Cleabo knew that they still had a journey ahead of them carrying all of the money, dope, and artillery. Tony and Cleabo made it to the subway station and as Speed said, the number two train was coming. They were on their way back to the Bronx. Tony stayed eye distance away from Cleabo. The train ride was long, but they made it back with no problems. They went to Speed's place and used the spare key and waited impatiently. Finally they heard a key in the door. It was Speed, Larry, and Slim.

All of them started hugging each other, saying "We did it! We did it!"

"Hey Speed, how long you think it's going to take PeeWee to get here?" Tony asked.

"I don't know, maybe another forty minutes, just enough time to see what we came out with."

Speed hugged them again, "Maybe we have enough to sit back and retire Cleabo! You are kind of young to retire though, aren't you?"

"Hey, Speed the way I feel right now," Cleabo told him feeling great relief it was over, "I'm going to retire regardless how much we have. I don't ever want to do this again."

Everyone started laughing. Speed weighed out the dope and counted the money. He said that it was $150,000 in cash and about $75,000 worth of dope at street value.

Slim said, "Damn, we hit the jackpot and that's a lot of dope!"

"Yeah, and I can't get rid of it here. I have to go some place far away, and you know a hit like this is going to make a whole lot of people dry. So, there is going to be a lot of talking on the streets, so keep your ears open and mouth shut." Speed said seriously.

"I will probably have to go to California to get rid of this smack. Here is what we are going to do. I'm going to give each of you $25,000 and I'll take some of my money to pay for the trip. We have trusted each other so far, I'm sure that you can trust me to make this transaction and come back. I'll be back in about a week."

Everyone said, "Yeah, Speed, we trust you."

"Hey, man," interjected Cleabo. "We have no choice but to trust you and if you try to do something stupid, I don't think you want us to come looking for you after what you have taught us. We are now the Magnificent Five," he added laughing.

Everyone started laughing again and Speed said, "Don't laugh too hard, the fifth one isn't back yet."

Soon as Speed said that there were two knocks at the door.

Larry said, "Hey, right on time."

It was PeeWee. "Hey! Let me in, man. It's cold as hell out here! What's up? How are we looking?"

Slim said, "Brother man, we are looking real good. We have a yard and a half big ones and seventy five-G's worth of smack, maybe one hundred worth if it's cut right."

PeeWee said, "Oh, yeah? No shit? Damn, give me some now, I could use a toot or two."

"Hell, no! That smack's not getting touched!" Speed shouted.

"Come on Speed, after what we been through, you should give me some, just a toot or two."

"Man, I'm giving you twenty five-G's to sit on until I unload the smack."

Tony said, "Hey Speed, we've been through a lot today. Let's relax a little. If Pee Wee wants a little smack, why don't you let him have some."

"You know, you are right." Speed said, relenting some. "I've been kind of uptight and we need to relax a little." Speed changed the subject but giving into PeeWee. "Hey, did you see the look on that guy's face when we came in? It looked like his whole world had ended."

Tony laughed. "Yeah, it looked like all the money he had was tied up into that dope. His wife is sho gonna kick his ass!"

Speed gave PeeWee some of the white powder and he started snorting it in his nose. Speed warned them to keep a low profile because the streets would be dry and the word couldn't get around about what had went down.

Everyone then left Speed's house and Cleabo felt $25,000 richer. Speed said that he would get back with them in a week. Cleabo felt pretty cool about the money. It was a lot of money, especially for a young boy to have. He went to a few stores and bought some new clothes, but he was careful; he didn't want to purchase extravagant items that would lead to a compromising situation. After all, the entire neighborhood knew that his family wasn't well off.

One day, soon after the heist, Cleabo was walking past the park and noticed how PeeWee was flaunting a lot of cash while shooting dice. He thought to himself, "Look at that fool. Speed said to be cool and stay out of sight, but PeeWee is just acting a fool, showing off his money to everyone." Cleabo had also heard that PeeWee was throwing a party.

Cleabo thought to himself. "Damn, I have to go to this party and talk some sense into this guy's head!"

That night he dressed himself to impress by putting on some of his new clothes and he went to PeeWee's party. There were masses of people there, the party was congested. A young lady named Jeanie approached Cleabo and said that PeeWee had some good powder; surprising since it was so hard to find right now. It was difficult to find PeeWee in the thick smoke filled apartment. Finally, he caught sight of him and PeeWee was out of control. Cleabo knew he had to get him away from the crowd of females that were gathered around him like vultures.

Cleabo called PeeWee off to the side and calmly said, "What are you doing, Pee Wee? Don't you know you are showing off too much? The other day I saw you gambling with a lot of cash in the park and now the party? You are really going overboard. Speed said to be cool!"

"Hey, Cleabo, relax! Everyone is so uptight. Let's just relax and unwind."

"PeeWee I was there! I know what's happening!"

"Yeah, and I was there too, so be cool!" their conversation was escalating and some people started looking at them. Larry came over and said, "Hey! You two are getting kind of loud."

Cleabo told Larry, "Maybe you can talk some sense into him. He has been loud and now this party. He's blowing our cover. Just look at that ho over there," he pointed at a female drinking out of a bottle in a brown paper bag. "Ain't never had nothing and probably never will. This is a low lifer's party and I'm not going to be a part of it!"

Cleabo grabbed his jacket and left, saying to himself, "If Speed was here, PeeWee wouldn't be acting like this." At the front door of the building he ran into an old friend named Cynthia. "Hi, Cleabo," she said with an inviting smile.

"What's up?" Cleabo answered, eyeing her quickly.

"Oh, nothing much, I haven't seen you in a long time. Where have you been?" "Nowhere." He said, "Just hanging loose."

"Nice party, isn't it?" Cynthia asked, then she laid a hand on Cleabo's arm and stroked it gently. "I'm glad PeeWee is throwing this party. We haven't had a party like this one in a long time."

Cleabo said, "I guess you're right." The more he looked at Cynthia the better she looked, and he was getting her message clearly. He hadn't made love to a young lady in quite sometime, so it must have been time; for sure he was long overdue.

It wasn't long before they were at her parent's place. Her parents were out of town, and Cynthia always took advantage of that; when she could. Cynthia liked to ride on top when she made love. Her favorite position was to be held by her small waist line while she rode, her movements while she made love to him were like she was mounted on a horse.

Cleabo complied to her wishes and caressed her in the heat of passion until they both reached total fulfillment. After ecstasy was achieved they looked at each other, and they both knew sharing a moment like this would never occur again; but the memory would always remain. She asked him to see her the next day, but he never did.

Two days later he met Tony. He said that Speed was back and wanted to see them at seven o'clock that night. Cleabo said he'd be there, he could hardly wait for seven o'clock to come. He was pacing the floor so much that his mother told him to get the hell out of the house.

It was around four thirty when he left. When he was coming around the corner of Dawson Street he saw a gray van going into the park. Sensing something may be wrong, he squatted down and stayed out of sight. He watched as three men jumped out of the back of the gray van wearing ski masks and armed with machine guns. The entire park cleared out when they saw the men holding machine guns. Larry, Tony, Slim and PeeWee were there. The three gunman pointed their weapons at Larry, Slim and Pee Wee and told them to get up against the wall and asked where Tony was. Tony was about to run but they caught him and shoved him against the wall. Then the men asked where were the others, a Speed and a Cleabo.

"I don't know," Tony told the men. Tony was still trying to uphold his gangster type image in front of the little kids that were looking from across the street, anticipating their brutal murder.

PeeWee started spilling his guts. He said, "Hey man, let me go, please! I'll tell you everything."

The gunman said, "We don't need your help!"

The masked men then gunned them down; their bodies splattering against the wall from the piercing bullets that echoed the sound of death as they ricocheted off of the wall. Cleabo turned around and ran like a rabbit. He ran to Speed's house to let him know what had happened.

When he arrived at Speed's, the door was open. All he did was push on it and he saw Speed in a chair with a bullet in his head, and a stream of blood running down the side of his neck. There was no sign of a robbery, so he knew that it had to have been a professional hit and they'd probably be looking for him. Subsequently, he knew he had to move quickly. Regardless of the money he had stashed away at home, he had to go and he knew it had to be at that second.

Cleabo had to run with the clothing he had on, and the little money that was in his pockets. He searched Speed's pockets to see if he had any cash. He thought that whoever shot him wasn't interested in his wallet. Speed had a little over $300, Cleabo took it.

While taking the money from Speed's wallet he looked at him for the last time. Speed had his eyes open and it looked like he was trying to tell Cleabo to run as fast as possible, and that's what he did.

CHAPTER VII

KIND OF HOT GOT TO RUN

Port Authority Bus Terminal in Manhattan hadn't changed. He was frightened by the large terminal when he first came to New York and now he was scared as he was leaving. The first bus he saw was to Atlanta. Cleabo said to himself, "Look out Georgia, here I come."

The bus was standing room only and smoke filled from the people in the back that were smoking reefer. He pretended to be in his own little world. Darkness began to set as he started thinking, "Who do I know in Georgia?" he questioned himself. "Not a damn soul," he answered. Then he remembered his grandmother, she had left New York a few years ago. "Maybe I can go stay with her a little while," he thought.

So he changed his plans. "Momma would feel much better knowing that I was at grandma's," he thought.

The bus arrived in Washington, D.C. and the atmosphere there made him feel like he was still in New York. He started thinking about those guys being splattered on the wall and the look on Speed's face. "What a waste," he thought, "Trying to be somebody the hard way; living life in the fast lane."

There was a thirty minute break in D.C.; he was trying to relax from all of the killing that had just gone down earlier. It was difficult to rest; the thoughts of his friends being massacred in such a manner made Cleabo feel so uneasy.

Cleabo knew that a town like D. C. had to have a liquor store near by. He needed a drink. Cognac was his favorite liquor, so he had to find a store. He found one on the corner across from the bus terminal.

Cleabo went inside the place and initially the cashier didn't want to sell him the alcohol because he looked too young. However, this was D.C. and when Cleabo waved a twenty dollar bill in the man's face as a tip, the man said, "What the hell! I can use that kind of a tip!" Cleabo knew that D.C. was his kind of town.

When he walked out of the store, he turned around and looked behind him. There were two guys holding a knife to a man's throat. It was the same man that was in front of him in line at the liquor store.

D.C. reminded him of the Bronx. He walked back to the bus terminal and recovered his seat on the bus.

"Damn, it must be my lucky day. I didn't get killed and now on the bus here is a pretty girl sitting in the seat next to mine."

A lot of lowlifes had entered the bus in D.C. and they smelled bad. Now, he knew why his mother always tried to keep him and his two brothers clean. He sat down next to the girl and he began to converse with her. Cleabo tried to throw one of those gangster raps on her, as his voice became deeper and smoother. Kihisha was the young lady's name. Her hair was kind of dry and braided in the dread-lock fashion. He later learned that she was a revolutionist of some sort. Kihisha generated the conversation and she seemed to be well educated. Her conversation was geared around the differences between the whites and the blacks, but Cleabo's mind was on getting away from the people that he had ripped off. He took a big hit from the Cognac he bought; it really relaxed him and calmed his nerves.

Kihisha took out a joint and said, "Here, my brother. You look like you need some of this." Cleabo's face lighted up like a Christmas tree. It seemed like the more they smoked the more she talked about the struggle and the depression of people. The way she talked had a certain poise. Kihisha was so sophisticated that he began to understand the psychological part of her conversation.

Kihisha said to him at one point, "Cleabo, you see that star and you know what a tree looks like. A tree is bigger than the star with the naked eye, even though scientists have taught us that the star is bigger. Therefore, things that we see may be an illusion by sight until we learn differently."

Hearing that, he grabbed his Cognac bottle and turned it up, thinking that this girl was crazy. Cleabo managed to fall asleep after sipping on the Cognac. Virginia was Kihisha's stop, she was going to visit her grandparents. When she stepped off the bus, he noticed again how fine she was. She told him to look her up and he said he would if he could. He knew that he could have picked up Kihisha, however, time didn't prevail. For some reason he never had any problems being a ladies man; it seemed like he always did the right things and they would come on to him.

The bus arrived in Orangeburg, South Carolina. It was cold and the station was closed. In the city all he needed was his three quarter length leather jacket to keep warm. He didn't have any bags, only his Cognac bottle to keep him warm and it was stuffed down his pants next to his belt.

There weren't any cabs in sight to take him to his grandmother's house. Around the corner from the bus station there was a telephone that he could use to call an all night cab station. There was an advertisement at the bus station with the number to the cab company on it. When he called it seemed like it wasn't a cab company. It was more or less some guy at his home trying to make a dollar. It sounded like the person answering the telephone was in bed. He told Cleabo in a sleepy tone of voice that he would be there in five minutes. The five minutes turned into thirty and he still needed a ride.

While waiting for the cab he looked around to see if he could see anyone on the street. The streets were empty and the wind was blowing harder. He kept seeing police cars go by every so often and he hoped they wouldn't stop. He read somewhere how the country policemen always tried to harass people in the south late at night when they were all alone. He wasn't in any mood to be hassled. At this point of time, he knew that he would retaliate if the police tried to harass him.

Some college kids drove up across the street from the bus station. One of them exited the car and went inside his house. The other two guys stayed in the car and began to eyeball Cleabo. Cleabo thought that maybe he could get a ride from these guys.

He walked over to their car and said, "Hey, can you give me a ride?"

The driver looked at the other guy like they hit the jackpot, but Cleabo was ready for anything that could've gone down with these two guys.

"The damn bus took all of my money, can you guys give me a ride?"

"Are you from here?" one of the guys asked.

"Yes and no. I came to live with my grandmother. I just left New York and as you can see, I don't have any bags. I guess you can say I left in a hurry, you know what I mean?"

"Yeah man, sometimes you just have to travel light. We know the deal." The driver said as he nodded his head up and down.

Cleabo looked at the two guys and he remembered how Speed taught him how to read people. These guys had the expression of being scared of Cleabo on their faces, but they realized that it was two against one so they said, "What the hell? Get in man."

Cleabo sat in the back and the reefer they had smelled good to him; he took a few hits off of it. They were drinking a quart of beer, so he pulled out his Cognac and saw their eyes light up, so he shared it with them. They mellowed out and took him straight to his grandma's house. He knocked on the door numerous times and finally she opened the door. "I've come to live with you grandma, is that okay?"

"Child, let me look at you!" Grandma Sadie Bell exclaimed on seeing Cleabo. "Your Momma know where you are?" she asked suspiciously.

"No ma'am, I'm going to call her.

"I'll be, you in some sort of trouble, aren't you?"

"Just a little bit grandma, but I'll be all right here."

Grandma Sadie Bell put some coffee on the stove and then she telephoned Cleabo's mother. She told Sara Cleabo was there and he was safe. The next day Grandma Sadie Bell outlined the work he had to do while he would be staying there. From the way it sounded, she had needed help for quite some time. Most of the work was chopping wood and things of that nature.

Grandma Sadie Bell told him to stay away from trouble and don't be 'nobody's fool.' Across the street lived the Johnstons; they had three girls. Cleabo fell in love with Pumpkin; she was the yelling baby. In other words, she was the second to be born. In the south the second child is called the yelling baby. His grandmother told him that the yelling baby would always cry out of jealousy when the mother picked up the first born and they would cry again when their mother picked up the youngest. The yelling baby needed more attention and most of the time they had to have things their way.

Pumpkin was a round-eyed, young girl with a nice figure. He treated her like she had a lot of class. Like the old saying goes, "Treat people like you would want to be treated," and that was how he treated her. Pumpkin was so remarkable that he never asked her to put out for him. She thought he was too scared to ask her to make love. Cleabo's reason for taking things slow with Pumpkin, was because he really fell head over heels over this young lady and he wanted to learn how to love from the heart. She became his girlfriend, but most of his time was spent on the basketball court. Perhaps he neglected her a little too much, because Pumpkin found another boyfriend by the end of the summer. Cleabo had no choice but to understand why. "I should have spent more time with her," he thought as he soaked in his sorrows over the first young lady he had truly loved.

Cleabo started school again that fall; he played on the basketball team and his style of basketball playing was different than the southerners. His athletic abilities were idolized by some of the basketball players and he made a great impression on the coach.

It was kind of hard for Cleabo to make the adjustment from the fast lane to the slow lane. Back home he seldom played any ball. It seemed like here in the south that was the only thing to do. Crime in the city was different than in Orangeburg. It seemed like the only people doing any crime were the lowlifes and he couldn't deal with them; they carried a bad rep.

The air in the south was different, it was kind of smoggy and sticky in the mornings. He also noticed that whenever he walked down the street, people would wave hi even if they didn't know him. Coming from the city he wasn't used to people waving hello to him. At first it was hard for him to understand why the people there would say hello to him when they greeted him, then continuously say hello to him during the course of the day. This was tediously stupid to him and he didn't want to be a participant of the great southern hospitality way. Cleabo refused to speak to a person more than one time in the course of the day.

After about a week, though, Cleabo realized that the people of the south were just trying to be friendly. He felt relieved to know that there were people that would speak to him with a smile on their face. He didn't miss the cold shoulder and the nasty look from the people in New York. Cleabo's mental attitude about people and life began to change.

His last two years of high school were difficult for him. The school's policy stated that all basketball players had to maintain a two point seven average. All of his classes were complicated to him, but he continued trying to apply himself. For hours at night after

123

basketball practice, he'd study until he would fall asleep at the kitchen table. Endlessly, he continued trying to study.

One night he had to do his History homework. Now, this was a subject that was agonizing to his brain. There was no way in the world he thought he could relate to it. He labeled the subject as being boring; he didn't realize that it was just laziness on his behalf. With all of the street knowledge Cleabo had, this subject wasn't sinking in no matter how determined he was. Cleabo felt like he was a victim of the "2 b bored" syndrome. He actually felt like he wasn't interested as fatigue began to step all over his body.

Perhaps he felt that he was too smart, but he couldn't see that ignorance was beating his head, like the raindrops thump on the top of a fool's head while he stands outside in the middle of a thunderstorm. Cleabo's head began to nod in a downward motion and bumped the kitchen table, leaving the lumps and bruises from an obvious fight between the thick history book and himself. He lifted his head and wiped the side of his face trying to disconnect that long string of saliva that was drooling out of the side of his mouth. He looked like a bulldog, with the lights on but with no one at home. Cleabo was sleepier than a wino in a Harlem version of Rip Van Winkle.

Anyway, that's when the strangest thing happened. Cleabo always heard of strange occurrences happening to people, but he never in his wildest dreams thought that he could be a participant in a bizarre event in his own home. In between nods and trying to stay awake, an indescribable mist appeared and made its home around his head.

Wrapped around his head like an Arab turban, it made him feel like it was a part of his inner self; he received vibes like this mist of a turban actually belonged to him at one point of his life. Cleabo was trapped within this bubble like mist that only he could see. He had no idea what was going on, but when the mist left, he felt relieved, in a state of contentment, with eagerness to learn any and everything he could get his hands on. Things that were boring before became stimulating. Learning was like a battle or a chess match and he wanted every challenge. Cleabo developed an obsession with the need for knowledge of everything.

Cleabo woke up one morning feeling fresh and well rested. The sound of the rooster's cock-a-doodle-doos was better than an alarm clock he thought. Unusually excited about going to school, this particular morning he dashed to the closet to put on his clothes.

Miss Smith, his English teacher had given his class homework the day before. The assignment was to write about something that influenced them and relate it to a part of history. Cleabo entered the classroom with his bookbag hanging off of his shoulder. Glimpsing at the females, he tried to catch an eye or two. The students were loud, which was normal until the second bell rang. Miss Smith was at her post, standing by the doorway in the hall. All of the teachers stood outside their doors in the hallway to monitor fights and to close the door when the second bell rang. Anyone trying to enter the classroom after the second bell was sent to detention. Their parents were notified whenever this happened. The second bell rang and Miss Smith shut the door.

"Good morning class." Miss Smith said. There was no response.

"I said good morning class!" shouted Miss Smith.

"Good morning Miss Smith," said the class, simultaneously.

"Now class, I know that I told you to have the assignment about *something that was a major factor in your life, and relate it to history,* turned in today. But, I have a surprise for you."

"What is it? We don't have to turn it in anymore?" asked Jimmy.

Jimmy sat in the back of the classroom. Most of the time he would make sarcastic remarks at the teacher or try to be funny. He was more or less the class clown. Although some of the things he said were smart and witty, it didn't help him any in the popularity contest at school. He was smart, however, he just needed to leave the comedy alone.

"Listen up class, I have thought of a fun way to start our day off. I have chosen three students to come to the front of the classroom and read their assignment to the class. The order that I call your name is the order you will come up. Maryland Digsbey, you are first. Carolyn Cobham you are second."

Cleabo's heart was beating fast at this point hoping that he wouldn't be called. It would be a total nightmare if he had to get up there and read his assignment. Cleabo was getting more nervous as Miss Smith hesitated with the last person's name and finally she spit it out of her mouth.

"Cleabo Jones."

Cleabo exhaled, thinking that she hadn't called his name and then he noticed that the entire classroom turned around and was looking at him. Now it had dawned on him that he had to read his assignment. His palms began to sweat as the anxiety of standing in front of the class set in. While the first student began to read her assignment Cleabo couldn't even hear what she was saying. His mind was strictly on his assignment and his nervousness. After the second student read her assignment it was Cleabo's turn. He wondered what everyone would think of him after he read his assignment, that was meant to be for the teachers eyes only. How embarrassing it would be if they disliked what he had written, he thought.

Cleabo stepped out of his chair and it seemed like he was walking in slow motion as he made his way to the front of the class. Looking down at his paper he cleared his throat and began reading.

"Hum, hum, something in my life that I can compare to history," he said hesitantly, then continued. *"My life has been full of ups and downs, in retrospect, I can see that I could've been a far better person than I am standing here today. Regardless, I think that it's never too late to change. Last night I worked on this simple homework for the longest. It wasn't difficult, all Miss Smith asked me to do was to basically express myself, and I wasn't used to doing that. Finally, my mind was able to relate to something that had happened in history, comparatively to something that happened to me in New York. The Quartering Act was the act that made it possible for the soldiers during the Civil War to help themselves to sleeping quarters at civilian's home. It was easy to relate this to a situation with Ned, the wino, in the Bronx. Ned would help himself to our fire escape as sleeping quarters. My mother didn't mind, she said he was a deterrent to burglars. Ned also considered himself to be the neighborhood philosopher.*

Ned once said, 'Sophistication without simplicity is nothing. Versatility is the key to growth. A person should be able to understand, adapt, and have empathy for the numerous levels of people in society; just be able to get along with people.' Those were influential words coming from a person that had been an outcast from society. I respected Ned. His speeches were explosive and generated a positive impact on my way of thinking. Ned's street words for research was to get what you need when you need it, and your problem will be solved. His words weren't of an extensive comprehensive level, but they were meaningful to me. The End. Thank you for listening."

"Thank you Cleabo, that was interesting," Miss Smith said.

Cleabo closed his notebook and began to walk back to his seat. It was obvious that some of the young ladies were impressed with Cleabo as they eyeballed him. He pretended he didn't notice the looks they were sending to him.

"Man that shit was heavy, give me some of what you've been smoking." Jimmy said humorously. Some of the class began to laugh at what Jimmy had said.

"Okay, let's simmer down! I'd like to thank the students for sharing their homework with us. I really enjoyed their stories. Cleabo, I need to talk to you at the end of class."

"Yes ma'am," Cleabo replied in a shallow tone of voice.

The bell finally rang and Cleabo almost forgot that he had to talk to Miss Smith. Miss Smith walked to the door, then she crossed the hall to get another teacher to cover her position as hallway monitor. Cleabo stood at her desk until she returned as the other kids exited the classroom.

Miss Smith was a nice looking teacher. In fact, she was more than that; nice looking would have been an understatement. She was fine. She always wore her hair up and it was straight with a couple of blond streaks; a northerner look for a black woman to Cleabo. She was always dressed to impress with her long creamy legs. Her eyes were light brown, and the color wasn't from fake contact lens either. With her unblemished skin and the way she pranced around the classroom, there wasn't a male student in the school that didn't want some of her. Everyday Cleabo would say to her in the absence of the other students, "Damn Miss Smith, you are so fine."

"Why thank you Mr. Jones," she would say.

But today was different. She said to see her after class. Cleabo knew she just wanted to talk to him about his assignment. Just the thought of getting into those drawers was a complete turn on to Cleabo. Having that creamy brown flesh all over his body would make him feel like the luckiest person in the world. Cleabo started thinking about having Miss Smith eyes looking up at him as she licked his hairy chest.

"Cleabo, what in the world are you thinking about!" shouted Miss Smith. "Boy it better not be what I think you're thinking about. Wipe that silly look off your face."

Cleabo just smiled as he realized she had beauty and she could also read facial expressions as well. Miss Smith sat down at her desk and began to talk.

"Cleabo, I want to talk to you about your assignment." Said Miss Smith, as she continued. "I thought that it was excellent how you were able to express yourself, your choice of words were powerful. But, I want you to know that you don't have to use big words to get a point across."

Cleabo noticed that while Miss Smith was talking to him he wasn't listening to a thing she was saying. The only thing that was on his mind was watching her. Miss Smith was rolling a pencil with one hand and with the other she was twisting a small portion of her hair. At the same time she was moving her legs sort of like working her knees back and forth and clinching her love nest from time to time. "Shit," he thought, "These are all the signs that Speed told me about when a woman wants to give you some; her body motion. He told me she won't come out and say it but she will show it. Damn! Miss Smith wants to give me some? If I try, I may get suspended. I know she's got free period now. Wonder where she want to do it at, the supply closet?" Cleabo began to daydream while Miss Smith was talking to him.

"Cleabo? Cleabo are you listening to me?" Miss Smith asked in a soft tone of a voice.

"What? Oh, I'm sorry Miss Smith, you are talking to me about my assignment, and my mind is on something entirely different."

"Cleabo, what are you thinking about? Maybe I can help you. After all, you are a senior now and this is my first year out of college. I think that I can relate to whatever is bothering you."

"Are you sure that I can talk to you about anything and it will be between us Miss Smith? I won't get into any trouble?"

"Yes, I'm sure. Your secret is my secret and we'll never tell anyone our secrets."

"Miss Smith, I've been thinking about you passionately."

"Oh, really?" she seemed to act unsurprised.

"Yeah." He responded in a soft tone voice.

Cleabo leaned toward Miss Smith and took his index finger and rubbed the side of her face by her ear and down to her neck. She gasped, and then closed her eyes as she breathed heavily now. Cleabo slowly rubbed his index finger across her smooth, rosy lips and she breathed harder. Suddenly, she grabbed his finger and slowly sucked it. He took his finger out of her mouth and kissed her, then she wrapped her arms around him and thrust her tongue into his mouth. While trying to stay as quiet as possible, she rose out of the chair hugging him and grinding her body on his.

Pulling and directing Cleabo to the supply closet, she turned the light on, and gave Cleabo a full view of her perfectly shaped body. She took off every piece of her clothing, right down to her birthday suit. Cleabo in return did the same. They didn't care; he was a senior and she was still young. With the light on, Cleabo noticed how perfect her body was in every way and it was the first time he had ever seen light brown pubic hair on a black woman. She kissed his entire body from head to toe and slammed his precious male organ inside of her and they stayed connected like two dogs in heat for the entire period. It was the best he had ever had. Miss Smith knew he kept their act a secret. She felt that Cleabo was the only one in her class mature enough to do something like that with. Cleabo felt that the gangster mentality is what always helped him to be so fortunate with situations like Miss Smith. In his dream, it only happened once and it was good enough for the both of them.

They knew that if they went back for seconds it wouldn't be a sign of maturity. Things would have probably gotten out of hand and most of the time that is when immaturity tends to step out. Stick and move, was the sign of a true player. Cleabo learned that from Speed and apparently Miss Smith thought the same way, in his dreams.

"Cleabo Jones!" Miss Smith shouted loudly.

Cleabo came back to reality when Miss Smith cracked his knuckles with the pencil she had been holding. Miss Smith leaned over closely with her beautiful eyes looking intently into his.

"Cleabo Jones," she said softly, but intensely. "You haven't heard a word I've said have you?"

Cleabo shook his head silently, knowing he could be in trouble, but still smiling over his delectable daydream. Miss Smith continued to eye him a minute longer, then she too smiled. Cleabo, as bad as he was, was too likable for her to remain angry with.

"Get out of here!" she told him and she watched his tall good-looking self rise slowly, still keeping the 'come on' grin on his face. She watched him as he walked to the door, and just before he exited she added, "You keep the good work up Cleabo!"

Cleabo sighed as he went out, "I'm trying to Miss Smith, I'm trying."

In the late part of his senior year, Cleabo and his friend Bernard decided to double-date to the prom. Bernard and Cleabo were physically similar in build and almost the same height. Like Cleabo, Bernard too lived with his grandmother. Finding a young lady to go to the prom wasn't a problem for Cleabo, although Bernard did run into some difficulties. Cleabo thought that this would be his last and perhaps his only prom he would get to attend. With that in mind, he wanted to do something different or unusual for this prom. He talked to Bernard and told him that he had decided to take two dates to the prom. Bernard flipped out, but promised to keep it a secret. Bernard and Cleabo picked up his first date at 5:00 p.m. He told the other young lady that he would pick her up at 9:00 p.m. sharp, but somehow he knew that he would be late. Cleabo believed that it was in a man's nature to be intentionally late picking up a date.

He had convinced Bernard to go to dinner with him and his date around five o'clock in the evening. Bernard said, "Cool, as long as we go by and pick up my date first."

After picking up Cleabo's first date, Christina, the four of them went out to dinner and then to the prom. Time wasn't on his side, he soon had to go get his other date. He told Bernard to keep Christina on one side of the gym, while he went and got Beverly and he would have her stashed on the other side of the gym. Bernard said, "Okay, cool." Cleabo told Christina that he was going to the bathroom, and then pick up something to drink. He dashed out the door with his expensive tuxedo on, arriving at Beverly's house at 9:15. When he arrived, he had to get the other corsage out of the trunk of the car.

Beverly looked gorgeous in her gown. He always wanted to take her on a date. Her parents gave him the normal parenting speech. Little did they know their daughter was a total sex freak. Rumors said that she made out with older men. Cleabo was feeling impatient, saying mentally, "Yeah, yeah, please, can we get this over with?" He knew that tonight was his night, but he didn't know which one he was going to impress the most. He knew for sure that the odds were in his favor getting lucky with either Beverly or Christina.

Cleabo couldn't keep his eyes off of Beverly. Thoughts of how his night would end were written all over his face. They arrived at the gym and he gracefully opened the door for her. Cleabo escorted her to one side of the gymnasium, knowing he had Christina on the other side.

Playing a double role became exhausting for him, and it finally came to an end. Christina followed him to the other side of the gymnasium. She made a big scene when she figured out what he was up to.

"What the hell is going on here?" she shouted when she saw Cleabo and Beverly together.

Christina started yelling and cursing and she slapped Cleabo one time as he was laughing. She told him to take her home or give her cab fare. He told her that he had spent all his money on her corsage and that all he could give her was some pennies. She called him every dirty name she could possibly think of.

"Pennies? You want me to tell you what you can do with your pennies? I'll take those pennies and stick them where the sun don't shine! Then I'll beat the living day lights out of you and that low class heifer!"

Then Beverly jumped into the fray, "No you won't, and who you calling a heifer? There is nothing between us but air and opportunity and I'm going to take the opportunity to whip you like you stole something!"

Christina swung at Beverly, but Beverly ducked the blow and then she rushed Christina knocking her to the floor, then she started punching her. Cleabo and Bernard pulled Beverly off of her as the crowd of people instantly started to form around the fight. Christina left; he never knew how she made it home. He tried his best to enjoy the rest of the prom. Puzzled that Beverly remained in his company, he thought that she must really like him, or was horny as hell.

Maybe she had some idea that he made preparations earlier that day for a hotel room and the thought of making out with him was on her mind. Cleabo didn't know what to think. One thing was for sure, she was getting pretty drunk from the spiked punch he kept feeding her.

The last song was being played, Cleabo's and Bernard's faces were glowing. Both of them couldn't wait until they would get to the hotel. In the south, the mind-set or mentality of a young man was that on prom night, a young lady was granting her permission to make love to her.

When they arrived at the hotel, Bernard and his date exited the car and went into the room he had rented earlier that day. Bernard's date apparently had been briefed on what was going on, and it seemed she was more anxious to get there than Bernard.

Cleabo watched as Bernard's date practically dragged him into the hotel room. He thought that Bernard was lucky for having a date that was so eager to engage in extra activities. Cleabo angled himself around in the driver's seat and placed his hand over Beverly's seat. He looked into her eyes, while in hope that she would be in compliance with what was going on.

Beverly was acting cool, she knew what he was up to. It was amazing how calm she was. Cleabo gazed into her sweet brown eyes as he moved closer to her and began to whisper into her ear.

He asked Beverly to come with him to the room he had for them. Beverly said no she wasn't going and told Cleabo to take her home. Cleabo tried to smooth-talk Beverly, telling her how much he liked her and would like for her to become his lady. He had paid for the room in full, and he was determined that something was definitely going to happen in there that night. When she said no again, Cleabo became extremely frustrated. He bolted out of his side, ran around to her side of the car and attempted to open her door. Beverly quickly locked the door before he could get to her side.

She began to laugh at Cleabo, as he made every attempt to open her door. She then locked his door, and he was completely locked out. Cleabo was really upset then. He knew that she couldn't drive, so she wasn't going anywhere. After an hour of sitting on the curbside, she finally opened his door, and he took her home in silence.

Beverly gave Cleabo a different perspective of treating a lady like a lady. She only went along with his program until she was able to get even, or conquer the situation.

Nevertheless, at such an early age, it was probably to his benefit; entering the unknown consequences of sexual excessiveness without the proper education of parenthood, could have been a terrible mistake for him. Times were changing and what was easy to do before, started getting difficult. Now he started thinking about what would have happened if a young lady became pregnant. His friend Bernard found out the hard way. Nine months later his prom date turned out to be a date forever and it ruined his life. Cleabo had felt his luck was running thin, but once again, he found himself escaping another scene that he definitely didn't want to be a part of. Life was a learning process for Cleabo.

Sara sent Cleabo the remainder of the stolen money to start college with. Cleabo told her where to find the money in his secret hiding place. Cleabo paid for two years of college, and bought himself a nineteen seventy six Cutlass Supreme. It was a cream color car with a half vinyl top. He then paid two years worth of rent on an apartment and moved out of Grandma Sadie Bell's house. Cleabo started to feel his independence, however, at the time he wasn't concerned with the idea of no income.

Cleabo's freshmen year of college was indeed a challenge for him. The work was harder than high school, therefore, applying himself was a must. His sophomore year was a wild year. Although he made good grades, the partying life was taking its toll on his body. Cleabo managed to get a job in the college cafeteria washing dishes. Unlike the other students that also worked there, he was paid under the table, the money wasn't applied to his tuition. Working at the cafeteria was enjoyable to him. The girls that wanted to date him would leave their numbers and a brief message to rendezvous on their trays for him to read. There were plenty of dates, especially since he had his own apartment and his own car. All he had to do was to take a girl to McDonalds and everything else was history.

He was considered by the guys to be a homeboy of Orangeburg; he knew where all the party spots were. Guys hung out at his apartment almost all the time, and while everyday became a party day, his study habits began to diminish.

One day while riding in his cream on beige Cutlass Supreme, he was cruising through downtown. It was pouring down rain when he passed the courthouse. While slowly driving down the street there was a nice looking female walking underneath her umbrella. After building up the courage to ask this nice looking female if she needed a ride, Cleabo rolled down the passenger window and yelled towards the girl of grace.

"Hey! Do you need a ride?" Cleabo said leaning out the window with his left hand still on the steering wheel.

"No thank you." She said as she smirked her lips, and continued to walk.

"Hey! I know you've been taught well and you shouldn't except a ride from strangers, that's cool. But, it is pouring down rain and I'm not going to bite you." Cleabo said eagerly, waiting on her next response.

She contemplated, then said, "Okay."

"Hey, what's your name? I'm Cleabo, Cleabo Jones. Girl, I'm not going to do nothing to you, but get you out of this rain. Come on!"

"Thanks," she said as she sat her umbrella on the floor. "My name is Angela, and thanks for the ride again.

Angela was five foot four and petite. Cleabo could easily tell she was fine. Her skin color was brown and her face was perfectly proportionate. The dimples when she smiled were complimented by the sheen of her black silky hair. Her figure was firm and displayed all the possibilities of being athletic. "She is as fine as they come," Cleabo thought, and Cleabo knew she felt like she was a complete package. Angela presented herself to be shy and quiet and he could easily tell she was a respectable girl.

"No problem, you're quite welcome. Where are you going?"

"I'm going on campus, if that's not out of your way." Angela said, holding her head up and finally establishing eye contact with Cleabo.

"Okay, no problem, what college?" he asked as if he didn't know. Cleabo knew all of the females on his campus.

"To S.C. State if you don't mind." Angela tilted her head in question.

"No baby, I'm right next door at Claflin College!"

"You are?" Angela responded showing some excitement, but, quickly composing herself. "What's your classification?" she asked.

"I'm a sophomore," Cleabo quickly answered. "And you?"

"I'm a senior and I'm the Homecoming Queen." Angela said, acting like she really didn't care about the title and wasn't insecure with her beauty. She left Cleabo with the notion that she was always in a beauty contest or being nominated for something. Cleabo sensed that being Miss Homecoming Queen, somehow didn't impress her. She seemed to be of regal stature with a seductive sexual mannerism.

"Yep, a senior." She turned again at Cleabo, with the sign of enjoyment from knowing that completion wasn't far a way. "I'll be glad when it's over."

"I hear you lady. Here we are." Cleabo turn into the college and waited for direction.

"Keep straight or turn left?" Cleabo asked, as he glance at her then downward to her nicely shaped breast.

"Keep straight." Angela pointed. "I'm from Maryland, and you?

"I'm from Orangeburg. And you know, it's amazing how the people from out of town think that I know where everything is here?" Cleabo smiled at Angela trying to warm her up.

Angela was feeling comfortable; she continued to tell Cleabo who she was and where she was from. She was a northerner and extremely fine; probably the finest in Maryland, he thought.

"My car broke down and I was going to call my girlfriend." Angela said gazing into Cleabo's eyes. Cleabo almost ran off the road while looking at her.

"Whoa, damn, girl you sure are pretty!"

"Thank you, but get back on the street." Angela laughed as she pointed to the street.

"So, tell me Angela, why didn't you call your man to come pick you up? I know you probably hear it all the time that you are so pretty, but hey, I feel every woman needs to hear that at least one time a day. If I'm lucky, I could be the first to have said it to you today." Cleabo paused then pointed his finger in the air. "Then again, on the other hand, if I wasn't the first to tell you it still wouldn't matter. Just knowing that I said it to you, would be all that matters to me."

"That's so sweet Cleabo, thanks; and no, I don't have a boyfriend. I'm all into my studies."

"I hear you lady. But sometimes you need to do something other than studying. You may need to take a break or something?" Cleabo said with confidence.

"You're right, I was thinking about doing that in a couple of days. Maybe go to the library and look around after school."

"No girl, you need to go have some fun! Let me take you out. We could get something eat." Cleabo knew she would like that. One thing he had learned, females love to eat. Some wouldn't go to bed afterward, but a good conversation was definitely bound to happen. "Then we could take in a movie or just ride around." Cleabo said, hoping that she would say yes.

She thought for a second. "Thursday is a good day for me."

"That's cool with me," Cleabo quickly responded.

"Okay, just come by my dorm at five on Thursday. Here is my dorm right over here." Angela pointed indicating to him where to turn.

"That sounds good Angela, I can hardly wait for the next two days to pass. Can I have your number so we can talk before then?"

"Sure I'd like that, let me find a pen." Angela rummaged through her purse until she found a pen and she wrote her number down. "Here you go Cleabo, call me. Do you have a number?"

"Yeah baby, write it down while you still have the pen out. It's 531-6940, and I'm going to call you about eight tonight, okay?"

"Okay Cleabo, I'll be there, and once again thanks." Angela said as she began to open the car door. "Bye Cleabo."

"Bye Angel, it's been a pleasure. I really enjoyed talking to you, you made my day."

Cleabo called Angela that night and they talked until they both became sleepy.

Cleabo and Angela finally connected with each other. They walked through the park holding hands and shared each other's ice cream cones. Angela even talked Cleabo into going to Church with her on Sunday. After Church they went to the Botanical Gardens and walked through the endless paths of beautiful flowers. It was breathtaking to Angela, she enjoyed being in the midst of nature. Cleabo thought that she was perfect in every way. Angela displayed poise and sound judgment; something he had never taken the time to look for in a woman.

After about three weeks Cleabo made a move on her for sex. While in the movie theater his hand that was resting on her leg slowly began to creep up to her mid section. In between eating pop corn and watching the movie Angela grabbed his hand and placed it back on her thigh, close to the area of her knee. The movie was rated R and there was a love scene, so Cleabo felt that it would be a good time to try again. This time he threw his coat over her legs so no one could see what he was doing. With his hand camouflaged, he slowly massaged her leg again while the love scene was going on. Only this time Angel went along with his gentle assault. Cleabo's hand made it to the mid section of Angela's gorgeous body, and he began to caress and rub her love nest.

It was difficult to rub her with the skirt she had on, so he slid his hand underneath the skirt and he made sure that his trench coat had her covered up. It was fortunate for Cleabo that no one else was sitting on the same row with them. A love scene was taking place in the movie and Cleabo was slowly massaging Angela. She began to twitch restlessly in her seat as Cleabo continued to rub her wet silk panties.

Cleabo removed his left hand just for a second and put it around her shoulders, then angled himself facing her as his right hand continued where his left was. Angela was into passion now; she looked Cleabo in the eyes and tilted her head, giving him permission to enter a part of her he so desperately wanted. With that look, Cleabo kissed her. While he kissed her his right hand moved her panties to the side exposing her sweet pubic hairs and the swollen lips of her love nest. He entered her with his finger while they kissed, but she flinched as his middle finger made it's way inside of her. The kiss seemed to last for quite sometime as Cleabo continued with his finger; but Angela couldn't stand it. With both of her hands she pushed Cleabo's hand out of her.

"I can't take that." Angela said, taking in a deep breath. "Can we go to your apartment after the movie?" she asked.

"Okay baby, I understand." Cleabo moved back into his chair. "Are you okay?"

"Yes, just a little uncomfortable." She sighed. "Lets just finish watching the movie, please Cleabo?"

"Alright baby, we'll finish watching the movie, then go to my place." Cleabo said, knowing that when they get there he would be able to have his way with her.

The movie was over and Angela seemed to have enjoyed it, at least the parts she was able to concentrate on while Cleabo wasn't up in her with his finger. After putting on their coats they held hands as they walked to the car. It seemed like it was a long drive to his apartment. They shared small talk on the way with his right hand again resting on her thigh. Angela rested her head on his shoulder while he was driving.

"You know I don't normally do this, don't you?" she asked.

"I'm glad it's with me baby," Cleabo said softly. "Angela you know we're not rushing into this, it's time. It's been almost a month now and besides, how many times we have to see each other before we do this; is there a number?"

"I don't know how many times Cleabo. I know I like you and all, but I don't want you to think that I'm something that I'm not. I'm not a trashy kind of girl!" Angela leaned up and turned her head towards the window.

"Hey baby, I know you're not. I can feel you, but I know it's time."

"Oh really, and how do you know that?" she breathlessly questioned.

"The way you respond to me, it's easily to see we were meant to be together. I don't think there is a number of times we have to see each other. If that was the case I would have knocked on your dorm door continuously counting the times. You know like knocking and each time you open the door I would say okay that's one. Okay that's two, then okay that's three." He laughed. "So you see it's not the number of times, it's just when we feel comfortable with each other."

"You're so silly Cleabo." Angela smiled. "But I understand the point you are trying to make."

They made it to Cleabo's apartment and he escorted her in. She had been there before but never did they reach the level they were at now. Cleabo played it cool with her; he didn't wanted to lose this churchgoing girl. He put on some music and set the atmosphere with some candles. It was Saturday and they were doing what two people that loved one another would be doing on a Saturday; spending time together.

With the wine from the refrigerator and the song, *'Reasons'* by Earth Wind & Fire playing, Cleabo could see that Angela had really started to loosen up as she talked about how much she liked the movie. Cleabo moved closer to her as their wine glasses sat on the table. Their steamy lips came together as one and after about thirty minutes of foreplay, they made it to the bedroom. After stripping to complete bareness, they kissed their way to the bed. Like a true player, Cleabo reached to his nightstand for a condom. Angela gave him a surprised look for being so prepared, hoping that he was only being ready for her.

"Wait a minute, Cleabo." She said softly. "Can you put some ice in a bowl and bring it here?"

Frustrated, but not wanting to show anger Cleabo said, "Okay, I will be right back." He stepped out of the bed and went into the kitchen wondering what in the world she wanted with some ice.

Cleabo brought the bowl of ice cubes back and sat it on the night stand, still puzzled at her actions. "Here is the ice, baby."

"Fill the condom up and do what you were doing at the theater to me with it. I read about that somewhere and I couldn't wait for the day I could have it done to me."

"Sure baby," he said before he began to fill the condom up with the block cubes of ice. He then slowly ran the condom up her leg and unto the inner sides of her thighs. Angela was shivering and began to shake from the coldness. Her sexual moaning became louder as he reached her pubic hairs and her swollen, sweet smelling lips with the condom full of ice cubes. Like a wishbone, she spread wide open waiting for him to enter her with the ultimate foreplay object. Slowly, Cleabo entered her with the ice cubes inside of the rubber. Her response was immediate. A loud scream sounded as she began to clinch the sheets with her hands. She shook hard; it was like she was having convulsions. After a few minutes, he noticed how the ice cubes melting inside of her sent her into a renewed frenzy. He could easily tell she was on an entirely differently level now. She grabbed him and pulled him into her, and they made love the entire night. Angela was never the same after that. Although Cleabo wondered if she had turned into a sex freak, he kept on seeing her. They kept dating and seeing each other off and on; Angela was too pretty for Cleabo to just let go.

After about two months of Angela and trying to keep up with his schoolwork, Cleabo was sitting at home when there was a knock at the door. It was Angela. She had her long hair wrapped and was wearing some tight, cut off jean shorts that had fringes at the end of them. Cleabo told her to come on in.

"Hey Angela, what's up?" Cleabo said, surprised to see her.

"Cleabo, we need to talk!" she said in a sad voice as she looked him in the eyes.

"What's wrong, are you alright?" Cleabo asked worriedly.

"Cleabo, I don't know how to tell you this, but I'm pregnant," she said, while looking at him into his eyes as the shocking news reflected off of him and onto her. "It must of happened the time when you thought the rubber broke. Cleabo what are we going to do? My father is going to kill me, and my mother, what is she going to think of me? They sent me off to get an education and look what I've done. I just don't know what to do."

"Damn Baby! Pregnant? Hold up, let me get it together." Cleabo said as he took a seat and placed his hands on his face, rubbing his forehead. "Baby where do we go from here? I mean, I've never been here before; what should we do?"

"I don't know Cleabo, it's just all messed up, I don't know." Angela began to cry. Cleabo quickly held her in his arms, comforting her.

"Hey baby, we are going to work this out, okay?" he said as Angela gazed into his face with her beautiful brown eyes.

"Okay Cleabo, but I've got some thinking to do. I just don't know what to do Cleabo!"

"First of all I want you to go into the bedroom and get some rest. I'll wake you up and take you back to the dorm, okay?"

"Alright, I could use some rest, I feel so weak, baby."

"It's going to be alright baby, trust me, I will stand by you." He told her staunchly.

"Thank you Cleabo." Angela smiled at him hesitantly then she went into the bed room and fell asleep as Cleabo tried to decide what he needed to do. He remembered in high school, his old friend Bernard had to quit school and find a job when his date became pregnant. His mother would definitely want him to be a man and take responsibility for his actions. She wouldn't want him to be like his father; a womanizer, or a deserter like Benny. Cleabo decided the best thing to do was to quit school and get a job to support his baby. After Angela woke up he told her what his intentions were. She was shocked, but thought that it was a good idea and wanted to think about the situation a little more.

A week had passed and Angela's morning sickness was becoming unbearable to deal with. Cleabo went ahead with his plans. By now his Uncle Jack had moved back to Orangeburg from New York, and had a job at the local chemical plant. He consulted him about getting a job there.

With only three months left in his sophomore year, Cleabo started working at the chemical plant. He worked swing shift, and made cool money. Two hundred dollars a week was good money back then. Working at the chemical plant was dissimilar to school, he was the youngest guy there, and everyone there expected a lot out of him, since his uncle had a reputation of being a good worker.

After two weeks of working at the chemical plant, Angela finally came by his apartment. He had been calling her dorm, but couldn't catch up with her. Cleabo opened the door and again Angela had that sad burdened look written all over her face.

"Come on in, I have been trying to get in contact with you for the longest." he said, while inviting her in. "Where have you been, and what's been going on?"

"I've been around, morning sickness been kicking my ass. They all think that I have the flu." She paused for a moment. "How is the new job?"

"Just a job baby, just trying to make things work for you and the kid you know."

"Really?"

"Yeah, I figure you can move in here soon." Cleabo said while waiting on a response.

"Cleabo we need to talk."

Cleabo didn't like the look on her face and said cautiously, "Oh really, what's going on baby?"

"Cleabo, I'm sorry. I didn't mean to come into your life and disrupt it," she apologized.

"No, baby it's not like that. I'm a man and sometimes a man just has to do the right thing."

"I know the feeling, because being a woman, we are sometimes pressured into making wrong decisions."

"What are you hinting around baby?" he asked, waiting for her to say what was on her mind. "Come on tell me."

"Cleabo, I should have kept it a secret, but eventually everyone would have known."

"You told someone?"

"Yes, my girlfriend." Angela said as she fidgeted. "She is cool though."

"Okay, if that's what you wanted to do, it's cool with me. After all, you are right; sooner or later they were bound to find out."

"Not only that Cleabo," she started, then paused a long moment before blurting out, "I have decided to get an abortion."

"What!" Cleabo was stunned. He hadn't thought she would do that. "Don't you think that I have any say so on the matter? I done quit school, got a job for you and you come here like this, talking about getting an abortion!" Cleabo thought her getting an abortion was much worse than him having to quit school.

"But Cleabo," Angela reached out putting a hand on his arm. "You can go back to school now. You mentioned something about me moving in with you..." she paused again. "Cleabo, well really, I would've never been able to do that. I want more out of life; more than you working at a chemical plant and living in a apartment. I really think my dreams are bigger than yours."

"Damn, baby you are laying some heavy shit on me." Cleabo felt like he was whirling in circles.

"I know Cleabo, I really am sorry, but for what it's worth, I did love you. But, not anymore Cleabo. I'm hurting so bad knowing that I'm hurting you. The feeling I have for you now is feeling sorry for you. I'm sorry, because I had something to do with you changing your life for me. What you did was admirable to the situation, but it's not what I want. I want to get my master's degree and I want my mate to be more educated than I am."

Her words hurt him badly, but he wasn't about to let her know it. "I understand, you feel like I'm beneath you. But you didn't feel that way when I was pleasing you good, did you?"

"Oh, there was nothing bad about the lovemaking Cleabo, and I doubt if I would ever get it that good again. But, I have come to face myself, and although I'm ashamed to say it, I'm a little materialistic."

Mentally he agreed with her, then he said slowly, "I see you have your mind made up. At least let me take you to have it done," he added, hoping he could still talk her out of it.

She dashed his hopes. "No Cleabo, my girlfriend is going to go with me. I couldn't stand you being there."

"I want to be there for you though." He really wanted to be there for himself.

"You will be in my heart, Cleabo, and in my mind. But can you pay for it Cleabo? It cost one hundred and fifty dollars."

"Sure," he said reaching for his wallet, then said what he was thinking, "And if you change your mind, let me know, okay?"

"Okay, but I won't. Don't feel sad Cleabo. After all it is my body, right?"

"Yeah, you're right." Cleabo said sadly, but it was also his child.

Angela walked out the door leaving Cleabo feeling sad and lonely. Never in his wildest dreams had he ever thought something like this would happen to him. In New York he walked all over women. Now here in the south he had fallen in love with Pumpkin and Angela and they had both broken his heart. What was he to do now? He decided he wasn't going back to school; his pain was too excruciating. How embarrassed he would be if they were to find out why he quit school and then he was dumped. There was no way he was mature enough to handle the situation and return to school; so he continued to work at the plant.

One night on the twelve to eight shift, a pipe line broke on one of the reactors and the material in the line was shooting up like a volcano. His co-worker, Harry, was working with him while the chemical was erupting out of the line. The hazardous chemicals were metalline chloride and heptane. The fumes from the chemicals sent him sailing. Cleabo and Harry were so high it was pathetic. The foreman came to their location and said, "Let's go outside and get some air," after shutting off a nearby valve.

They must have stayed out there all night long. He had never been so high in his life. He knew that it was some powerful stuff because his foreman didn't smoke or drink and he was high as a kite. Eventually though, the job at the plant became repetitive. His mind was still on Angela and the shocking news, and because of his situation with her, he began to slack off on his job responsibilities.

One night he came to work and his foreman told him to come into the office. When Cleabo went inside the office the supervisor and the foreman were there. They told him that if he didn't shape up he would be given his walking papers. They told him that his job performance was insufficient. He said to himself; "Damn, I've been working my ass off here and they think that I haven't been doing nothing. That's a trip!" all he could say to those people was, "Alright! Is that all?"

They asked why he was taking it so lightly. "If that is what you think of me you are going to keep on thinking it. There may be nothing I can do to change your mind. I'm going to keep on working hard, no matter what anyone else may think," he then looked over towards the foreman.

The foreman and the supervisor looked at each other and said, "Cleabo, we just need to see more production out of you."

"Yeah okay," Cleabo lifted himself out of the chair and left. He went back to the centrifuge and told Harry what had happened. Harry shouted, "Man, them guys are crazy! You work harder than a lot of people here."

"Maybe they're just trying to do this because I'm young and black, and I have my whole life ahead of me," he said.

His shift was over and the sun rose from the east as it normally does, while daylight and reality were hitting Cleabo dead smack in the face. He realized he had become slack on the job. He couldn't work there with his mind consistently being on Angela. Perhaps he just needed to get away and just start all over, he thought. It seemed the more he aged the more the pain of being dumped became devastating and harder to deal with.

One morning, when he finished his night shift, Cleabo and the fellows went to the courts to play some basketball and drink some beer. This was a normal activity; it was sort of a celebration after working five night shifts and having four days off from work. Basketball and beer helped welcome what was called the long weekend. In the south a person really didn't have to worry about being drunk in the daylight hours. The police wouldn't stop anyone unless they had an accident or was driving crazy. Cleabo and the fellows were so drunk they looked like zombies. After the games were over and they were sitting around, his friend Tommy suggested they all do something really crazy.

"Yeah, like what, man?" Cleabo said.

"Let's go join the Army!" replied Tommy.

Without thinking, everybody said, "Yeah, let's go to the recruitment center!" They arrived at the recruitment center drunk as skunks. The sergeant there told them to come back when they were sober. They argued with him and told him that they knew what they were doing. The sergeant finally gave in and gave them the test and they all passed.

Cleabo and his friends changed their minds about the Army; they decided they would rather join the Air Force instead. The test seemed to be relatively easy, however, Cleabo was so drunk that he fell asleep during the test. When he woke up he only had thirty minutes left to finish it. By using the learning skills he taught himself in school he was able to finish the test and made a decent score. One of his methods for taking any test was to answer all the questions that he knew first. When he would come across something that he didn't know he would put a dot next to the number of the question and then come back to it.

A week went by and he had forgotten all about the Air Force. One night, while he was at home, the people from the Air Force called and asked him to come down to the recruitment center. When he arrived, they told him that it was time for him to decide what he was going to do.

CHAPTER VIII

INDUCTEE

He decided to join the service, but he had changed his mind again and now wanted to join the Army.

Cleabo notified the chemical plant of his intentions to go serve his country. He was trying to sound patriotic when he handed his written two weeks notice to his foreman. The human resources manager told him that his job would be there for him when his tour ended with the Army. Cleabo knew that would be the last place he would ever want to come back to.

Cleabo told his grandmother that he was going into the Army and she was sad. She asked, "What the hell you want to do that for?" she shook her head and continued. "Now, Cleabo, you know you ain't the type to listen to those folks in the Army. You are hardheaded, lazy, stubborn, and you only want to do things your way. You probably won't make it out of boot camp." From that point on he knew he had to finish boot camp, even if it was just to prove his grandmother wrong.

When Cleabo arrived at the Army reception station, it was like something he had never seen before. The air was clear and everything around him was extemely clean. There wasn't a sign of paper or trash anywhere. Fort Jackson, South Carolina is one of the hottest training posts in the U.S. It was so hot there the place adopted the reputation of people dying from heat exhaustion.

One of the soldiers told Cleabo about the long six miles or so hike, on a hill called Tanker's Hill. A couple of soldiers died there while marching with thirty pounds or so on their backs, as they attempted to convert themselves from being boys into soldiers. The soldiers would collapse from the extremely hot weather and the gear inside of the backpacks. After so many deaths, the Post Commander decided to do that type of road march (or hike) at the latter part of the day, preferably when the sun went down.

At the reception station there were about thirty new inductees being processed for the new Army life. The barracks were like something you would see on the Gomer Pyle show. They had long hallways with shiny floors and you could see your reflection in them.

When they arrived, a sergeant lined them up in the barracks and started talking as he walked up and down the shiny hall. To Cleabo, his voice sounded like a loud, hard bell.

"Welcome to Fort Jackson!" the sergeant shouted. Cleabo later discovered that the sergeant never said anything that wasn't a shout. "You'll be here for the orientation portion of your enlistment. Any questions you may have shall be answered here prior to going off to boot camp, or as some of you call it, Basic Training. They call it boot camp because that's what it's like, a summer camp. You can really enjoy a whole lot of sporting activities; hunting, fishing, etc. but, there is an exception to all of that fun. If you fuck up, you will get a boot in your ass. The post exchange is located down the street and off to the left. Corporal Sutler will show you the way there."

The sergeant then turned and pointed to this corporal who was standing by the door. The young black soldier quickly locked his feet together and stood in the position which is called attention. He had his arms down to his sides and his legs were together. Cleabo thought that he was trying to impersonate an iron board. Nevertheless, he was merely trying to display an impressive form of discipline. He was sharp and mean looking. Cleabo remembered that he was the same young man that had greeted his group in the day room when they signed in. Cleabo had already programmed himself to use the silent trick and never, on any occasion give up any type of information voluntarily unless asked; even then be sparse with details.

This corporal was sharper than a knife. He just stood there looking mean as hell and Cleabo heard someone whisper, "I ain't asking him shit."

The sergeant continued to shout, "You must stay in the barracks and the only places you can go is to the post exchange or to the mess hall."

One guy said, "Hey, Sarge! What is the mess hall?"

The sergeant replied in a sarcastic tone. He said, "You better hope that someone can call the MP's to get me off of your ass. If you have the guts and the balls to raise your right hand and be sworn in the United States Army tomorrow, I'm going to beat the living shit out of you everyday, midget brain! The mess hall is a place where good little soldiers like you eat."

"Hey Sarge, where do you eat?" asked the soldier.

The Sergeant was suddenly in this soldier's face, so close he was touching his nose. "I eat your Momma out every chance I get, you ignoramus! What's your name, soldier?"

"Miller, Sir."

"Mr. Miller. For the time you're here you'd better get your act together, or me and you will become the best of friends. You don't want that, now do you?"

"No, Sir," he replied.

"Sir! I work for a living soldier! I'm part of the backbone, the bulk of the United States Army! When you talk to me the first or the last word that comes out of your mouth better be Sergeant! Do you understand me?"

"Yes Sergeant!" Miller responded.

The Sergeant then stepped away and continued his shouting, "Everyone listen up! From this point on, you will call all enlisted soldiers by their rank and all officers sir, or ma'am for a female officer. The rank structure is posted outside of this building. Get to know it! Especially those of you who will be hanging around after your physical. That's all I have to say to you knuckleheads and good luck with all of you in processing. Oh yeah, welcome to the United States Army; the real thing!"

The Sergeant went toward the door and the Corporal yelled, "Attention!" and everyone came to attention like they were in the Army already. Almost everyone came to attention except for this guy named Smith. The Corporal ran up to him and put his face directly in the face of Smith's. Cleabo had thought the Sergeant was loud, but the Corporal was even louder. He started yelling at the top of his lungs. It hurt Cleabo's ears listening to him.

The Corporal said, "At the position of attention, your head and eyes will be straight forward, your chest will be up and out! You will stand tall and look good! Your legs and heels will be together and your feet will form a forty five degree angle! Your arms will be locked in joint at the side of your body with your hands cuffed and your thumbs on the seam of your trousers! Do you understand, Private!"

148

The word private hit Cleabo like a ton of bricks. It sounded so degrading to him; he rationalized that all of them standing there were privates. He hated the word private; it sounded like dirt when the corporal said it.

The corporal then said that bed check was at twenty one hundred hours. Everyone turned around and looked at each other wanting to know, what the hell was twenty one hundred hours?

Some fool said, "Excuse me, Sir, but what is twenty one hundred hours?"

"For you civilian minded ignoramuses," the corporal answered sarcastically, "Twenty one hundred hours means nine o'clock p.m."

At that moment Cleabo knew how bad the Army was going to be and why he absolutely had to complete it. He could just see himself going home and hearing his Grandmother Sadie Bell say, "I told you so!"

"No, that isn't going to happen. I'm here to stay, no matter what," he thought to himself.

Cleabo settled into his bunk ten minutes to nine. The sheets were so clean he could smell the cleaning agent used on them. He couldn't sleep a wink thinking about the situation he had himself into. Down the hall, the latrine light stayed on. Latrine is the word the Army used for the bathroom. Cleabo could see everyone's bed; the bunks were in rows. At nine o'clock sharp, the corporal stood at the end of the hall for about two minutes before he came walking down, checking the bunks to make sure that everyone was in bed.

Laying in the bed, Cleabo felt like he was finally in prison for all the bad things he had done in his life. All the robbing and illegal things were coming back to haunt him. That night he had a dream that someone jumped on him and was trying to choke him. He couldn't move; he tried to push this invisible force off of him and he tried to yell, but it seemed like no one could hear him.

He told his grandmother about it when he called her and she said that it was just the devil riding him. Cleabo thought that he was already in a hellhole, now the old southern metaphor of the devil riding him made him more fearful to go to sleep.

The following day, that damn corporal came and woke them up at zero five hundred in the morning. No one was used to getting up that early. The corporal said, "Line up by your bunks. At zero six hundred hours you will be dressed and at the mess hall. At zero seven hundred hours you will start your in-processing."

Going through the breakfast line was a trip to Cleabo. They called it the chow line. Everyone was in uniform except for them and the ones who were in uniform acted like they were robots; they weren't allowed to talk. He tried to talk to one of them, but the guy wouldn't say a word. Finally another guy told him that after they received their uniforms and raised their right hands, they would be the same way. At least until they were shipped out and then they might be allowed to talk on the bus on the way to basic training.

There was a sergeant watching them as they ate, just like they were in prison. Cleabo felt like he couldn't breath; he was experiencing claustrophobia. He wanted to get out of that mess hall right away, but he couldn't.

After chow, the corporal marched them to the building to take their physicals. The doctor had them line up in rows. They were instructed to pull their drawers down and bend over. The doctor stuck his finger up their butts, saying he had to check for something, but Cleabo thought they were just checking to see if some of them were homosexuals. This was a painful test for him. When the physical portion was over, those that passed were marched into a large room that displayed an oversized flag and a large engraved replica of the constitution.

The new inductees were instructed to raise their right hand as they were being sworn in. After being sworn in, they made all of them put on uniforms within a certain time limit. Everything from that point started to have a time limit. From the time they woke up until the time they went to bed they were on a time schedule. "All hell broke loose after we raised our right hand," Cleabo thought.

Now it was time to get their hair cut. He had a nice groomed afro; back then an afro was the style. When they left the barber, the corporal was waiting outside for them. With all of his hair cut off, Cleabo looked like a monk.

Some of the other guys were crying as they stepped outside of the barber shop because they had lost all of their hair. Cleabo was used to the bald hair-cut style. Before he had his afro, his grandmother would cut his hair like this when they couldn't afford to go to the barbershop. So, he just laughed at them and from that point on, they regarded him as the type of person who didn't give a damn about anything.

They gave them uniforms that didn't fit. Later he learned that they did that because privates aren't supposed to look better than the corporals or sergeants. His uniforms were baggy and his boots and cap were also too big. After getting all of their uniforms, they returned to the barracks to put them away; there was a time limit to do this also.

The sergeant then took them outside and began teaching them movements. They called it drill and ceremony, or marching. Cleabo called it a bunch of mindless fools moving the same direction in the hot ass sun. Finally, some of them caught on; but for some, the movements were difficult. It started getting hot in the sun. A couple of people started falling out because it was so hot, but the sergeant didn't care. He would just shout at the corporal, "Take care of that piece of shit!"

The other soldiers didn't want to collapse and be called a piece of shit. The sweat poured down Cleabo's face, but he knew that he had to make it. There were a couple of females in his platoon and the sergeants would 'dog' them out royally; Cleabo knew why. They figured that a female was like any type of system. If abused, eventually they would break down. That's when the sergeants would seduce them sexually. After the females would give up and then give into the harassment, they wouldn't have any more trouble from the sergeants. It was incredibly noticeable. If a survey had been taken back then, seven out of ten females would engage in sex for favors with the sergeants.

After a few days at Fort Jackson it was time to move on to basic training. They had to get on a bus and travel to Georgia. It was a long bus ride and they had little freedom. When they arrived in Georgia there were about twenty other buses there. A big mean sergeant stepped on the bus to greet them. He said, "Welcome to basic training, I will be your momma, your daddy, your sister or your brother. You've got ten seconds to get your goat-smelling asses off of this damn bus and nine of them are gone. The last lowlife, whale shit-eating, motherfucker is going to do more push-ups than you can count. Now get off the fucking bus!"

Everyone started running off of the bus and getting their duffel bags from the bus, while the sergeants were yelling and screaming at every last one of them. This was the intimidation portion to the introduction part of basic training. Cleabo saw about fifty sergeants yelling at all of the privates. There must have been a sergeant for every private. Cleabo thought, "if a private has his own personal sergeant to yell at him; it is going to be a long day." They made them do push-ups in the hot sun endlessly; it was continuous harassment. Cleabo hung in there and was glad to go to bed that night.

One of the females there was named Susan Shine. Sunshine was her nickname. She was about five foot two inches tall, with sandy colored hair. Her skin was gold and it complimented her shape. Cleabo thought she was fine in all aspects. Sunshine had dark brown eyes and some sweet juicy-looking lips. When she walked the whole world stopped to take a look.

Sunshine was a 'sho nuff' heartbreaker and she knew she had it put together. Cleabo and Sunshine became friends, but he wondered why she chose him to be her friend. Everyone wanted to have her in so many ways, even the drill sergeants. One thing they didn't like was him befriending Sunshine; since they all wanted her. The drill sergeants tried to break Sunshine down, but she displayed excellent physical endurance. On the day they went to the confidence course, Sunshine was the only female to climb to the top of the tower. Some of the guys were scared and shaking like a leaf once they had reached the top, but Cleabo and Sunshine used teamwork to come down. Finally, the drill sergeants decided that she was too much for them, so they left her alone.

After coming down from the tower, they had to crawl on their knees and forearms under some barbed wire while the drill sergeants shot live rounds over their heads. Crawling underneath the wire as the bullets were piercing by his head was nerve-racking. Sunshine crawled the fifty yards or so like it was nothing. She was a true soldier. At the end of the day everyone was tired, which seemed to be one of the drill sergeant's main objectives.

The next day, he met Sunshine *under the green tree* where they had established a rendezvous point. In a dreamy tone of voice she said, "Yo, Cleabo."

"Yeah Sunshine, what's up?"

"I would like to have the world at the tip of my fingers and not work and have you in a huge ass house. I would treat you like a king, just because you are a true friend."

"Oh yeah, thanks girl, that sounds real cool."

"You know what else Cleabo?"

"What's that Sunshine?"

"I've finally figured out why we sit our asses underneath this damn green tree and rap." She paused for a moment. "You see, the tree represent growth. Just like we grow in life and learn. The limbs that stretch out are us trying to reach our goals. And the leaves are merely money; you know, currency. But, it's up to us to reach out and get it."

"Damn baby, that's some deep shit." Cleabo responded looking somewhat puzzled at Sunshine.

Those were some good times spent with Sunshine, but he knew that all good things must come to an end. Talking to Sunshine every night *under the green tree* was the best thing that could've happened to him. She made him feel like someone real. Cleabo had finally realized he could have a true friend that was of the opposite sex and was beautiful without thinking of having sex. Sunshine really opened his mind up to understanding people instead of selfishly thinking of himself all of the time.

Although Cleabo hated basic training, he was surprised to find he felt sad when it was time to be shipped out. He had received orders for Airborne and Ranger school while Sunshine's orders sent her to Fort Ord, California. He was going to miss her. They knew that they would probably never see each other again but they accepted it. Cleabo couldn't forget the days he spent with Sunshine. It seemed like everything they had done together had been perfect.

His days started early at Airborne school; it seemed like running was the ritual. Three miles was an easy day, and when he didn't have his pack on his back it made the long run easier. The military's main concern was conditioning his body to be able to take the fall from an aircraft. Push-up and sit-ups were done throughout the day. While running in the hot sun of Georgia, he felt his body turning into a machine. He was being programmed to kill the enemy. Never in his wildest dreams did he think he would actually have to kill anyone.

The closest he had ever gotten was during the heist and even then it didn't set right with him; the thought of killing.

The six months he spent at Airborne and Ranger school was indeed challenging for Cleabo. He had learned how to survive off the land and jump out of planes, and also reconnaissance techniques. Females or any type of illegal activities were far from his mind. The pain he had suffered with Pumpkin and Angela somehow dissipated from his mind; perhaps Sunshine helped to ease his discomfort. One thing was for sure, having her in his life turned him into a totally different human being. Cleabo's character began to change; no longer was he looking at females as objects or something to do. The females that were in his platoon at Airborne school were brave, but he easily detected the fear in their hearts as the door of the C130 slid open. The wind gusted in as he watched the lips of the jump master move while speaking on his first jump.

Not hearing a sound coming from his mouth Cleabo knew what he had to do, so it really didn't matter. He glanced to his side and watched as the females and some of the guys shivered with fear, and he wondered why he wasn't scared. "Could it be I have no fear of dying?" he thought, as he sympathized with the females by nodding at them and saying, "Everything is going to be all right." None of the females fit the bill of being a companion for him like Sunshine. They only shared casual conversations and he helped them out in anyway he could. He started taking on the role of a leader and was setting a good example for others to follow. He answered their questions in the absence of the sergeants, and he even showed a few of them how to polish their boots.

At Ranger school his training became even more demanding. The running escalated to about six miles a day. The combat training was intensified and survival techniques were taught by a professional in each particular field. Cleabo was in a whole new ballpark. Never could he ever compare the streets of the Bronx to what he was going through now. He had no idea the body could stay awake for such long periods of time. At one time he was up for four days with no sleep; only a nod here and there. He began to think that perhaps they thought that if they punished them hard some of them would quit. For some it worked, but Cleabo hung in there to the bitter end.

At graduation, Cleabo felt like everything was over, but he really didn't know what to expect next. After being strung out everyday for the past year, how could he possibly put himself into low gear? Cleabo now had muscles bulging out of places on his body he had not a clue existed on him before. But, like a soldier, he had to adapt to changes and moving on to a new duty station was one of them. He continued to write Sunshine and shared everything that was going on in his life with her. Sometimes he would reminisce those heart to heart talks shared with her underneath the green tree. She was a true friend, nothing more to him, and without a doubt nothing less.

Sunshine's life in California seemed to have gotten off to a good start. She had found someone and fallen in love. When she experienced pain in her relationship, so did Cleabo as he read her letters under his night light before going to sleep. He knew she would be able to handle her situation, therefore, he just wrote her words of comfort during her bad times; proving to be a friend that would always be there for her regardless.

The plane landed in New Orleans, Louisiana. He had a three hour layover, and of course, he had to check out the fabulous Bourbon Street. Bourbon Street was a trip and he fit right in. Cleabo spent so much money, the people there thought he was a star or something. Then Cleabo caught the connecting flight to Fort Polk, Louisiana. The aircraft was a twelve passenger airplane. It looked like one of those crop-dusting planes. Cleabo wondered what he had done to deserve to die like this. His stomach was bubbling, and he was getting nauseated; almost throwing up. The aircraft finally landed.

Fort Polk, Louisiana was a totally new experience for him. A fresh private and he didn't know what to expect of his new duty station. There were some sergeants there to meet him and they started asking him thousands of questions. Then they took him to where he would be staying. The place looked like it was set up for a World War II film. When he walked through the courtyard, he could see some people looking out of their windows yelling, "Hey, newby! Give me some fresh meat, newby. Hey newby!"

He wanted to tell them where to go, but the sergeants were with him and they were waiting to hear what he was going to say; to see what kind of person he was. Somehow he felt himself being tested from the time they picked him up, so he ignored the negativity and conducted himself firmly and sternly.

The sergeants weren't like the ones in boot camp, Airborne or Ranger school; they were more relaxed. Cleabo started to feel like he was at a home away from home. The barrack hallways weren't as shiny as the ones in boot camp. Cleabo thought they were relaxed there and he wondered if anyone did any work. The Sergeants took him to his room and introduced him to his new roommate.

His new roommate's name was Presswood and he acted like Cleabo was invading his privacy. He didn't say much and he talked in a low and deep toned voice. If a person didn't know Presswood, they would think that he was kind of slow, but he wasn't. He was from Oakland, California. Styles, another newby from Chesapeake, Virginia entered the room. He was a little short guy about four foot five, but he was excellent in the martial arts and quick with his hands and feet.

A guy named Phillipen also came into the room. He was dark skinned and wore glasses. Phillipen was a cool and funny guy. He told a few jokes that had Cleabo rolling. He was from Little Rock, Arkansas, and he was a true comical character. Then Alex came into the room, he was a Puerto Rican from New York. Cleabo felt real comfortable with him; he reminded him so much of New York. The sergeants exited the room and told Cleabo that he didn't have to be back to work until the next day.

All of them interrogated Cleabo trying to find out if he was cool. After answering so many questions they finally felt at ease with him.

"You drink beer?" Presswood asked with seriousness written on his face.

"I haven't had anything for a while, being in school you know." Cleabo paused, "But I could use a beer to unwind."

"Cool, me and the fellows were about to pick up some beer and drive down to the lake." Presswood looked around at the other guys. "You want to come and hang out with us?"

"Sure man, I need something like that. I've been stressing for a long time now." Cleabo said as he sat his duffle bag on his bunk. "I'll unpack this stuff later."

Presswood felt more comfortable after finding out that Cleabo wasn't a square or some creep.

"Hey man, there are some fine ladies at the lake." Phillipen said.

"Cool, been a long time since I seen a real live one in a bikini." Cleabo smiled and they walked out of the door.

The lake was beautiful. There were people paddling aimlessly around on paddle boats, while others were fishing off of the grassy bank. Cleabo's companions whistled and tried talking to the beautiful females that walked by. He was fascinated by some of the black women speaking French, noticing that a few had green eyes. Cleabo thought they might be fake contact lens, but later found out that it wasn't unusual because of the high yellow Cajun blood line. The men returned to the barracks with talk of obtaining different females telephone numbers. Cleabo thought this game was beneath him, his thoughts were on family and his friend Sunshine. Being with a woman was far from his mind at this point of his life.

The incident with Angela taught him well. Sunshine once told him that there was a good possibility that Angela was never pregnant. She said it was a game some college students played on underclassmen, just to get some money. Cleabo was shocked and didn't want to believe her. He couldn't imagine being taken for a fool like that. Cleabo felt he would have never let his guard down for such treachery. He knew Speed had taught him better and he told Sunshine she was mistaken.

Cleabo was assigned to the only Airborne Unit on the base. His field was in telecommunications. He worked hard everyday and displayed a great deal of motivation. He was dependable and took the initiative to do a good job even in the absence of his sergeants. If he was told once to do something, they knew it would be done. Cleabo treated the Army as he had Speed's organization. He may have not known it, but he was a soldier even back then. His weapon was kept clean and his uniforms were sharp.

He cleaned the vehicle that was assigned to his communication shelter like it was his own personal vehicle. Everything he did was well above average, and his superiors started noticing his behavior as he grew into being a model soldier. Cleabo was special and different.

He really dazzled his sergeants one day when they had an inspection and discovered that instead of the normal wire hangers that everyone else used to hang their clothes up with, Cleabo went out and bought all plastic burgundy hangers. Every garment in his wall locker was pressed and starched. Everything was neatly in line when the general walked into his room. His floor sparkled like a mirror and it almost blinded the general when he stepped in. In an unmilitary fashion, Cleabo also had a three foot ivy plant in the corner of his room; demonstrating he thought that his room had life.

After that they promoted him to corporal, and continued promoting him. He became an example for the other soldiers to follow. They sent him to the soldier of the month board, where he competed with other soldiers about military knowledge. Cleabo's study habits assisted him in winning the soldier of the month and then soldier of the year. After three years Cleabo was promoted to sergeant. Having those three stripes on his shoulders was one of the greatest accomplishments of his life, he thought.

He was thrilled when he became a sergeant. He enjoyed the idea of having a little bit of power. Unlike the other sergeants, who treated new recruits like animals, Cleabo treated his subordinates as human beings, which resulted in making him popular among the lower ranks.

Despite the fact that he was a leader now, Cleabo had to keep up his military knowledge even more so. His superiors started sending him to boards again; first sergeant of the month, which he won, then sergeant of the year. His reward for sergeant of the year was a four day weekend trip to New Orleans to the Super Bowl. Although he had to carry the flag of Louisiana on the fifty yard line, he didn't care. The hotel expenses were free and he was able to watch the game; being a part of the pre-game show. He arrived in New Orleans by bus on a Thursday. The streets were filled with people as if there was a festival going on. Professional football players that didn't make it to the championship game were walking down Bourbon Street. A retired football player known to be so mean that had been renamed *'Mean,'* was in the congested crowd and his wallet was lifted.

'Mean' felt the bump that occurred as the thief made the lift, and he ran the thief down. Grabbing him by the collar, *'Mean'* lifted the man up in the air, throwing him against a wall and holding him there. The thief had *'Mean's'* wallet in his hand and was shaking like a leaf. *'Mean'* told him as long as he was in New Orleans the thief had better never try that again. He let the relieved thief go as the crowd stared and watched, waiting for the well-known celebrity's next move.

The crowd quickly dispersed when someone shouted, "Look, there goes Spike!"

Cleabo didn't recognize the individual; Spike tucked his head and picked up his pace, eager to get away from the desperate crowd that was so in need to be in the presence of a celebrity.

Rehearsals at the stadium weren't long at all; the flag stayed in its case. Cleabo, along with fifty-one other most outstanding sergeants from all across the world, walked across the beautiful green grass. The lights were bright and every color was so vivid. Cleabo was astonished as he stood on the fifty-yard line glancing at two humongous helmets that would be used for the two teams to run through. While Cleabo stood there, a husky African-American man wearing jeans along with a cut off jean jacket, came walking out. He walked up to the podium and began to test the mike.

Cleabo watched as the man waited for his cue, then began to sing the first few lines of the Star Spangled Banner. At first Cleabo thought that the man worked for the ground crew, but later he learned that the guy was a famous singer. The other guys at the hotel told Cleabo that he was a country and western singer. It was the first time Cleabo had ever heard of an African-American country and western singer. Cleabo enjoyed it; that guy really sang the hell out that song, he thought. The two teams that were playing that year were San Francisco and Denver. Cleabo thought it was a good game but he felt the excitement was overwhelming. It was kind of hard to concentrate with all of the noise.

It was a partying weekend for Cleabo and he visited places like Pat O'Brien's and a few other bars. He was careful with his drinking in a town like New Orleans. He also made sure that he picked up a postcard for his dear friend Sunshine. Sharing this kind of news with her just made his day, and hers too he thought. It was a long ride back to Fort Polk on the bus, but he enjoyed the time for reflection. The memories he had stayed with him forever.

CHAPTER IX

SAVE LIVES AND GOT LIFE

A few months after returning from his trip, Cleabo was sitting at home one night when he received a telephone call. It was his First Sergeant. The First Sergeant is normally the highest rank an enlisted soldier can achieve while being assigned to a company size unit, which consists of anywhere from one hundred fifty to two hundred people, under normal circumstances. He is considered the pioneer, the bulk or the backbone. His First Sergeant told him to come in with all of his gear.

"What's going on?" Cleabo asked.

"Alert Status," his First Sergeant stated briskly. "Contact your next in line, and Cleabo get in here fast. There are a few things I need to go over with you," he demanded.

"Okay, I'll be right in."

Cleabo was trying to figure out what was going on. He thought that maybe it was just another one of those alerts in which everyone had to come in the wee hours of the morning to show their faces, and sign their names and go home. Little did he know going in that night would change the whole course of his life. He jumped into the car with all of his bags, and sped down the highway.

At the post gate, the guard told Cleabo that the entire Post was in a state of alert.

From the tone of his voice, it was easy to comprehend that something serious was occurring. At his unit, there were soldiers putting on their war gear with their heads hanging down, similar to people that were about to attend a funeral. Cleabo spoke to one of the head hanging soldiers.

"Lift your head up, private, you act as though someone is about to die or something," Cleabo said.

The soldier said, "Yeah, Sarge, and it might be me or you."

Cleabo said, "Yeah okay, but if I'm going to die, I'm going to die with my head up and fighting."

Cleabo walked straight into the First Sergeant's office and said, "Hey, what's up?"

"Hey Cleabo, I want you to get your team together. No one is to make any phone calls to their wives, cousins or anyone else. They are to stay in this location."

Cleabo's grandma's and his mother's face flashed in his mind. After all the bad things he had done in his life, that old saying came back to him. Speed used to say it all the time, 'Once a man, twice a child,' and in regard to that statement, it was exactly the way he was feeling. Cleabo couldn't let his soldiers see him this way. He had to show that macho image.

Cleabo was given his mission from the First Sergeant; a drop zone somewhere in Panama. His transit times and manifests were all in his package. The First Sergeant also told him good luck. After getting his team together, he instructed them to board the bus that was waiting for them outside. Private Simpson came to the front of the bus where Cleabo was sitting and said, "Hey, Sarge, you got a minute?"

"Sure." Cleabo answered.

"You know as much as I'm acting all big and bad in front of these other guys," Simpson said, "I'm not ashamed to say to you that I'm scared as hell."

"Simpson, there is nothing wrong with being scared; fear is based on the unknown and we don't know what we'll be getting into." Cleabo told him.

"You know, Sarge, I'm bigger than the rest of those guys and I know that you will be depending on me a lot in Panama. But, I'll tell you what Sarge, when I fight, I'll be fighting for you and those fellows back there, because I don't think that my country gives a shit about me, and I don't give a shit about them either. I'm going to try to get my black ass back to Chicago and get a peace of mind. And you know what else Sarge? Don't nobody know what the hell we are doing here and we don't know ourselves. This mission is so top secret it's pathetic."

"Let's just be thankful, it's a privilege for you and me to be called on to do such a task."

"Yeah," the Private said shaking his head in disbelief. "I'm sure that you are thankful for going somewhere and you don't even know if you're coming back. Tell that one to the birds, Sarge."

"Yeah man, you're right." Cleabo said, nodding his head in agreement. "But we've got to do the best we can."

"Yeah, I know that's right."

They shook hands and then they hugged as a tear rolled down Simpson's eye. Simpson strolled to the back of the bus and sat down, as the other soldiers watched him. What they saw on Simpson's face was the fear of death. Knowing that big, bad, Simpson was scared made them feel a little paranoid.

The bus stopped about a hundred feet away from the aircraft. It was a C-130. Cleabo stood in the middle of the bus and said, "All right, here we are. This is what we've been training for. The next time you step down on the ground it will be on the dirty ass soil of Panama. So get your gear together and file your ass off this damn bus."

They sounded like they were ready to fight and proud to be a part of such a unique team. The lion roars they made were only to cover the fear. When the bus was empty and all of the guys were waiting outside, Cleabo said a quick prayer to the Lord, asking to give him the strength to bring everyone home to their loved ones.

One soldier yelled to Cleabo; as he turned around, he could see a figure like a shadow, but he couldn't make out who it was. Then another soldier said, "It's Private Smith. He left all of his gear and is trying to go AWOL."

Cleabo looked at Smith, and according to regulations he started to shoot him for desertion, but he didn't. He said to himself, "If a man is too scared to fight, then why make him?" he just watched Smith run like he was in a hundred yard dash. Cleabo told himself that if he had to, he would swear he'd never even seen Smith.

The team entered the aircraft with their packs on their backs. There were plenty of sad faces and it was extremely quiet. Cleabo was tired of seeing the soldiers so downhearted, so he said, "Listen to me men, we are going to kick some ass and whatever it is we have to do, we are going to do it in the name of the United States Army!" it didn't exactly cheer the men up, but it seemed to help a little.

One soldier jumped up and yelled, "Yes, let's do it!"

The plane ride was long and exceptionally shaky. It had been over a month since Cleabo had been in an aircraft, but he tried to make the best of it, trying to overlook that his stomach was feeling wheezy.

He thought about the drop zone that was yet to come and also the fear of the unknown. Just the thought of jumping into a small country without knowing if they were going to be fired upon; was frightening. It felt like they rode on the plane for days. They started to receive the countdown to the drop zone. Now that it was time to stand up, hook up and shuffle to the door, his fear escalated.

Cleabo prayed that his main parachute would open, despite the fact that he had a reserve. The last thing he wanted to do was to land in a tree, but little did he know that should have been the least of his worries. The door opened loudly, wind was blowing everywhere. He knew that it was getting close to jump time. His knees were shaking and his ears were popping. His life was in God's hands.

He was airborne on the count of four; all the other jumps he had ever taken before this one had gone by quickly, but now it seemed like this one took forever. While riding downward in the sky he could remember all the bad things he had done in his life, it was like a flashback. He said to himself, "Oh man, I'm going to die." Those fears became reality when he felt the whistling wind of a bullet zing by his head. Then all of a sudden, there were bullets screaming all around him. Panic punched his stomach; he didn't know where the shots were coming from. He prayed all the way to touch down.

The jump only lasted for a few minutes, but it was one of the hardest jumps he had ever made. Bullets continued being fired upon them once they were earthbound. Thankfully, the grass they landed in was tall; it was to their advantage. The tall grass made it difficult for the ambusher to take out his targets. Cleabo had to find out where the firing was coming from. He was pinned down, all he could do was lay there on the ground and hope that all the men landed safely until he could get himself situated.

He low-crawled to an immense rock, then he held his head up on the side of the rock, only to see that the weapon that was firing at them was a fifty-caliber machine gun. "Jesus!" Cleabo exclaimed softly. A fifty-caliber bullet can crack the engine block of any truck; it would sear completely through a man.

Looking off to the right then left, he saw Corporal Mapp. He wanted to make sure that the corporal saw him. A hand signal from Mapp indicated where the firing was coming from. Cleabo nodded his head. He spotted some more of his men watching and waiting on his signal to flank the ambushers. The grass was tall, Cleabo gave the hand signal to the other men to flank the ambushers; they crawled and fired. The sound of bullets pierced their ears and the thought of dying made them tremble.

Cleabo implemented a V-shape offensive tactic on the ambushers to take out the gunmen. He lost two men, but could have lost more. Once they killed the ambushers, he decided to camp out there. They waited to see if anymore of their people would come to see what had happened to their surprised attack team. Cleabo and his men stayed well-hidden and camouflaged for about an hour and nothing happened. From his pack, Cleabo retrieved the map that had been given to him on the aircraft; he had to get the soldiers to a certain point on the map. The soldiers were hungry, so they opened some C-rations. When chow was over, it was time to move on. It started getting dark and their next point was somewhere outside of Colon, Panama.

That first incident made him realize how things were going to be in Panama. The night started to settle in and they were surrounded by trees. In the jungle it's enormously dark at night; if a person held his hand up he couldn't see it. The sound of crickets was totally different than the sound he was used to in the United States. Cleabo was getting impatient waiting for his contact and the darkness didn't make it any easier. After hours of waiting, finally the sound of a vehicle was heard coming toward them.

Cleabo instructed Private Washington to go to his guard point. The sound became louder; it was a jeep carrying three American soldiers. They stopped and peered around like they were looking for something or someone. Cleabo's soldiers surrounded the men in the jeep. "Halt!" Private Washington shouted at them and told them to identify themselves. An older guy said that he was looking for Sergeant Cleabo Jones. Washington walked up to him and asked, "What do you want with Cleabo?"

The soldier answered sharply and quickly. "We need to talk to him."

"I'm Cleabo." Cleabo spoke up loudly from a distance with his weapon in his hands.

Come over here and let's talk."

The three men identified themselves and said they thought he and his men had been killed in the initial gunfire. The men took out a map and pointed where they were and gave Cleabo and the team their mission. The mission was to go inside Panama City and rescue whatever Americans they could find at the university. A terrorist group had taken over the university and was holding hostages.

One of the men said, "The reason we need a reactionary force of talent and capabilities such as you and your team, is simply because most of the troops here are preparing for other ground and air missions. Things are getting kind of heated up here and everyone at the embassy would like to keep this matter under control. You do understand?"

"Yes, I understand," Cleabo answered.

The man continued to talk. "Apparently, some Americans went into an area inside of Panama City where they didn't belong and they were shot down in cold blood. Other American students are being held as prisoners at the university. You and your men have two days to get in and out before the air attack starts."

The soldier also said there would be someone joining them in a day and his code name was Moses. Moses would take them to get more ammo on the way to Colon. He indicated on the map where they would be meeting the native called Moses. Their job was to rescue any Americans and kill anything in their way.

Cleabo wasn't surprised at what his mission was. He knew that there was some reason why airborne rangers of their caliber were there. The men were trained to eat off of the land and exceptionally knowledgeable at survival techniques. After the men left, Cleabo had to let his team know exactly what they would be doing.

Cleabo and the men sat around in a circle in the dark and discussed their long journey. At zero four hundred he decided they would depart to meet Moses, hoping that they would reach the promised land. From that point, they would make more plans.

"Let's take it one step at a time," he told his men. "But realize the situation we are in and expect a lot of surprises. I want Williams at the point, Simpson with the fifty-caliber and Mapp, you help with it. Johnson at the rear with the .60 and Styles in the middle with the grenade launcher. The rest of us will fall into place."

Cleabo continued…for a moment he thought that he sounded like Speed.

"We will be traveling in a staggered wedge formation, watching over-bound in full effect, two rock n' rollers at the wings, snipers and semi-auto in the rear. You know who you are," he finished.

Morning came quickly and it was time to move out. Cleabo hoped to find Moses somewhere in the jungle. As the men gathered up all of their equipment, he could see that some of them were a little nervous. They traveled about five miles before they ran into Moses. One of the men in the rear heard a noise and passed the signal on to everyone. They instantly took cover.

Cleabo noticed a tall, dark-skinned man wearing only a loin cloth. He said in a disturbing tone of voice, "I'm Moses and I've been following you for quite some time now. You travel well in the jungle, however, the journey you have ahead is much more difficult."

"It's good to see you Moses, we could have killed you for sneaking up on us like that."

"There's no need to fear me. I will be your navigator. We will be traveling east to a little village about ten miles from here. The place is heavily guarded and there are a few civilians in the area that are aware of the hostages. They were transferred out of the city and they're no longer at the university. You can get more ammo about five miles from here."

The journey was long and terribly hot. They had to cut down bushes with their machetes to make a path through the thick forest. The stop for ammo was quick. It was hidden in a camouflaged cave. The men quickly took what they needed and continued on their mission.

Upon arriving near the perimeter of the village they had to recon the area. There were patrols all around but they knew they had to get in. Cleabo stated to the men that he didn't want to use a lot of firepower unless it was necessary. He wanted to get in and get out.

The sun had slowly drifted away and the darkness made it's appearance taking away the soldiers vision; forcing them to wear their nightvision goggles. It was time to move out. Everyone had their own individual tasks. After breaking the perimeter and they were inside of the enemy's territory, the signal was given. There was gunfire all over the place and people running fast, trying to save their lives. Cleabo and two other soldiers made their way to the hut where they found three hostages that looked like they were suffering from malnutrition.

They gathered them up and made their way outside, as grenades began blowing up. They escaped while dodging rocket launchers. He noticed some of his men coming out of a hut that wasn't in the instructions issued to them. While wondering what they were doing in there, he called for them to get to the rendezvous point.

A lot of his men were injured and a few were left behind for dead. It was sad watching those young guys shaking like leaves, as they thought about their buddies' bodies being splattered open. What a sight, Cleabo thought.

Moses disappeared. No one knew what happened to him, but the mission was done and it was time to make it back to the drop zone. A chopper was waiting for them; they boarded it and expeditiously flew to the area to get on an aircraft.

The flight back home was long on the C-130 aircraft. As they looked at the hostages they had rescued, they realized that it hadn't been an even trade. Their buddies' were left behind with the insides of their stomachs exposed, and their intestines hanging out on the ground. Their blood flowed a red trail onto the earth and down to the coil of hell.

The men were happy to be alive even as they thought about the demolished bodies they left behind. Cleabo never imagined in all of his days that he would have so many bullets pass by his ears and survive.

After having a couple of drinks from a bottle he had stashed away, he managed to get some sleep on the aircraft. While he slept he started dreaming about what had happened. During his dreams Cleabo was perspiring heavily, moaning and shouting, "No, no!" he was dreaming that he was back there in Panama with his leg shot off.

One of the men woke him up and said, "Sarge, wake up! Wake up! Damn Sarge, you're having flashbacks too soon."

Cleabo sat up and brushed the sweat from his eyes, glad to be awake. "I'll be all right," he told the soldier.

When the plane arrived in the United States, they were greeted by his First Sergeant and it wasn't a pleasant greeting, either. The men were sad from losing a few of their buddies' and Cleabo was depressed because he was in charge of those dead bodies. Cleabo and his First Sergeant exchanged greetings and he told him and his men to take the rest of the week off. He wanted to see them the following

Monday in his office to fill out some paperwork. Cleabo and the men needed some rest after what they had gone through. Cleabo spent most of his off days at the bar.

Monday morning came and he had this funny feeling in his stomach like something wasn't right. Cleabo arrived on the post at zero five thirty hours. It was dark and there was a full moon. When he arrived at the gate, six military police cars surrounded him. All of the officers pulled their guns out, locked and loaded, ready to fire at his slightest move. They told him to get out of the car slowly with his hands in the air.

Cleabo didn't know what was going on. One of the officers said, "Lie on the ground, face down, with your arms and legs spread, fully extended."

Cleabo carefully complied, while the officers handcuffed him and searched his car for weapons. They kicked him in the mid-section and called him a murderer. Cleabo didn't know what was going on. All he had been thinking about was coming to work and asking for a discharge.

The cell they put him in was cold. Some of the common lawbreakers, like the DUI offenders were in the cell next to him. But, he knew that his offense was more serious. The facts hadn't reached him yet. He knew that he would be hearing them tomorrow.

It appeared there were three Panamanians killed and some illegal money stolen. Cleabo's .45 caliber was the murder weapon. His fingerprints were all over it and three eyewitnesses saw him confiscating some money during the involvement of the hostages rescue. The witnesses were three of Cleabo's soldiers. They all had matching written statements. The local police conducted a search of Cleabo's house and five thousand American dollars were found.

Cleabo was behind in paying some of his bills and the First Sergeant told the authorities that bill collectors were calling for their money and he had talked to Cleabo on several occasions. Cleabo knew that he had been set up. Why, he didn't know. All he could think of was how Speed would get himself out of a situation like this. He remembered losing his weapon and how the Army stressed on keeping your weapon. He was going to file the report that morning but it was a little too late. Tomorrow he would get to see his lawyer.

Dinner was some thick potatoes and some sweet peas. He gave the guard his pork chops but he drank his kool-aid. Cleabo could barely swallow the thick potatoes; eating was far from his mind.

The guy next to him said, "Hey man, we heard what you did and it's good for them motherfuckers."

"Hey man, I didn't do nothing. They sent me to rescue some people and now there is no one to rescue me. But that's all right. I just have to have faith." Even as he spoke the words, Cleabo wondered at his lack of it.

The next morning, Cleabo woke up freezing. The wind was rushing in from the long hallway in front of the cell and the thin linen he had didn't help him at all. The toilet bowl was stopped up and the smell of manure was in the air. Cleabo knew he had to get the hell out of there. His court appointed lawyer showed up after he finished his breakfast of cold oatmeal.

Mr. Jacourski was let into the cell. They shook hands and the lawyer started talking about the treatment of the holding block. Cleabo told him to cut the small talk and get to the nitty gritty.

"You are in here for three counts of murder and the taking of illegal money. Your weapon is the murder weapon and three of your soldiers stated they saw you kill the three civilians and take the money."

Cleabo denied it and explained to him what happened in Panama. He recalled the night before the mission, his .45 being missing and a couple of soldiers being out of their sleeping bags when he woke up in the middle of the night. He just thought that they were on their guard point. The news was shocking to Cleabo. The lawyer said he could be facing twenty to forty years in prison.

"Man that's too long for nothing! Hey man, I know you heard it before, but I'm innocent."

His lawyer started asking him in detail about everything that went on in Panama, and Cleabo told him. The lawyer said that a military trial was arranged for the next week. Cleabo told him to find his close friend, Sunshine, and let her know what was going on.

Unfortunately, the night was long inside of his cell. Cleabo had a lot of nightmares and somehow he didn't think that he was getting out of this one.

Sunshine finally came to visit him and Cleabo told her what had happened. Sadly for Cleabo, there was nothing Sunshine could do for him except give him support. To Cleabo it was enough that Sunshine had come. He felt that when a person is incarcerated, no one wants to see them in that capacity anyway. He was just pleased that someone he knew came to see him. Feeling like he was backed up against a wall, he knew that he had to use the tools Speed had given him for survival.

The following week at Cleabo's trial, things went fast. It was practically '1,2,3 you're guilty.' He was given a forty years to life sentence. As the judge delivered the sentence, Cleabo displayed no emotion. He was hard and stern as his eyes stared the judge down. He knew there was nothing he could say or do that would get him out of this situation. He was pinned down and backed into a corner he had never been into before. Cleabo needed time; time to figure this one out, he thought.

After the lawyer's final visit, it was time to move Cleabo to a different jail, other than the holding cell. The ride was long everyone had shackles on their feet and their wrists were chained. The military prison was a little different than normal ones. Most of the people were there for hard crimes. When they said hard labor, that is exactly what it was.

CHAPTER X

ESCAPE

The bus entered the gates of the compound as the guards stood and watched the new load of inmates. Sweat dripped from underneath Clayton's cap and rolled down the side of his face, making it's way to the tip of his chin.

Clayton was a military prison guard. He stood about five foot ten and weighed about one ninety five. He was a sensitive, but on some occasions, hard guard; who was just waiting on his time to get out of the Army. He had thick eye brows and despised his occupation. He lived alone with his dog Max, and his small apartment was trashed with paper from typing up numerous resumes for a job in the civilian world. His enlistment time was near expiring. He was a pleasant man, unless you pissed him off, then you had hell on your hands.

It was hot, and the dust from the tires of the bus as it came to a shrieking halt didn't ease Clayton's discomfort. With the mild case of diluted mud on his face Clayton stood with the rest of the guards. Appearing to be mean, he was an authoritarian figure while waiting for the prisoners to exit the bus. With the sun beaming on their backs, the armed towel guards stood anxiously; locked and loaded with their weapons pointed at the new arrivals. They waited, itching for the opportunity to squeeze the trigger if one of the prisoners made the wrong move. They often bragged about shooting prisoners down when they would try to escape. It had been a long time since they had any excitement like that, so their weapons were pointed on the bus as it entered the gates, in eager anticipation.

The driver exited the bus, slapping his cap on his leg to get some of the dust off of his clothes, and the prisoners began to shuffle their way off of the bus. Twelve of them lined up in the middle of the court yard, as the commander gave his little speech about the rules of the camp. Clayton's eyes zoomed in on Cleabo and at the same time, Cleabo's left eyebrow raised as he held his head up. Their eyeballs locked in on one another. Clayton instantly noticed the pain and suffering Cleabo displayed; his brown eyes had a gray line at the bottom of the eyeball, a look similar to cataracts. His eyes were blood shot red with tiny veins in the white portion of them, from drinking too much. The sizzling sun rays of Panama had left him with crackling dry skin, and his complexion that was once brown, had now turned black. His lips were dry and chapped and it was easy to see the skin peeling off of his black and pink lips from a distance.

"There is something different about this one. I know he isn't trying to stare me down. Surely he wasn't in a position to try to intimidate me," Clayton thought.

After the commander finished his speech, the guards marched them into the in-processing area. Some of the guards smacked the prisoners on the leg with their *billy clubs* as they walked in a single file. One of the prisoners was struck on the knee cap and he dropped to the ground screaming from his pain. Cleabo looked at him, feeling sorry that he couldn't get up and continue to walk. So did the older prisoners, as they stood from a distance and shook their heads. They knew this inmate was about to really get messed up. Around the same time his knee hit the ground, he was jumped on by three correctional officers, who whipped the day lights out of him. Their clubs rippled on his back, and all Clayton did was watch and ensure that the other inmates didn't try to get involved.

Cleabo knew these guys weren't messing around, they meant business. They talked to the prisoners like they were dirt. Cleabo thought boot camp was strict, but it didn't have anything on this place. The guards unsuccessfully tried to intimidate Cleabo. They made remarks to him insinuating that they were going to get another inmate to kick his ass, but it didn't phase him.

Clayton noticed the bloodshot eyed inmate, Cleabo. Cleabo was looking at Clayton as he watched the guards brutalize the new inmate. Finally, a few minutes after the commander turned his head away from the incident, the beating stopped. The guards began to yell at the fallen inmate, instructing him to get to his feet. With his bruised lips and broken ribs, he was indeed a good example of the type of treatment that would come to those that stepped out of line. It was normal for one of the new arrivals to get beat up. Even if they all would have followed directions, one of the guards would have tripped one of them up with their club just to have a victim.

The new inmates were placed in a huge gymnasium. The floor was covered with little black pictures of every article that was in their bags. They went through this trip of unpacking all of the items from the duffel bag. Each item had to be placed on it's particular picture on the floor.

When all of the garments were out of the bag and neatly folded on the black piece of artwork, they had to re-pack it in a certain order. That game went on for about four hours. One inmate was complaining so the guard took him out of the line up and beat the living daylights out of him in front of everyone.

After the in-processing, the guards took the prisoners to the side of the building and hosed them down with a high-pressure hose. Regardless of what time of year it was, the tradition of getting a bath outside couldn't be changed. It was like a baptism; they would have to state their name and stand fast to the high pressure hose as the coned shaped force of water made it's attempt to knock their tiered bodies to the ground. After the bath the guards would then march their dripping wet bodies to their new home, the cell block. Clayton learned that the blood shot eyed prisoner was named Cleabo Jones and he was indigenous of the *"Big Apple."* After a couple of weeks Clayton started to get to know this Cleabo.

One day as he was passing by his cell, Cleabo stopped him. "Hey guard, I'm innocent you know?"

"Yeah Cleabo, that's what they all say."

"No, I'm for real," he took a deep breath, "I'm innocent and I can prove it."

"How in the hell are you going to prove it from here? Didn't you have your chance to prove it?"

"No, I didn't have a chance; that was a damn lynching mob." Cleabo leaned his head downward and continued. "The only way I know to prove my innocence to you is by telling you my story. Then you will know who I am and then you can pass judgment."

"You know how many people here have stories, Cleabo? What make yours so spectacular? I could lose my job messing around with you."

"If you would just listen to me," Cleabo begged earnestly, "I'm sure you will find it interesting. Let me tell you from the beginning to the end."

"Okay Cleabo," Clayton stopped and leaned sideways to the wall next to Cleabo's cell. "I will listen, but you have to give it to me piece by piece, I can't be caught standing here too long."

Cleabo started rapidly, he wanted to tell as much as he could as quickly as possible.

"My mother always told me the story of our lives from the time I was born until the time I could remember on my own, so I will start there." With his crackling, low toned voice, he began to tell Clayton his story as told to him by his mother.

Most of the guards felt intimidated by the presence of Cleabo. They knew how dangerous he could be after reviewing his background. To some of them, his record was similar to theirs. The type of mentality that was required to be a prison guard of a military facility basically was the resume of a ruthless individual, and they knew that Cleabo fit the profile.

When Clayton first saw him getting off the bus, the first thing he noticed was the survival instinct. The pain that was in his red, blood-shot eyes gave Clayton the feeling of a person with a hole inside of him. Hardness wouldn't have given him total justice as a description. Cleabo delivered a threatening demeanor with a painful expression.

Clayton was a prison guard; however, his background was more or less pretty strait-laced. He always managed to keep his nose clean. However, like Cleabo, he started breaking some rules, too. He wasn't suppose to socialize with the prisoner, but Cleabo became his friend. Everyday Cleabo would tell him bits and pieces of his life story until Clayton managed to put them together. Being able to share some of Cleabo's joys and most of his pain made a major impact on Clayton's life. They became friends and Clayton became convinced Cleabo was innocent, but he couldn't do anything about it.

It became hard for Clayton to go to work everyday feeling sorry for Cleabo. There were times when Clayton found it hard to even look him square in the face. One morning when Clayton stepped out of bed, he knew something was different about the day. Sometimes things can be in place and everything as normal as can be. But this particular morning was different. His dog, who normally slept at the foot of his bed, wasn't there, and his watch was mysteriously in the kitchen instead of on his dresser.

"Wait a minute," he thought to himself. "What the hell is going on here this morning? I hope my car is still outside."

After getting dressed in his silly-ass uniform, Clayton dashed out the door, running late as usual. He opened up the car door and started the old 'always want to get rid of' car of his. Clayton raced down the freeway trying to make it to work, receiving a speeding ticket was far from his mind. His car was going 70 miles an hour in a 55 mile an hour speed zone. He didn't care; his only concern was to see what Cleabo was going to talk to him about this morning.

"Damn, his stories are good and I don't know if he knows that I'm jotting them down when I come home at night. Maybe I'll tell him today," Clayton said to himself while driving.

As he pulled up to the compound, it looked like all hell had broken loose. He normally listened to the news coming into work, but today was a different day in so many ways. Clayton had a 'Third World' tape in, instead of the news. He was listening to this song called *'Now that we found love, what are we going to do with it?'*

There were fire trucks and police cars, and all of the armed guards were going mad trying to round up prisoners. He quickly pretended that he was of the same capacity as the other guards, truly faking the funk; although in actuality he really didn't care. Clayton was only hoping that one of those crazy inmates wouldn't be trying to kill him. He was trying to protect himself in all of the confusion.

"Damn a prisoner, half of them were innocent anyway!" he said to himself sarcastically.

Guards were stabbed and part of the compound was blown into pieces, like someone had set off a serious bomb.

"Damn, who could have done some shit like this?" he puzzled in his mind.

With all of the smoke and fire going on, he managed to get to the cell block area. Clayton had to push bodies out of his way to get to the ground level.

"Damn, let me see if Cleabo is alright!" Clayton said out loud at this point.

He made his way to Cleabo's cell and to his surprise, it was empty. So many people were killed in this incident that the Army refused to have a whole lot of publicity. They just wrote it off as six men killed, 20 injured and 12 were missing in action.

"Don't that beat all, missing in action!" Clayton thought.

Clayton knew that Cleabo had never told his grandmother or his mother where he was. He had hoped to get out of prison and just go see them. "Oh well," Clayton thought, "He must have, because his body was never recovered."

Cleabo was smart enough to know that if he ever surfaced, he would be detained by the police and his fingerprints would put him right back into military hands. The "missing in action" was just a bunch of hog wash; Clayton knew it and he knew Cleabo did too.

The government would back off looking for the MIA's, and let the local authorities handle them. Cleabo knew this and he also knew that he would have to go underground. Cosmetic surgery would take care of the fingerprints and a set of dentures would perhaps decrease the chance of him being identified by his dental work. Where could he be, Clayton thought to himself?

After gaining Cleabo's life story, Clayton knew what type of individual he was. He knew that Cleabo would be able to survive and blend in with society and walk the same streets as everyone else without getting caught.

As the ambulance crew carried some of the prisoners out on the stretcher, the smoke and flames began to diminish. The smell of dead bodies made Clayton's stomach turn; it was a nasty odor. Not having the opportunity to experience any combat, he wasn't used to the appalling odor. Some people had told him about the smell of dead bodies. Maybe they should have told him about the repulsive chemical smell of burnt dead bodies that lingers in the air for days.

That scene at the compound of burnt separated limbs all over the place was something he would never forget. The main building was destroyed, and bricks crushed the weight lifting area in the courtyard. Dust filled the air while guards rapidly attempted to ease the chaos. Fire blazed from the cafeteria while inmates hid behind barricades from the guards. The precision timing of the explosions had been definitely planned. Alternating explosive devices had been set off in three different areas of the compound.

Only a person of great experience could have done such a treacherous thing. The expression on the men's faces were somewhat different as they passed by him on the stretcher. The ones that were just wounded had odd smiles on their faces; like they knew that the explosions were going to happen. It seemed like all of them had conspired with a leader and they were willing to take the chance of living or dying. Why not? These were the same terms that were issued to them when they had gone into combat.

All of the prisoners weren't crazy, but they were all soldiers and willing to obey orders from a leader. Someone must have injected into their minds to treat the compound as a prisoner of war camp and Cleabo had taken advantage of it. The military had taught every soldier ways of escaping, and they consistently stressed that the quicker you try to escape the better your chances were.

It was stupid for the Army to have put all of those master criminally minded soldiers in the same compound. It was like a time bomb waiting to explode. Clayton felt fortunate that the explosion started at four in the morning, long before his time to come to work. He could have been one of those guards he saw being carried out with a hole in their forehead. Some had the backs of their heads completely blown out from being shot at point blank range, execution style.

The prisoners showed no mercy when they were in control of the compound; he could easily assume it had been a mad house. Somehow, Clayton thought this episode was trying to tell him that he needed to get out of the Army or his life would be cut short. Clayton always thought there was a fine line between being stable and being insane. What happened at the compound demonstrated to him that these soldiers had crossed the line a long time ago.

For the next two weeks, he tried to keep a low profile. The dead and the missing body count were kept on the down low. The higher ranks didn't want any more publicity than they already had. The compound was located in a secluded area. The media could only stick their nose in from a distance and that was by chopper.

Some of the men were caught by the FBI agents and the local authorities, but the majority of them escaped. Unlike ordinary escapees from regular prison, most of these men were trained to live off the land and to blend in with the terrain. One of the local perimeters that was set up in the woods by the local authorities, ran into some problems. They found two dogs with their throats cut open and blood splattered all over the place. Traces of the dog's blood were scattered in three different directions sending the other dogs in circles.

One of the dead dog's legs had been amputated; it was assumed that one of the prisoners ate them when he was hungry. The FBI was no match for these soldiers and Clayton's time was running short at the compound. After seeing how things could get, he couldn't wait for his last month to end.

Military life as a prison guard was cool while it lasted for him. His search of finding himself and what he wanted to be was over. Clayton now realized that he wanted to be a writer. Cleabo's story had given him the confidence he needed, despite what his friends said. As Clayton burned his green uniform in the large sized metal trash can, he gave it a final salute.

He packed all of his belongings in his car and headed to his home town of Los Angeles. After sending out numerous resumes, Clayton landed a job as a supervisor for the distribution department at the *L.A. Times*. After arriving there, he found out that his job was basically handing out bundles of newspapers to be delivered. Although he was still trying to put together Cleabo's story for publication, he somehow thought that he would one day write articles for this huge newspaper company.

Clayton managed to get Cleabo's story published and it received enormous popularity. His job gave him a better position and a promotion; he was now writing small articles. With the aid of a spell-check and grammar proofreading on his computer, Clayton was able to stay afloat with his competitive comrades in his new office environment.

Clayton's words weren't as extensive as theirs; but the editor told him he had a way of expressing with meaning, and they received a different type of feeling from his articles. Clayton thought they were just bullshitting him and he was given the newly created position due to the popularity that arose from the publication of his book of Cleabo's life.

One summer day, after leaving his crowded cubicle, Clayton was thinking about how he had to work twice as hard as everyone else; but he was learning more about writing than he had ever dreamed. L.A. was a busy city with so many people on the streets. As he stopped his car at a red light, just before the entrance of the ramp to get onto Ventura Freeway, a bum, or transient, dressed the way Cleabo would describe them, thrust his body onto the hood of his car.

With his head turned to the side, Clayton could see his matted, gray beard and uncombed hair. Clayton rolled down the window only to smell the aroma that almost gagged him from this hobo of a man. The man's face was turned away from Clayton, only exposing a side view. Clayton yelled at him, "Hey! Get the fuck off of my car!" to his surprise, a familiar voice said, "Can I wash your windows for you?" the transient turned his head looking him directly in the eyes.

Despite the beard, his hair, and the way he was dressed, Clayton looked this man squarely into his blood shot brown eyes and recognized him. He said to himself, "Holy shit, it's Cleabo!"

Cleabo looked at him with a grin, as he reached into the inside pocket of his coat. For a moment Clayton thought that he was going to pull out a weapon. Cleabo retrieved a copy of Clayton's novel and placed it on his windshield and said, "Thank you."

The cars behind him started blowing their horns after the red light turned green. Clayton turned his head for a quick second to tell them to hold on, but by the time he turned around to talk to Cleabo, he was gone; just as quickly as he had fallen on the top of the hood of his car.

This felt like no coincidence to Clayton; this man truly had the talent and ability to mingle in with society. Clayton could never forget Cleabo; his life, and the things that helped shape his world. His lifestyle was one that truly exhibited good and bad. Clayton only imagined that he was making his way to see someone that was never a part of his life. Perhaps his father, he didn't know. He only knew whoever became involved with Cleabo, had better be on their p's and q's.

CHAPTER XI

THE A O

Cleabo hitchhiked his way to California after someone set off numerous amounts of explosions at the compound. Some people were killed, and that was too bad, but he had to get the hell out of there. Several people escaped and they all went their separate ways. Clayton, the prison guard, used to listen to his story about his life through the bars of his cell. Cleabo knew that he was going home at night and writing his stories down.

"He thought I didn't know what he was doing." Cleabo thought to himself, "But I did, and I just didn't say anything."

Cleabo thought that if this was Clayton's way out by writing a novel about his life, it was cool with him. Now, Cleabo began to write his own journal about what happened to him after the escape from the compound.

"Maybe I will send it to Clayton and he will do a reprint of his novel; my life. I hope so, but, I know he will have to put what I'm saying in his own words; I can't write worth a shit," Cleabo smiled.

Cleabo had tracked Clayton to L.A. and he gave him his thanks for bringing his life story to print. As quickly as he found him he left him; Cleabo was taught to maneuver in such a manner.

While showing his face to Clayton as he lay on the hood with his cleaning materials in his hands, Cleabo told him thanks as he displayed a copy of the book. Little did he know his life story was just beginning. Clayton knew that if he ever mentioned seeing Cleabo, Cleabo would kill him quickly. He knew he couldn't hide, Cleabo would track his ass down. With all of the teachings he had from the streets of the south Bronx, and the military training of survival techniques, killing could have easily become second nature to him. Clayton knew who he was and Cleabo wasn't at all worried about Clayton turning him in, they had become friends at the compound.

"Sure I'm glad he published that book, but shit, I could use some of that money now," Cleabo thought, as he sat in his corner with a can of day old potted meat that he retrieved out of the garbage can around the corner.

L.A.'s Hollywood Boulevard is where Cleabo found refuge in an abandoned office space. Couldn't use the front door, he had to go in through the back. A small dark alley and a door with two by fours nailed across it in an x fashion, yellow tape with the words *'Condemned'* wrapped around the two by fours couldn't stop him. This was his new home; he needed shelter, a place to stay out of the rain, an "A.O." As the Army would say, "Area of operation;" Damn, how those words lingered in his mind.

Cleabo's new space was small and dark with no running water. Unlike other transients, he read the newspaper to find his new home. Strange as it may seem, he knew that in the Sunday papers he could find a condemned building or an abandoned office space in the classified section. Being the first in a condemned building helped him avoid fighting for his territory. However, there could be a time when a bad ass would come around and attempt to throw him out, but he wasn't going for that. This was his space now; they could share the bathroom, but that is as far as it would go. Turning the water back on was an easy task; the city never traced the water, just the electricity.

He laid claim to a large room and all of the junkies knew it. He was the first one there and therefore, Cleabo was considered to be the landlord; but he had to be a bad ass in order to maintain respect. If he was a softy, he would get tossed out of the old office building. Cleabo pretended to be cold and unpleasant and he was hard on the junkies in the other three rooms; they really found it difficult to understand him and Cleabo wanted to keep it that way.

It was difficult for them to understand why he wasn't shooting up, smoking or snorting dope. Cleabo understood how confused they may have been, especially since he would never reveal his past. Shooting dope was all the other transients did, day after day.

"What a waste," he thought. Continuously they tried to figure him out. Most of the time he would just yell at them, "Pick your partner up out of the hallway, and carry his ass inside your room!" It was much like Mrs. Doria did for her son Richie in the Bronx.

Yes, he had rules. Cleabo was just a sergeant in the Army a few months ago, before he was sentenced to forty years for something he had nothing to do with. He escaped though; busted the hell out of that lock down. So, when he came to the hallway to set the junkies straight it was in a direct and forceful manner. They learned to respect him, and he usually treated them pleasantly. However, landlords rarely become friends with their tenants.

The junkies would try to steal the drawers off of a person if they slept too hard. Cleabo kept his room door locked; although a locked door doesn't mean a thing to a transient or a dope fiend. Therefore, he turned his little room into a serious booby trap. Although he had nothing inside of his little room, it was all that he had in the world and he made it his business to protect his domain. Having a junkie snooping around and trying to steal from him while he was gone, was most definitely out of the question.

If someone tried to enter his room while he was out for the day, they were in for a surprise. Cleabo had traps that would activate CO2 canisters at the door and the two boarded up windows; a nasty gas for anyone without a gas mask. Another canister was in the ventilation system to clear out the entire office space.

All jokes aside, he wasn't to be messed with. He had become hard and bitter. Revenge on the person or people that set him up to take the fall was the only significant thing on his mind.

"Forget those junkies. As long as they stay their smelly ass out of my room, they will have no problem with me," Cleabo would say when he thought about his new arrangements.

Sometimes a junkie can be the smartest person in the world; at least they would think so. Cleabo heard some of their conversations when they were on that stuff. He had seen a transformation that was out of this world. They would talk about politics, world issues, and things of that nature. Cleabo knew they had to be out there, hell he didn't even talk scholastically, and they were *'mainlining'* too. Cleabo had something for that smart junkie that would try to break into his room while he was out for the day. If the junkie was smart enough to get a respirator, Cleabo's back up would go into effect.

Deviously minded with hood and military knowledge, he carved into several blocks of wood a channel, or a gully. Then, he placed the fat portion of a car radio antenna into the gully of the blocks of wood. With the antenna placed on the wood and secured, Cleabo placed a twenty-two bullet inside the opening of the antenna. He made six high-pressure hammers that would pound the end of the bullet, sending it's deadly messenger in the direction of whoever was messing with his territory. Three blocks set for the window and three set for the door, both firing at alternating intervals at a ripple effect.

Cleabo really didn't think those junkies knew who they were messing with if they were to ever cross him. The security aspects of his room had created a reputation for itself after a junkie tried to break in while he was out one day. When he returned Cleabo discovered bullet holes in the walls and in the hallway as well.

A drugged out neighbor of his greeted him; he was anxious to tell Cleabo about the unknown intruder. Cleabo remained calm, knowing that his territory was protected, and he would probably never have a problem of this nature again. Cleabo's *"AO"* gained a reputation of being a trap as it was intended. How relieved he was to hear the excitement in the voice of the junkie name Kenny, as he described how the intruder was dodging bullets as he fled. Kenny said that gas went off in the ventilation system during the commotion.

"It just messed up everyone's high, and we had to clear out of the building to get some fresh air." Kenny shook his head and then continued. "Man we won't mess with your stuff, and we'll make sure no one else will. We can't enjoy getting high like this man, and besides, you don't have anything in here to steal anyway." Kenny said as he glanced around Cleabo's room. He had the facial expression that clearly said, 'I can't wait to get back to my syringe.'

Cleabo sighed relief as he realized from that point on, he wasn't going to have anymore problems with anyone trying to break into his room.

"I hear you Kenny; yeah you guys keep an eye on my stuff. The next time there's going to be a different surprise."

"Yeah, okay C."

"All right. Later Kenny."

'C,' is what they called Cleabo. He wasn't at liberty to tell them his real name, Cleabo Jones. When they would ask what the 'C' stood for, he would merely tell them it was none of their business. He couldn't give his real name to anyone; especially to those junkies. He looked and dressed like they did to disguise himself. His real name didn't matter. Besides, it would just be a way for the Army or the Fed's to track him down. Just the thought of how things went down at the compound left him confused more than ever. Prior training had taught him how to play the undercover game, only this time he had to play it for life.

Being an escapee had made his life difficult; it placed a lot of restrictions on his everyday activities. Pulling his share of duty on the corner was something he had to do, in order to be accepted as one of the regular transients. He panhandled and pretended to be intoxicated with some of the others, so that his face could be seen and be familiar to the police. Staying out of trouble was a priority; he couldn't get arrested. Cleabo had managed to confiscate identification from another transient that was dying of AIDS. He had passed away in the alley about four blocks around the corner. He had no criminal record, only a sad story of being a doctor and after his wife died, whatever sanity he had left was lost to the streets and drugs.

Prior to going on to the other side, the transient told Cleabo about some of his old friends that could do plastic surgery; he wrote the address and a message down for him. He also told Cleabo some of the underhanded and illegal activities they shared together. While drinking together Cleabo managed to obtain more information from the man about these doctors; things that he could use for blackmailing.

Although the doctors lived in another state, he still knew that the cosmetic surgery could be done. He wasn't worried about his teeth, Cleabo knew that if he didn't brush them they would eventually fall out, then he would get some dentures. The change of dental and fingerprints were indeed necessary, so that he wouldn't be traced in any form or fashion.

Now that he had blackmailing material, he walked away from his friend as he noticed his chest rose no more. Without a strong mind a person can surely snap and end up in the streets. Cleabo often wondered why some people avoided walking on the cracks or lines in the cement blocks of the streets. Now he knew; half of them were his friends at this point of his life.

Protecting his identity was no longer a problem. It seemed like with time the answers to all of his prayers just fell into his lap. Now he needed time; time to sort things out and figure out why he was set up. He also needed to figure out how he could get some money to get the cosmetic surgery for his fingertips; to include money to help him get revenge on the individuals that conspired to put him away. Washing windows and panhandling wasn't getting it.

Lucky, his friend, slowly walked over to him with hunger saddled on his back, wearing his little puny ass out. Lucky was a stray cat that took Cleabo to be his friend; hell anyone that would have fed him probably would've been his friend. Cleabo guessed he was first. Lucky was hungry and dirty when they first met; a brown and black big headed cat, with a huge appetite. Cleabo guessed Lucky didn't realize that he was so ruthless at this point in his life, if money was low and he was hungry, Lucky's ass would definitely be supper.

Crazy as it may sound, Bar-B-Q cat can be '*Gooder than a mug*,' to Cleabo. A smile came to his face when he thought about how this greedy cat looked at him, when he said, "Come here and let me fatten you up."

While sharing his food with Lucky he thought that the cat must have known the deal, and somehow this cat was just hanging around until the time would come for him to be digested. It was the military that introduced Cleabo to the consumption of animals. He'd often heard of people eating dogs and cats in Korea, but, never in his wildest dreams did he think he would partake in such a primitive method of eating. It was at guerilla warfare training that he had to learn to eat off the land. With only a knife and a map he had three days to be at a specific point. Cleabo ate whatever he could get his hands on. Most of the time it was rabbit, their traps were easy to make.

On one occasion, his first day in the jungle, darkness came and he was all alone; he was frightened and intimidated. "Why in the hell did I volunteer to put myself in this position?" he thought.

He was told by some of the other fellows that crickets would be a good snack and he would get used to them. It was true; they had a crunchy and gooey taste to Cleabo. By the second day they were his snack and the rabbit was his only meal each day. Cleabo had to kill a copperhead snake that startled him. The snake brushed against his jungle boots and quickly crawled into the bushes. Out of fear, he could hear the rattling sound of the deadly creature of the wild. After establishing eye contact he slowly bent down into a squatting position to pick up the stick he had been carrying with him through the thick forest of a jungle. Instantly the snake struck, and so did Cleabo;

catching his aim in mid air. Cleabo swatted the snake's venomous body to the ground and continuously beat him with the stick. He stopped beating him only for a second to retrieve his knife that was at his side.

With the blade in his hand he threw the knife hard, connecting to the serpents head. As the knife stood three inches into the ground surrounded by snake's head and body, Cleabo thanked God and himself for remembering to carry a staff in the wilderness. He was told to always have distance between animals and himself. With distance they may feel intimidated and would probably go away.

The blood from the snake dripped into the soil, the smell could spread like a wild fire in the jungle, Cleabo thought.

He had to make distance between the snake and himself quickly. He ran fast and swiftly but staying on his course, knowing that if he strayed away from the correct path, it would take a week for the military to find him. Cleabo was being trained to learn survival tactics and to track guerilla soldiers that lived in such terrain. With plotted evidence of their presence along his path, the majority of his trail was full of booby traps; including the wild animals that he had to deal with. His camouflage was good; the snake had no idea that he had brushed against his boots. He blended in too well, at least that is what he thought.

The darkness of the night landed in his lap and there was no time for sleep. He had to keep moving at a careful pace. Cleabo ran in the dark for quite a distance, then he found an area that apparently looked as though soldiers had camped out there. He didn't have a clue if the military was using real people for the task of simulating guerillas.

There were cans of C-rations located at the camp site and footprints were all over the place, but they were too obvious; it was easy to determine their direction of travel. Fortunately for him he found a pair of night vision goggles. Whether they were left there intentionally he didn't know. Cleabo knew he had to travel parallel to their tracks, so he walked a distance of about twenty yards, constantly looking for signs from the leaves, bushes, or anything that would let him know which way they went. Most of the time when there were no tracks, his instincts would direct him on the proper course.

He knew they could've hidden their tracks by sweeping; toe tipping, scattering, or other techniques. One thing was for certain, they wanted him to find their camp. The lack of any smell told him they weren't in the area. Cleabo noticed movement in the trees, which indicated to him the animals felt safe. The animals would generally go away when humans would come around, so this was a good indication to him that the soldiers weren't near. What their intentions were was another question, he was puzzled.

By using the north star as a guide and the nightvision goggles, he was able to swiftly travel all night and stayed on his course. Sleepy as hell as the sun rose, Cleabo knew that every animal in that jungle was aware of and threatened by his presence. That morning he found himself looking in the face of a wild boar, about twenty feet away. His body was huge; his horns stood erect, and he had such a vicious look from an animal Cleabo had never seen before in his life.

Cleabo was in his territory and they glanced at one another before the boar came charging at him. He didn't have time to think; only run. The boar was on his ass! Cleabo zigzagged and crisscrossed trying to lose him. But damn, that boar was fast as hell! He managed to find an overhead limb, and with a vertical leap while still in stride, Cleabo grabbed it and swung himself onto the tree. He watch the boar continue his run, looking baffled, wondering what had happened to Cleabo. After ensuring himself distance from the wild boar, he continued his journey to his destination.

The crunching sound of the leaves underneath his feet only reminded him of how much quieter he needed to be. Wooded trees and bushes obstructed his path to safety. There were broken branches and footprints; a good indication that someone else had been on this route. At this point he didn't really care if he were caught. It was only simulation with the humans, but to the wild life it was a matter of life or death.

Next to some of the footprints there was an apple core.

"Perfect," he thought, "This will be bait for my meal."

With his knife he sharpened a twig into a spear. Using his bootlaces and belt he set up a snare with the apple core. Around a tree Cleabo tied the spear. He tied off the apple core with one of his shoestrings, leaving it hanging down. After ensuring that the spear had plenty of spring action when the core was tugged, he tested his snare. He pulled on the apple core and the spear expeditiously snapped it's way to the apple core. The snare was now ready to prepare his next meal.

Cleabo climbed up a tree and patiently waited for 'Peter Cotton Tail' to arrive. After about thirty minutes a huge overfed rabbit approached the apple core. He pretended he knew better than to grab the apple; however, with his small teeth he began to nibble on the core.

"Damn," Cleabo thought to himself. He watched the oversized rabbit that he knew he would make a good meal. The size of his legs were so appetizing he made Cleabo's stomach growl.

The rabbit hopped away with a small piece of apple in his mouth, nibbling on it as he went. Halting about a foot or two away from the snare, the rabbit seemed to have been contemplating whether to go back for more. Cleabo knew that this rabbit could smell him, but Cleabo's stillness left the rabbit confused. He was unable to see Cleabo and the aroma of the apple core threw Cleabo's body scent off just a little. The fat, juicy rabbit decided to bring his greedy ass back and get some more of the apple. He should have left well enough alone. His second nibble was more or less a tug.

The spear sprang from the tree with force. Stabbing the rabbit in his side, it prepared him to be Cleabo's main course. He was some good eating. After Cleabo finished most of the rabbit off, he went on his way. Cleabo finally made it to his objective point, earlier than expected. He infiltrated the instructor's camp at around five in the morning. There were three of them; one was supposed to have been on guard duty. Outside the perimeter Cleabo gathered twigs, and with the night vision goggles he was able to collect enough twigs to tie two sticks together; two for each men.

He formed a cross or plus sign with the twigs; when the men woke up they would see the twigs tied together. Then they would realize that with the knife they had issued Cleabo, their throats could've been cut. Cleabo had won the game.

With a nice, warm fire blazing at sunlight, he was heating up some of his left over rabbit. The men woke up and to their surprise they saw the twigs at their feet made into a cross. They became conscious of where their grave could've been. Cleabo learned to enjoy those little training exercises. They were exciting and horrifically adventurous, being in the jungle by himself was a lesson of it's own;

survival was the only thing he could think of. Cleabo was scared, but too scared to think foolishly; sort of like the streets. But, in the jungle he was all alone, hungry and nervous, unaware of what may happen next.

Now sitting down on the floor with his cat eating the day old potted meat, it seemed as though Lucky was reading his mind as he reminisced about the Army. It was cold as hell on the floor. Cardboard helped a little, but it didn't stop the cold air from seeping in from the floor.

"I'd better get some shuteye," he thought, "I need to try and make some money tomorrow. Damn! I got to piss."

While getting off the floor to use the bathroom, he hoped he didn't find one of Kenny's friends nodding in the restroom; he was about to burst from the pulsating pain of his bladder being full.

Walking with his legs twitched together, he made it to the bathroom and it was empty. Like a waterfall he began to flow, shaking his manhood dry so that he wouldn't feel the piss on his legs. His only pair of underpants were long gone. Besides, it didn't even matter now; transients don't wear drawers!

The sound of the police siren, and the long cone shaped light from the Police helicopter as it shone down, made Cleabo paranoid. He trembled as he hoped like hell they would never come there. If the person they were chasing came there, he was *'sho' nuff'* in for a serious beat down. "I'd kick his ass back onto the streets," Cleabo thought out loud.

After peeping out of the boarded up window, Cleabo was able to see the guy as he dashed by. The Police were right behind him. Although the brother was giving them a run for their money, lady luck wasn't in his favor that night.

Instead of the usual 'Dunkin' Donut cops' these officers looked like they had served some time in the hood, or at the gym. They were in good shape and ran faster than the accused. They gave him a serious beat down after they grabbed him from behind. The helicopter flew away while they were beating him down, letting the police below know that the next chopper would be the news reporter's.

"Didn't he watch 'Roots?' Brothers need open fields and trees to run in. The chances of getting away in the city are slim to none. There are too many buildings and people watching you as you run by, directing the police in the direction you ran in. They have all kinds of help! Including the dog that would be running at top speed to catch and detain a criminal until his partner arrives; while he tries to bite a hole out of them. The odds weigh too much against a criminal," Cleabo thought to himself as he watched the excitement from his window.

"Time to lie down again, and if this big headed cat thinks that he is going to hog my cardboard, he is in for a serious awakening!" Cleabo thought as he crawled under the blanket.

It was cold, and the little blanket he had wasn't helping the situation at all. At this point Cleabo would've given anything for a bed. Something soft, but the ultimate would've been to have a woman at his side. It had been a long time since he had been with a woman. He was getting kind of tired of whacking it. The women that hung out in Kenny's room were out of the question. There was no telling what they might have! All of them had cradles or holes in their faces. He liked slim women, but in the streets when a woman was slim, it wasn't because she worked out.

Most of the women of that lifestyle did aerobics; elbow aerobics. This was the kind where they toke the pipe up to their mouth. Or maybe they had the AIDS from the needle. Cleabo knew one thing, he couldn't trust them to leave him without some sort of disease. He thought he'd better get some sleep, tomorrow would be a new day and full of surprises. Unaware of what to look forward to, was actually kind of sad. One thing was for sure, soon he had to get his priorities together.

He pushed Lucky's ass off of his cardboard and assumed the fetal position. He had never in all of his days heard a cat snore before. It was quite an unusual noise; Lucky was snoring like he was human. "Damn, this cat has got issues!" he thought.

Sunrise, and it seemed as though all of the transients and homeless were doing the same ritual. At dawn was when everyone would go to the lake to wash their faces and bodies. The homeless that had cars would get out and wash also. Their cars would be filled with all of their earthly belongings. There were about 20 to 30 cars on the side of the street in lined by the lake.

"Why would they want to keep all of that stuff?" he wondered.

Cleabo thought that it just identified how they were living, he preferred to keep his way of life a secret. Some of the people had kids and some were alone. Yet their cars were filled with whatever memories and possessions that hadn't been taken away from them. To most he did give credit for the way they raised their children. Although they didn't have anything, their children were the most respectable kids he had ever seen. They were well mannered.

The kids that attended school dressed well enough to make it difficult to know that they were homeless. Occasionally they bathed at the 'Y.' Most of the time the lake was their main bathtub. Although they couldn't have friends visit them, they seemed to be happy most of the time. He found out that the families generally used P.O. boxes for their children's address for school. Some of them owned tents and would live on campground sites. Most of the sites had rules and regulations. They couldn't live there longer than three weeks at a time and they would have to move on to another campground site.

The familiar faces he would see at the lake would be the ones that were in between their time period before they could go to another campground site. One family had two vehicles. One was an old beat up car and the other was a brand new Toyota four by four. The father used the new four by four to go to work with and he would leave his family the beat up car. Why he didn't put his family into a home or an apartment Cleabo didn't know, nor could he understand it. However, Cleabo was a good judge of character and from the look in the gentlemen's eyes, Cleabo could easily see this guy was a runaway with a new identity.

Being prejudiced, or thinking that you were better than someone else, didn't exist at this level of life; there was no room for it. Survival was everyone's main objective. They bathed in the same water, and if the kids woke up too early and walked down to the lake, they would see grown ups with their naked asses in the water. It didn't matter, nor did it phase the children. Everyone just minded their business and went on with life.

After the city finally figured out how to track and turn off Cleabo's water, he had no choice but to utilize the lake, just as everyone else did. Using his hands as a funnel he scoop up some water to wash his face. The hazel black dirty water with all of its pollutants felt good as it ran down his face. Dripping down his salt and pepper matted up beard, the cold water felt refreshing.

"Oh, that feels so good. It's been a while since I washed my entire body," he thought as he began to take his clothes off. Partially camouflaged behind a four foot bush, he knew he could wash up without his privacy being invaded. There were weeks of dirt between all of his cracks and unmentionable places.

"Oh, how disgusting I've become!" he thought. Even with the absence of soap he felt cleaner now. The clothes that he wore were his dry towels, and the big leaves that were on the ground he used as a wash cloth. It felt so good getting his body all cleaned up.

As he was exiting the lake, to his surprise this beautiful creature startled him. She was around five foot six with a creamy skin complexion. She was exceptionally pretty, and she stopped in her tracks; staring at his totally nude body. He didn't move, fearing he would startle her and perhaps she would think that he was trying to rape her while she was walking her dog.

"Perhaps she'll scream and the police will come. That would be the last thing I need!" he thought as he froze in his tracks for a moment.

He kept his distance and continued to dry himself off. However, he noticed how she continued to look at his nude body. Her eyes wouldn't let go of him. She was mesmerized.

"I'm sorry." She said apologetically.

"That's quite all right, I didn't mean to frighten you, I was only trying to wash up."

"No, no, it is I, who bumped into you. Have a good day," she said, leaving just as quickly as she came, while he continued to dry himself off. Cleabo started to wonder why such a clean looking lady would stop and just stare. Could she have liked what she saw? Or, maybe she had been in shock? Exchanging of names was out of the question. He was a bum; but maybe she saw who he really was in his eyes. Perhaps she thought a transient couldn't have a body like his? He disguised his physical conditioning in order to blend in. The sit-ups and push-ups really helped out. The small little stomach pouch he had was from the contribution of drinking beer. After all, what else did he have to do but drink?

As he put on his clothes, Cleabo continued to think about the beautiful creature that had stood in front of him. Her dark black hair had the sheen of silk. It was well groomed and preserved. Her nails and haircut were a good indication she was a high maintenance woman. Even the dog's hair was cut and trimmed. His paws were full and his tail shagged. The dog also wore a beaded collar around his neck, a gold-colored dog, probably a golden retriever, one of those pampered show dogs. The look on the woman's face had expressed total surprise while he stared into her pearl-glossy eyes. She was elegant without a doubt; and her eyes glanced down at his cold, shivering, dripping wet body.

"Could she have been walking her dog and stumbled upon me? Or was this an everyday thing for her to do?" he wondered. "Did she always wake up early and strut her classy self to the lake to look at the homeless transients as they bathed their bodies every morning? No, her poise and the way she strutted herself away clearly signified she wasn't that type." Cleabo thought. A mystery lady he had to assume; yet a little freaky he could conclude. The womanly manner she presented was tall and strong. He sensed the dominant side of her character that displayed strength.

Perhaps a Kung Fu lesson or two she had taken could've given her this inner strength that was appealing to him, it was easy to tell this was no ordinary lady. As she walked away her aroma followed her. It was like a mist of the sweetest thing he'd never smelled before.

"Damn, she smelled so good!" he shook his head back and forth.

Cleabo wanted to follow her. He sat on the cold ground to put his jeans on, making sure that his foot didn't go through the hole at the knee. Thinking of her, he watched the sunrise. He had to get his mind off of her; soon people would be there and the sight of transients at the lake during daybreak wasn't tolerated.

All of the homeless people with cars hastily drove off, and the ducks gracefully swam to the edge of the lake. Out of nowhere they would fly in and look for someone to feed them bread. Cleabo thought most of the homeless people departed the area quickly because a fat duck can be tempting when you have nothing to eat. They knew it would be against the law if they killed one, and for some reason it seemed as though everyone was trying their best to stay above the law.

While walking down the path of the lake on his way to get something to eat, he stuck his hands into his jean pockets. His mind was still bamboozled from the lady he had just bumped into. He should have remembered that his jeans had a hole in the left front pocket. Instantly Cleabo searched the right pocket, looking for some change from the day before. If it was only a dollar it would be good; he could make the rest by panhandling to get some food as soon as he hit the streets.

An egg McMuffin to start the day would be all he needed.

"Damn, ninety cents. Better check the inside pockets of this long overcoat." He mumbled.

The collar was ripped and the edge of the sleeve was torn. The shoulder seam was beginning to separate from the body, but the dirty brown coat kept him warm. Searching inside the pockets, he already knew nothing was there. He felt some papers and like a blind man, he had the ability to distinguish the difference between paper and money. He knew it wasn't money. But, like anyone else, he would be surprised as shit if it was.

The paper that was inside of his old beat up overcoat was the information that his dead doctor friend had given him. It read: "Dr. David Wesley...We removed organs from patients that were dying. Only from the patients that we knew no autopsy would be performed on. The specific organs were packaged and shipped to different customers abroad. We received large amounts of money. Dr. Wesley is still doing it." His doctor friend also gave him the address. It was in Phoenix, Arizona. With Phoenix only being the next state over, it would be easy to hitchhike he thought. Cleabo's friend had also told him to tell Dr. Wesley that he had sent him; and if he didn't help him out, he was going to pull the rug from under his feet. He said that David would know what he was talking about.

Cleabo held his head up after reading the note, carefully and cautiously he made it across the street. A coffee shop that was taboo to his kind was staring him in the face. Around the corner and a few garbage cans away stood Mickey D's. With only ninety cents he knew he needed more. Most of the time, if he stood in front of an establishment and panhandled, the people wouldn't give him any money. Sometimes they would say, "Come on in and I'll buy you something to eat." However, some of them would think for a second then change their minds.

Just the thought of having a smelly, nasty and poorly dressed stranger in line with them was indeed intimidating. Perhaps they wondered what everyone else would think? Or, maybe the fear of doing something decent influenced or accelerated their way of thinking. So they just handed over the quarter or fifty cents and said, "Here," in a cruel and cold way.

The people that did invite him in would sometimes lecture or scorn him. Cleabo would feel so embarrassed as everyone would stare and listen as the person who thought he was doing Cleabo such a big favor continued to fuss at him. The people looking at him would have pity written all over their faces. The person buying his food would fuss at him for being homeless, jobless and living on the streets. They just absolutely degraded him in front of others for a damn Egg McMuffin. Unfortunately, Cleabo had to push his pride aside and think about his stomach.

Then there were the people who treated him as their pet. While they stood in line the manager would run from behind the counter and ask him to leave. Either the lady or man, whom ever it may have been, would tell the manager that he was with them. On this occasion he felt like he was a puppy that wasn't allowed into the restaurant. But he was submissive to their behavior in order to receive a meal.

The morning air was a little chilly that day, as he pulled his coat tighter around him to stay warm. Across the street he noticed Willie. With eye contact, they waved at one another. Willie was into cans; he collected them and sold them at the aluminum yard, off of Claremont Avenue. Rules of the street said that he couldn't cross the street into Cleabo's area of operation during a mealtime. For him to enter Cleabo's established turf at mealtime would be disrespectful. Cleabo had claimed the spot; a better one than Willie's. While leaning on the side of the building of Mickey D's, he detected a slight nod from across the street.

Willie had indicated to him that he had a potential customer approaching. Willie knew that after Cleabo received enough money to eat Cleabo would move on. Then he would be able to get the hot spot. Whenever panhandling by places to eat, your spot had to be shared, these were the rules.

A man approached Cleabo's arena, away from the door of course. Cleabo noticed the man picking up his pace after a quick glance at Cleabo; his head and eyes instantly turning away into another direction. The man hoped Cleabo didn't see him as he pretended to be invisible. How could he have ever thought Cleabo didn't see him, was ridiculous. It always amazed Cleabo how people would think he wasn't a part of their world when they crossed his path. But he was; he did exist. For whatever reason he played this hand, it was only because of the cards that society had dealt to him; it could happen to anyone. For this man to think that he could just turn his head and Cleabo would disappear was even more stupid than the way the man was dressed.

The way Cleabo was dressed didn't hide his miseries, but the man was easy to read. The Florsheim shoes were a good indication of a 'wannabe.' His insecurities were plain to see. The button down shirt and tie with the London Fog coat, placed him in the world where he wanted to be. His change of pace in his walk only made Cleabo assume there was fear and uncertainty in this man's life. He definitely had the need to belong with other people in order to feel secure. His body language and movement was indeed a good indication that he thought he was 'All that.' It was easy to see this man was heading for burnout. Stress and his life style was wearing his ass out.

"Excuse me sir, can you spare some change please?"

"No, I don't have any."

"Thank you."

When the door closed Cleabo could tell he glanced back at him, only seeing the naps of his hairline that were protruding from around the old sweater cap on his head. Within a few minutes another prospect arrived at his location, only this time a dollar was given. He only had to make one more hit and the first meal of the day would be accomplished within an hour. The next person was a female. She had pale skin, blonde hair and blue eyes. Her opened heart was easy to see when she said, "Here you go, mister." Mister; a term used so loosely. Even though he had nothing, she made him feel like he had something, or that he was somebody. Out of all of the things in this world that was taken away from him, she made him feel that the title of mister was something he could never be stripped of.

Across the street he noticed Willie moving his feet from side to side; he clicked them together as he waited for Cleabo to leave. He turned his head back and forth, anticipating a potential customer, while hunger jumped on his back and rode the shit out of him. A skinny fellow Willie was, and missing his front tooth. A thief and a dopehead, how he managed to be up and about so early was amazing. The crack was slowly destroying him; it was a slow death that everyone who did it knew would come soon. They needed it like a baby needs milk. Cleabo always thought that it was bad enough that he was out in the streets trying to survive, and panhandling for something to eat. But, he would never let drugs be the reason for him being there. Only revenge; revenge on the group of people who set him up.

"Damn!" the thought of it made him upset.

Willie delivered another nod from across the street. He knew that after this customer Cleabo would be able to eat. This time a brother that was in a rush tossed him a dollar, and he said thanks. Cleabo became a familiar face to the manager behind the counter. When the manager was new he threw Cleabo out, even though he had the money for food. Cleabo didn't make a scene that day; he left quietly. Continuously he came each morning and finally the manager gave in; Cleabo thought he just wore his ass down. As long as he was out by seven and had money, it was cool. He couldn't block the doorway though, those were the rules. During the course of the day the manager would let the senior citizens eat and relax. They would stay in the joint from nine until about three o'clock, drinking coffee and reading the newspaper. Cleabo envied those people for being able to relax in some place warm.

The hawk greeted him with his Egg McMuffin in his hands, and Willie was making his move. Before he could step off the curb Cleabo noticed him being greeted by Angel. Angel was a puny looking thing; it was easy to see she could've been fine and a work of art, at one point of time in her life. Now she looked like *'Who did it and what for?'* Her tight-ass jeans fitted her well, and from the neck down she could be desirable. But her mug was in pretty bad shape; only a plastic surgeon or a croak sack bag could help her. The front view was nice to look at though, her pelvic protruded outward, and her gap at the "*y*" was noticeable as it set the tone for her slightly slender bowed legs.

Between Willie and the streets, they had just worn Angel's raggedy ass out. Cleabo was always taught to look at a female's shoes. Someone once told him that if a woman's shoes were run down at the heel or if they weren't well maintained, generally that told him what kind of woman she was. If the shoes were run down then so was she; and when given the opportunity, she would just bring her mate's ass down right along with her. Willie was Angel's victim. He hadn't a clue what her intentions were. He should have known by the dirty-ass, brokedown, run over Converse sneakers she wore. She started working on him with the weed first, and eventually they went to another level, the pipe. Willie's ass was into so much trouble behind her; until he finally gave up. His life had become the streets. He talked about it sometimes; he'd tell Cleabo how much he just couldn't leave it alone; the pipe or Angel.

Angel was Willie's problem, she had left the pipe alone when she did a six months sentence. A dike turned her out and now they said, '*she goes both ways.*' Angel started doing speed, or crank in prison. Cleabo was surprised to see her ass up this early; he thought that shit kept people up all night long, and they would have to sleep during the day like Vampires. He remembered the time when Kenny had her and Willie over and they were doing their drugs. He had to go to the bathroom and she noticed him pass by. He saw her in the room firing up, while Kenny and Willie were laid out, she followed him to the bathroom. Angel confronted him about giving her some sex, but he merely told her that she was Willie's and he didn't want no parts of her. She told him how much she wanted him and that Willie did too many drugs and he was unable to get it up; she said she needed a real man.

His response was hard and cold. He just said that he wasn't the one. She knew that her secret was cool with him, and he never said anything to Willie. Just the thought of making it with Angel left him with a weary feeling, no matter how desperate he was. She just didn't excite him.

The Egg McMuffin went down good as he noticed Willie trying to get rid of Angel. Willie knew he had to panhandle alone. Having a female at his side would only complicate things for him. From the way she looked, he guessed Willie told her to leave him alone. Willie was hungry at this point and it was easy to see. He must have told her where to go. When she turned and walked away she had a serious attitude. Angel spotted Cleabo as he was walking away, while he was biting down on his Egg McMuffin. She waved and he waved back, then Angel began to yell from across the street towards Cleabo.

"Hey, what's going on C?"

"Nothing much, how are you doing?" Cleabo yelled back.

"Just chilling, and checking in with Willie with his old tired ass."

"I hear you, just handling your business, huh?"

"You know that's right C; aint nobody gonna do it for me."

"Yeah, I hear you babe. Haven't seen you in a while."

Angel crossed the street to talk to Cleabo as Willie took his spot by the wall. With his right hand he saluted Cleabo, as though, he was saying take that scamp away from here. But, Willie knew Cleabo didn't want to be bothered with Angel's shit this morning.

The quicker she was out of his sight the better off he would be.

"Don't know why she is crossing the street. Hell, she probably on some shit and just want to talk." Cleabo thought to himself. He could easily assume she was asking Willie for some money. "Damn, can't she see that we are trying to get our hustle on? Damn! Here she comes."

"Hey C, where you been lately?"

"Just chilling babe, trying to get my game plan together."

"Oh really, what is it you gonna do?"

"Can't speak on it babe, you know how I roll."

"Damn C, you always so damn secretive and you don't even have a woman; shit!"

"Yeah, and gonna keep it that way too. I'm kind of choosy, you know what I mean?"

"Hell C, in our damn shoes we can't be too damn choosey, you know what I mean? What you think, you too damn good or something?"

"No, it ain't that, it's just that I got too many other things on my mind. Can't let a woman get in my way. You do understand?"

"I hear you C; you are a serious brother. Hey C, let me hold something on a drink."

"Girl I ain't got no damn money! Shit, Willie and me been standing out here for a while now, and you come springing your little happy ass out here."

"Come on C, I know you got something."

"I had enough for breakfast! Now I'm going to go and make enough for lunch and maybe a forty. You know the deal."

"Okay, C."

"And besides, you know you don't want nothing to drink; ain't shit opened this time of the morning."

"I got my connections, I can get something to drink anytime. But you take your broke ass on C."

"Later Angel, you be tripping."

After walking away from Angel he began to laugh to himself. "That girl is really messed up."

She had dragged Willie to the curb and now she would do anything just to get another hit. Her game was weak, and Cleabo knew Social Services would be taking her two kids away from her soon. She lived in an abandon building three blocks away from Hobo Junction. Hobo Junction was a place where people of his kind would hang out and socialize underneath the freeway as the cars rolled above their heads.

Totally away from civilization, it was a world of it's own. Dressed with shopping carts and home made shelters, this is where they hung out. Most of the time when he was there, he had to share whatever drink he had. Tucked away in the inside pocket he had a half of a pint of some cheap brandy. Cleabo tried to save his liquor and not drink on an empty stomach. He couldn't get sick out on the streets; he had to think about his health. For sure, he wasn't going to let either Angel nor Willie know he had something.

CHAPTER XII

HOBO JUNCTION

Cleabo walked three blocks to get to Hobo Junction. Underneath the highway in a corner, local transients stood. Fire was blazing out of the cans and the people were trying to stay warm. Brown paper bags were passed around; backwash going down the throats of whoever was last. In the corner there was a shelter that was made with a tin overhead roof. The sides were insulated with cardboard. Pots and pans were visible but if someone cooked anything; there were a lot of mouths to feed. The fire kept everyone warm and Cleabo loved the socialization with people. They became like family although they stunk; it really didn't matter, so did he. Just like any other group of people, someone has to bring you in. Willie had introduced Cleabo to the crew.

Zeak was the landlord at Hobo Junction. He was a skeptic that didn't tolerate nonsense from anyone. He stood about five eleven and was medium built. Zeak kept things in order at Hobo Junction. His matted beard, twisted up like a nappy ass Afro, was complimented by the raggedy coveralls and the puffed snowman kind of coat he wore. Zeak was consistently into someone else's business and inquisitive about their past.

Cleabo gained respect from Zeak after being blunt with him one day. He told Zeak that his past was none of his damn business. Zeak admired his fearlessness and welcomed him into the pack. For most, the junction was a place to stop for a few hours, maybe, from eight to ten in the morning and then again in the evenings. From ten to twelve Cleabo had to make his lunch money, washing car windows as they stopped at the traffic light or collecting cans. It depended on what Cleabo's mood was that day.

He kept a little plastic thermos cup in his overcoat. Just the thought of drinking behind those guys made him want to throw up. They knew it; some of them thought he felt he was *"hot shit,"* as one transient put it one day. Without a doubt, Cleabo knew there would always be one bad ass in the crowd, and sooner or later he would have to kick his ass. *Damn*, how he didn't want the crew to think that he was a punk, especially since they had heard how he talked to Zeak.

Ricky was the punk's name, and he thought he was tough; especially after a few drinks. Cleabo really didn't have time this morning for any of his stuff, as he filled his cup up and started drinking over the fire. Cleabo's associates knew he had to finish his first drink and pour another one before he would share it with them.

The fire blazed out of five garbage cans, and Cleabo over heard Ricky talking to Zeak.

"Man Zeak, he acts like the police."

"No, I feel C. He's the kind of man that just handles his business and keep folks out of his business. C is on a mission; a serious mission, but he is far from being the law."

Cleabo's speculations were correct as normal; Zeak knew how to read people as he did. After Cleabo had read Ricky, he knew he wasn't worth the time fighting. Any type of confrontation would easily make Cleabo a prime suspect. Everyone at the junction knew they didn't get along, so Cleabo just hoped that nothing would happen to the fool before he accomplished his mission. Cleabo made him think that he feared him just to ease the tension. He had bigger fish to fry; Ricky just didn't know it. Zeak checked out Cleabo's moves as he did his.

"There is something about this brother," Cleabo thought.

It seemed as though people always wanted to be around Zeak. He had a controlling personality, yet laid back and relaxed. He reminded Cleabo of the leader of the Black Pearls.

After Zeak had calmed Ricky down, someone started talking about what had happened at Cleabo's room the day before. Zeak was laughing and Ricky said Cleabo was crazy. Cleabo just smiled and merely said, "Yeah."

At the Junction they would talk about anything under the sun. Most of the time it would be about how to make a dollar. But this particular morning, he noticed something he should have seen a long time ago. While standing underneath the freeway at the junction Cleabo noticed the eighteen wheelers as they passed by.

"Damn, some of them are heading east," he thought to himself. "Eastbound, that's where I need to go." While staring at the freeway it was then he realized this could be his way to Phoenix. Cleabo noticed that some of the tractor trailers were boxed and some were tankers.

Cliff, a twisted mouth transient whom he considered to be a friend, was one person he shared bottles with, and it seemed like Cliff knew everything. He always had his lips twisted to one side when he talked. Cleabo really didn't understand why his mouth was like that; he thought that perhaps it could be some sort of deformity. It looked as if Cliff had found himself a new coat as he strolled his way to the garbage can Cleabo was using to stay warm with. Cleabo couldn't wait for him to get near, so that he could ask him about those trucks. Cliff strolled up to the can with a dirty ass coat that had the checkerboard look.

"Yo, what up Cliff?"

"Huh wee, man let me get some of this fire," he rubbed his hands together. "What up C?"

"Nothing much, just hanging, you know?"

"Yeah, I know what you mean." He blew warm air threw the palms of both of his hands. "Gotta little nip C?"

"Yeah, you know I saved you some. Your turn tomorrow though."

"Okay, I got cha back homey."

"Here you go." He handed Cliff the bottle. "What did you do last night?"

"Nothing much man, still doing this street thing you know."

"Yeah, me too." Cleabo said.

"Man, you should have been here at the Junction last night." Cliff said excitely.

"Oh really, what happened?"

"Man, Red got some volts put into his ass!"

"Volts?"

"Yeah, like electric volts man."

"Really, what happened?"

"Ronald, you know the new fellow?" Cliff paused for a second. "The one that just got out of prison and found out his old lady was living with that crack dealer?"

"Yeah, I know who you're talking about."

"Ronald came up into the junction with two fifths and a damn TV set that was hotter than a hooker at a bachelor party." Cliff took a sip from the bottle.

203

"Oh, really, so what happened?"

"That old girl of Willie's, Angel, she came behind him like a hyena looking for a meal, and she had an extension cord in her damn hands. One of those orange ones about thirty feet long. And she was all hyped up; you know how that Angel rolls. Now you know Red never have anything. When he do, he owe too many people something to drink, so his shit be gone right away. You know what I'm saying?"

"Yeah, go on man."

"Red wanted to join their little party, so Ronald started cooking up some shit on a spoon, and Angel was waiting like a damn dog with his tongue hanging out."

Cleabo laughed, seeing it too clearly. "I hear you man, she is a stone trip."

"Red told them he would run the cord and hook up the TV. He ran the cord to that switch box around the corner. Now, you know something was wrong with that box, but he was trying to play Mr. Electricity man and get him some of that shit for a favor. He must have pulled the wrong wires or something, 'cause the box puffed up with smoke! Red had the wires in his hands, just a shaking. He couldn't let go. He fell on the ground shaking his ass off. While he was on the ground shaking, Angel ran and told Zeak what was going on. Zeak grabbed a two by four and swung it like he was hitting a damn baseball. He hit Red's hand and the wire went loose. Red was still on the ground, shaking and a trembling as we stood over him." Cliff looked around and continued.

"Somebody yelled, 'Go call 911!' but we all just looked at each other because no one had damn thirty five cents to make a phone call. Man we was so fucked up, no one was thinking that we didn't need money in order to call 911, everyone was just that tore down. So Ronald poured some liquor on Red's face. C, Red stopped shaking and started licking his lips! Zeak told him to get his good for nothing ass up and stop being so damn stupid. I laughed my ass off. After that they heated up the dope they had, shot it into their veins and sold that damn TV to get some more."

"Damn, I missed that. Hey, Cliff what do you know about trucks man?" he finally asked. Cleabo had no real interest in what he had just told him. He was just being polite before he asked about what really interested him.

"You mean driving them?" Cliff asked.

"No, the shit they be carrying on the back of them."

"I know a little about two kinds."

"Really, and what kind is that?"

"Box and tankers. See that one right there?" Cliff pointed towards the highway. "That's a box trailer, they be about forty-eight footers."

"Are they hard to get into?"

"Yeah man, most of them be locked and banded when they got something in them. And the driver mostly sleeps in the cab if he has a sleeper."

"Tell me about the other one."

"What, the tankers?"

"Yeah."

"Let me see." He paused to watch some of the trucks going by, then he pointed at one. "Look, there goes one." He looked to see if Cleabo saw, then continued.

"You see that thing on the top of it? That's called the dome. That's the lid of it. The tankers mostly carry liquids. Some carry milk and some carry some dangerous shit man."

"And how do you know which one carries what?"

"The ones that carry safe stuff aren't going to have anything in that little diamond on the side of the trailer. The ones that have dangerous chemicals in them will have something inside of that diamond. If it's red, it's highly flammable. The more decorations it has inside of that diamond, the more the shit will blow up or eat your ass alive. I think they are called placards or something like that. Why all of the questions about them trucks C?"

"I just wanted to know." Cleabo answered in his normal evasive way. Cliff knew he wasn't getting more from Cleabo, then he thought of more information.

"Oh, another thing about the tankers is that some of them have more than one hole up top. Some have three or even four holes."

"Really, do they fill all the holes?"

"No, they got to have one empty hole with those, something about the axle weight."

"Can a person fit inside one of those holes?"

"Sure, if they don't get caught."

"So if I wanted to hitch a ride, what would I have to do?"

"First know which direction the truck is traveling, then check the license plate to see where the trailer is from. Most of the time its final destination will be where the trailer is from. There's a ladder on the side of the tankers, or maybe in the back. I would climb up on top of it and get my ass into the empty compartment. Make sure the driver is away, because they carry guns for people that'll try to rip them off at truck stops. Wait until he goes into the truck stop for something to eat, then climb up top and tie a rope onto one of the lug nuts on top so you can always get your ass out of there." Cliff stopped for a moment to take a sip.

"Push one of the lug nuts down so that the lid won't completely close and suffocate you, and then ride quietly. Pull yourself up whenever he stops and look at your surroundings. Make sure it's safe to come out when he stops. Oh yeah, you will know when the driver is at the weight station. There will be a dispute over his middle axle because you will be in there. However, a normal human being only weigh about two hundred pounds, so they generally let them go for such a small amount. The driver will be a little puzzled but it will be no big deal. Why you asked about that C? You thinking about doing that shit?"

"I don't know man, right now I'm just weighing out my options."

"I hear you man, but if you decide to do it just be careful man, those damn truck drivers will try to put a bullet in you."

"Maybe that'll be my chance to get a piece too."

"Man C, you are out there; just like Zeak said. Good luck, and I won't tell anyone, okay?"

"Cool Cliff. Hey man, I've got to go now, I'll check you later."

"Alright dude, be easy."

After leaving Hobo Junction, Cleabo began his day on the boulevard washing car windows as they stopped at the traffic light. Some of his normal customers began to be familiar faces and so did he to them. On one occasion as he was panhandling, a man gave him a dollar. The man turned to walk away and said, "Don't you remember me? You wash my windows almost every day."

"Oh yeah, I remember you. How are you today?" Cleabo asked.

"Just fine, see you later," the man said as he hurried away.

Cleabo wondered why some of the same people would get their car windows cleaned every day. They would give him a dollar and some of the times they would even pull to the side, to make it easier for him. It was as though they were socializing with him. He was used to the nodding of the head from indicating no, they didn't want their windows washed. Even the waving of the hand as they shouted, "Get the fuck away from my car!" was understandable behavior, however, the regulars truly puzzled him. It seemed like they were once transients themselves. The sincere look they displayed was the look that is only shared between compassionate beings.

He could never figure out some of the people in L.A. Who would have thought that after a day of work a person would want to pull to the side of the road and get his windows washed? On several occasions when the freeway was severally congested, some of the young folks would pull over and pop their trunks. He'd see a cooler with cold beer in it. To his surprise, he would get a nice cold beer and a dollar, sometimes more, for cleaning their windows. "In an odd way, this life sure has it's perks," Cleabo thought.

Cleabo thought about the time Willie had his 'Will work for food' sign displayed with him on the boulevard. A lady in a candy apple red Porche picked him up. She said she had some yard work to be done, and she wanted to know if he could cut her grass. She took Willie home and made him bathe, then gave him the time of his life. This little spot by the corner of the entrance onto Ventura Freeway indeed had it's benefits. That lady wanted more cut than her grass. The way that Willie put it, it was more like she wanted her ass to be cut, especially with all of the toys Willie said he had to use on her.

After that incident, Willie must have felt that signs were his thing. That fool made a sign that said, "Will work for pleasure," and he misspelled the word pleasure. It was spelled *'pleshore.'* He received a lot of odd looks from people, especially the ones that didn't understand what Willie was trying to say. They would constantly ask him what was it he would work for. Willie was getting a little pissed off from being asked so many times. The police stopped by and warned Willie that if he received any money for pleasure or *'pleshore,'* they were going to lock his ass up. Cleabo laughed his ass off at Willie.

The cars on the freeway soared above their heads as they attempted to get their gig on. They were free lancing like an artist, only displaying the unwanted skills of a true panhandler in the form of an art. Perhaps it was an art the way they would manipulate the public in order to obtain their necessities.

Cleabo questioned himself whether being on the streets was better than finishing college. Along with the majority his answer was a *"Hell no!"* but still, the question sped fast through his mind. In college he learned how to pass classes in order to receive a piece of paper. A paper of which half of the people he once knew, probably had forgotten almost everything they had ever learned. But, here in the streets, everyday was a learning experience and it was life threatening. He had to remember and absorb every lesson that he learned, never forgetting the things that others would teach him in order to survive. For certain, this life style was far from having a college degree. It was hard as hell on the streets; sure he had his good days, but on the bad days he had no help. He was always on his own and would've given anything for some type of family support.

"Damn, it's hard out here, I would have give anything to have the IRS on my ass for back taxes. Anything but this would be better," he thought, as he looked down upon what he had become. "Raggedy to the bone, and dirty to the core I am. Had it not been for the discipline that was instilled into me by the military, I would've been lost to the other side by now." Cleabo thought.

"Just look at my shoes; and I have the nerve to talk about Angel." He said out loud. "I'm no better off. At least she is always on a mission. Not the same as mine, of course, but she has one."

Cleabo had learned street terminology well. When the crackheads spoke to one another and said they were on a mission, they were referring to looking for some more crack to satisfy their *'Jones.'*

Angel stayed on a mission. At the moment Cleabo's mission was to drive pity out of his mind while he waited for another car to drive by so that he could wash its windows. Cleabo glanced down at his shoes again and a smile came to his face as he looked at the black Adidas sneakers he was wearing. He remembered as a child not having a top name brand pair of sneakers. His mother bought him and his brothers some pairs of Bata Bullets. They had holes underneath them on the bottom of the sole that looked like craters, just like on the moon. They were supposed to be like suction cups, and when air broke the vacuum they were supposed to make a person jump higher when playing basketball. "Damn, these are some good sneakers," he thought, when his mother gave him the sneakers. "And now, I should have known something was wrong with those Beta Bullets when the kids would always tease me about them!" not only did they not work as claimed, but the Bata Bullets also came with a whistle.

"Now what kind of sneakers comes with a whistle? What the hell was I suppose to do with the whistle? There was definitely too many bad things going on with that footwear." Cleabo thought, as a smile came to his face.

His last straw with those Bata Bullets was when he was playing basketball and a friend was going for a layup. He tried to block his shot. Cleabo jumped into the air knowing that he was just going to smack his shot away. He blocked the shot with the help of his incredible jumping abilities. When he returned to the ground the bottom sole of his Bata Bullets was in one spot and he was in another. Cleabo ripped right out of the sole; his sweat socked feet landed on the cold asphalt, and everyone in the park just stared with their mouths wide opened.

They started laughing and he picked up his Beta Bullets and walked out of the park. He tucked the soles underneath his armpits and walked his almost barefoot ass home. The top portion of the sneakers were still strung up, they just didn't have any bottoms. Everyone in the park was rolling with laughter. That day was so embarrassing.

Cleabo's crooked mouth friend, Cliff, arrived on the boulevard. He was always a joy to be around; it was always easy to assume that he had a little nip with him. Cliff made it simple for him to sympathize with his situation, especially after he shared his story with Cleabo. Cliff had spent some time in the Army too. However, Cleabo never shared any of his past with him. Cleabo truly related to what Cliff was telling him one day as they shared a bottle together. While in the Army, Cliff was in the field for thirty days. Being in the field is when the Army goes into the middle of the woods and train for war. A person had to sleep on the ground and play war games day and night.

After thirty days of being tired and dirty, Cliffs unit returned to their garrison location. With his duffle bag filled with all of his dirty belongings, he had to clean his weapon, the M16; before he or the rest of his platoon could go home. Before going to the field, Cliff was caught drunk while driving, so his privileges were suspended. His buddy and another friend waited for him so they could give him a ride home.

The war games ended earlier than scheduled and everyone was pleased to be able to return to civilization. Cliff caught his ride home. His buddy Jackson, drove and another friend Taylor, was sitting in the front passenger seat. They parked on the side of Cliff's house and he dragged his heavy duffle bag out of the back seat of the car. Cliff gave his thanks for the ride, then turned and went inside the house. Before the two friends could pull off, a stranger jumped out of the window of Cliff's house onto the hood of the car. His weight put a dent into the hood, and he stood in a squatting position with fear in his eyes. He looked at Jackson and Taylor through the windshield, then jumped off of the car and began to run. Jackson and Taylor looked at each other, wondering who was going to tell Cliff.

The two men decided that neither of them were going to tell Cliff. They didn't want to hurt his feelings; they felt that he would find out sooner or later. Six months went by and it came time for Cliff to go to the field again for thirty days. Surprisingly, the exercise ended a week earlier than planned. The aggressive tactics of his Colonel led the battalion to victory. There was a great celebration in the field and an early return to the garrison location made everyone happy.

Cliff's sergeant was filling out the paperwork at his desk in the shop at the motor pool, while the platoon waited for his permission to leave and be with their loved ones. By this time Cliff had regained his license, and he hastily jumped into his hoopty that was waiting for him, like a chariot out in the motor pool parking lot. He arrived home, noticing his wife's car was parked. Leaving the heavy duffel bag inside the car, he anxiously ran inside the house. With no one to greet him in the living room, Cliff walked down the hallway to his bedroom.

The smell of sex assaulted him and the sound of loud moans clogged his ears. He gently opened his bedroom door, only to find his wife's legs in the air, spread like a wishbone, and a huge black man pounding the shit out of her. Neither of them knew of his presence. The oversized man blocked her view, and his head was facing her as they continued their episode. Cliff stood in the door way traumatized, as he watched for a second that seemed like hours. He then turned and walked away and drove his car back to the motor pool. Still in a state of shock, he felt the need to talk to his sergeant.

Cliff's sergeant was still at the desk doing his paperwork. Cliff sat in front of his sergeant's desk not saying a word. His sergeant knew something was wrong, although the magnitude of the problem wasn't yet discussed. Cliff told his sergeant what had happened and he wanted his sergeant to give him some advise. Sergeants were trained to never give advice, but to only be an ear in these types of situations. After wiping his last tear, Cliff managed to compose himself. His sergeant told him that he needed professional help, and the chaplain was the person for the job.

Although the sergeant was trained to deal with problems of this sort, he didn't do what he was supposed to have done. Instead of escorting Cliff to the chaplain, he made a phone call telling the chaplain that Cliff had a problem and he was sending him over. The sergeant hung up the phone and directed Cliff to go to the chaplain's place of worship. Cliff lifted himself out of the chair, leaving the sergeant with the belief that he was going to the chaplain. Cliff burned rubber in his *hoopty* as he left the post; he was on his way home to reconcile things with his wife. He had loved her so dearly, and was willing to forgive her. In his mind he was glad the sergeant didn't tell him anything, such as to leave his wife. The chaplain was only going to be an ear, he thought the decision process would always be left up to him.

Cliff decided to forgive her and pretend as though he had never walked in on her. He made his way home and pretended to put on a good demeanor. The situation at home was still the same. They must have taken a water break or something and continued trying to find ecstasy. Cliff pushed opened the bedroom door and all he could see was this huge, black ass mooning him. The man was kissing his wife, as he pounded the hell out of her five foot two, one hundred and five pounds.

Cliff's wife was yelling at the top of her lungs, as the man continued to ask her what his name was. She screamed, "Ray! Ray!" Cliff gently opened the top dresser drawer where he kept his thirty-eight caliber. Without either knowing he was there, he pulled the trigger back and the cocking sound of the trigger was heard in between the name calling and the strokes. The man froze, then turned and looked at Cliff as his wife yelled, "No, Cliff!" The Mandingo looking man jumped off of Cliff's wife and put his hands in the air saying, "Please don't, please don't, man, she didn't tell me she was married!" He stood in front of Cliff totally nude. Why Cliff didn't shoot him right then and there Cleabo didn't understand.

Cliff told Cleabo he was in a state of shock looking at the huge man that could have been related to a horse. His male organ hung to his knees and Cliff wondered how his little, itty bitty wife was able to take all of him. For the moment that Cliff was in shock, the man ran for the window. Buck naked, like he had done it before, and knew exactly what window to go to.

"He was just lying; talking about he didn't know that she was married," Cliff said to Cleabo. Cleabo could remember him starting to get a little angry. As the man jumped out of the window, Cliff squeezed the trigger. Fortunately, he missed the man's center mass and shot him in the ass. That didn't stop him from running though. Cliff then turned to his wife. She was begging, "Please don't Cliff, please don't!" she sat in the bed trembling in fear. Cliff shot the remaining five rounds at his wife's legs. He told Cleabo he just wanted to cripple her for life. He said he wanted her to walk with a limp for the rest of her life, so that when another man saw her coming he would know something was wrong with her.

The Army discharged Cliff, and Jackson and Taylor told him what had happened when they took him home that day. They laughed as Cliff shared with them what he had done. Cleabo was the only one that knew Cliff's story at the junction; he must have felt that he could trust him. Cleabo felt kind of awkward when Cliff told him he couldn't do nothing but look at the man's male organ hanging down to his knees.

"Hell, I would have shot it off! Both of them was freaks. Her tunnel must have gone well up her back to be able to handle such large of a man, and be so damn small!" Cleabo said to himself.

Cliff walked over to where Cleabo was standing. "Hey C, what up man?"

"Just chilling Cliff, made enough for lunch and a little more, you know?"

"You still thinking about doing what we talked about at the junction, man?"

"Yeah man, I'm thinking about busting that move tomorrow night. I've got to get everything I need today."

"I hear you C, good luck man, you want a shot?" Cliff handed him the un-opened bottle.

"Thanks Cliff." Cleabo looked at the bottle then exclaimed. "Shit, this is some expensive stuff you have here Cliff!" It was Crown Royal, something that wasn't often seen in the hands of a transient.

"I know and it's so good."

"Where did you get the money for this kind of liquor Cliff?" Cleabo asked. He figured Cliff must have robbed a liquor store or something.

"Hey don't worry about it C, I've got something going on right now. Now go ahead and pour you a good one, 'cause I know how you roll. Here you are a bum and don't want to drink behind anyone. Boy, you try to give class to the word transient. Damn C, you are funnier than a *mug*!"

"Yeah you are too, with your crazy ass!" he laughed. "Damn Man!" he said in appreciation. "This stuff would give class to anybody." He took a drink and savored the rich flavors as he pushed slightly on Cliff's shoulder in a thank you gesture, and they enjoyed each others company. But, he knew soon he would have to put the things Cliff had told him earlier into affect. Cliff and Cleabo said their goodbyes as Cleabo departed the area. "Damn," he wished Cliff could've left that bottle with him. Crown Royal was one of the best money could buy; the sweet taste was so refreshing, and Cliff knew it.

It was around noon now, and the Egg McMuffin had totally digested in his stomach. It was time to get something else to eat. He couldn't go into the large grocery stores, too many people just stared at him and turned up their nose's. The grocery store around the corner from the boulevard was his next stop; most of the people of his kind utilized it often. The owner didn't mind as long as they had money. At the grocery store he bought some canned goods. They lasted for a long time and could be stored for a rainy day.

Potted meat, Vienna sausages and some bread were the items that he purchased. While standing in line he came to the conclusion that he wasn't going to wait another day to hitch hike his way to Phoenix. He had decided that tonight would be as good as ever. Cleabo now had food and he could even leave Lucky some of it to carry him over for a few days while he was gone.

"Damn, it's beginning to be difficult to have a pet," he thought, reluctantly admitting to a fond feeling for the ugly big headed thing.

Finally, he made it back to his "A.O." Kenny and his crew were hanging out in front of the building; bumming cigarettes from the people that walked by. They asked him what he had in his bag. Cleabo just told them it was none of their business. He carried his bag to his room, and a smile dressed his face from the thought of how happy Lucky would be to get something to eat.

He traversed down a long narrow dark hallway, with about four rooms adjacent from one another. His new domains had a wet mildewed odor. The smell of urine lingered in the air, but it was home for the time being. Cleabo could hear Willie and Angel getting their groove on as he attempted to open his door.

"How gross," he thought to himself, "For sure I didn't see neither of them at the lake this morning. I know they both could use a bath!"

His big headed cat greeted him at the door. Lucky meowed at Cleabo in a manner as if he was trying to tell him to change his litter box. Cleabo complied to the demanding little feline. Another meow indicated he wanted something to eat. Lucky was now beginning to be a pain in the neck. However, he knew he had to keep him fat for a rainy day. Two cans of potted meat and a full can of Vienna sausages was Lucky's meal for the day. Like a squirrel, he would store whatever he didn't eat. Cleabo thought he had the potential of being trained to be a soldier; a smart little cat Lucky was. Cleabo just didn't have the time to train him.

It was time for Cleabo to start getting ready; the truck stop was a few miles down the road and he had to get his equipment together. Cleabo always kept a rope, and his pocket knife would also be needed. After putting all of the necessary items into his back pack he patiently waited for night to fall.

After saying his goodbyes to his feline friend, Cleabo adopted the same feeling as he had during the *"heist."* The nervous and nauseating feeling in his stomach accompanied by fear, rode him like a jockey at the Kentucky Derby. Although the nearest truck stop was about three miles away, the walk seemed to have been quick. He wore a good pair of pants and a nice looking shirt that he had stashed away.

Cleabo knew they would come in handy someday. His disguise had to be different than a regular transient look. His beard was trimmed with his pocket knife now; he had to present a neat appearance in order to take care of his business with the doctor. Cleabo wanted to be taken seriously and not like a tramp, so his holey clothes had to stay behind.

Cleabo's back pack contained his rope, knife and some food, and a small pair of binoculars he had hidden in his room in a secret hiding place. He also packed about a third of half of a pint of brandy, with a few cigarettes to calm his nerves, and a *Jet* magazine. Like he would really have time to read! Stopping for a moment as he approached the truck stop area, he dug into his back pack to take him a little sip. Standing from a distance and out of sight, he squatted down near the gray and black rocks that surrounded the truck stop area.

Tractor trailers were lined up in some sort of formation. He noticed the box and the tanker trailers. With his small binoculars, he was able to get a better look as he scanned the area. Cleabo selected a hypothetical victim to train himself on. By watching him, he could figure out what he needed to do. The driver exited the truck and turned around and his lips were moving as though he was talking to someone.

"Damn! Cliff didn't tell me there could be two!" he said.

While expecting difficulties, knowing that things would never go smooth, he had to figure this one out. He needed to find a tanker that had three or more holes. Also, he needed to make sure there was only one hungry driver.

Moving his binoculars around the lot, he was able to see a driver on top of a tanker checking his lug nuts; ensuring that they were tight. A sigh of relief entered his mind, as he thought if someone was to see him, they would assume that he was doing the same. Now he had to wait until a hungry driver entered the truck stop so that he could watch his every move. If his lips moved, Cleabo could easily assume he was talking to his partner or to himself. If his lips moved as he exited the cab, for sure there would be someone else inside. The driver that held his head down and filled out his paperwork without moving his lips would be his ride, he thought, as he continue to survey the lot.

After thirty minutes of waiting for his ride, his knees began to ache. Stretching his legs and sitting on his butt eased his discomfort.

Shinny lights and a highly decorated Peter Built truck, with a rebel flag on the front, entered the truck stop. There were no colors in the diamonds on the side of the trailer; as Cliff spoke of. After backing the huge eighteen wheeler trailer into the available space, the driver seemed a bit exhausted as he rubbed his eyes. The tags were from Arizona and he picked up a clip board and began to write.

The driver seemed to fit the bill for being his ride, but he wasn't sure at this point. As he stepped out of the cab with a look of fatigue and hunger all over his face, Cleabo assumed that he could take him out if they were to fight. He was a short, medium built man. Cleabo was taller and out weighed him; he knew he could handle him. Cleabo wasn't in the attack mode though, his only concern at this point was getting a ride.

The driver walked away from the truck towards the truck stop diner. Quickly Cleabo walked into the lot trying not to be noticed. He waited a moment for the man to glance back at his truck, before he entered through the diner's glass doors. Just as Cleabo thought, the driver looked back at his truck and felt at ease before sitting down on the bar stool to order his meal. With his back turned and the menu in his hand, the only thing that was on this man's mind was getting something to eat. He had no idea that he would be carrying a stowaway when he left.

The ladder was on the side of the trailer just as Cliff had said. After climbing to the top of the tank wagon, he carefully walked to the number two compartment. The lid was cracked opened with a lug nut. Quickly he tied his rope onto the lug nut and lowered himself down into the compartment space and closed the lid on the lug nut. The little crack of space gave him the required amount of air while he waited for the driver to return.

There was movement from the cab as the door slammed shut. The vibrations were a good indication the driver had returned and was about to continue on his journey.

"A successful mission thus far," Cleabo thought.

As he rode in the tank wagon he could only see the stars, while the wind from the highway briskly seeped into the compartment space. It started feeling like a freezer; he was cold as hell. The noise was loud and the ride was bumpy; his butt began to hurt while he sat on the cold metal floor of the compartment.

After about two hours of riding, he could feel the truck coming to a stop. Grabbing the rope he elevated himself up to a standing position trying to see if he could see anything. Cleabo could only see the stars and the top of some buildings. There were a lot of lights in this area. He thought that they must have stopped at a weigh station; he could hear the men asking the driver some questions. Cleabo really didn't know if they weighed him in, but he heard them asking the driver if he had any weapons or fruits.

The sound of the truck's engine and the odor from the stack assured him that everything was alright. The truck was rolling again and they were on their way; hopefully the next stop would be Phoenix.

The billboards and the backward words of the highway destination signs, kept him informed of where he was at. After another hour of riding, he noticed a billboard displaying a strip-joint in Phoenix. The sign indicated it was fifteen miles to the bar, and twenty minutes later the truck stopped. Cleabo had no idea where they were. The driver finally exited the cab and slammed the door. Pulling on the handle, he checked the doors, to ensure they were locked. This was a good indication he would be gone for quite some time.

Twenty minutes later, Cleabo lifted himself through the man way, making sure the driver was gone. He saw a sign of a twenty four hour K-Mart with an arrow pointed in his direction from the road. For a moment he thought the driver was shopping in the K-Mart, but then Cleabo assumed he was just parking there to go to the strip club. It was time to get out of the compartment while he could. After climbing down, he noticed there were other eighteen wheelers parked in the street next to the all night K-Mart also.

"Damn, I made it," he thought to himself. "Now I only have to survive until morning. Being in a strange environment can sometimes throw a person off; especially not knowing anyone. "For sure, it would be a stupid idea to try and find the doctor's office tonight," he thought.

Being on the streets had taught him it wasn't a smart idea to be out at night, especially in unknown territory. In his own territory or turf, it probably would have been cool. But, in Phoenix, he didn't know what to expect. Traveling in the jungle he felt fine; the animals didn't pack weapons like an AK or a forty-five. Therefore, he could take them on, or just run for dear life. Here, he would be in the defense mode the entire night. So, he just found a nice quiet corner, behind some dumpsters in the back of K-Mart, to get some sleep. Cleabo gathered up some cardboard to keep himself warm and he slept until the break of day.

"What a night!" he thought to himself, as he drifted into his dreams.

"Hey, you better get your ass up from around here!" a man shouted at him, as he wiped his eyes, while the daylight practically blinded him.

"Oh, okay, I'm going." Cleabo responded.

It was easy for Cleabo to assume the man thought that he was just some old crackhead that didn't have a place to sleep. Little did he know that was the least of Cleabo's worries. With the spit from his mouth and his index finger, he washed the matter from the corners of his eyes. Then, after wiping the crusty white stuff from the corner of his mouth he was ready to go find the doctor. Cleabo retrieved the address from his pocket. After asking a couple of people for directions, he was told that he was on the wrong side of town; far away from the doctor's office.

"Damn, if my luck would have gotten any worse, it wouldn't have been considered to be bad luck, just fucked up luck," he thought.

The temperature was extremely hot. It must have been well over a hundred degrees in the shade. "Man, it is hot," he panted, wiping sweat from his brow.

Occasionally, he would stop and get something to drink and confirm his direction of travel. His sweat fell to the ground as it made the attempt to cool his body temperature. At times he felt as though he was going to pass out, but he knew he had to continue. At a park he filled his belly with water and released his golden colored urine. Far past being dehydrated, he was at another level, perhaps a delusional stage.

After resting on a bench *under a green tree*, he waited to let all of the water he had drunk settle down. It was now time to finish his journey; only twelve miles to go. It would seem like twenty four miles in the dry heat that made him feel like his skin was peeling off.

Around two o'clock he finally made it to the doctor's office. His office was a pink colored building that had large marble like steps leading up to the front door. As exhausted as he was, he felt like lying his tired, sweaty body down right there on the steps and sleeping for days.

It was cool inside the building; the air conditioning must have been at its maximum capacity. The water at the fountain was extremely cold and it tasted so refreshing. Cleabo wallowed his face in it, giving his head a bath. He received some odd looks as he shook the water from his face and head. The movement was similar to a dog shaking water off after he has been wet.

In the center of the hall there was an information board. Cleabo could see Dr. David Wesley's name and it indicated that he was on the second floor in room 204. Cleabo walked up the stairs. While standing in front of the door of the office he noticed Dr. David Wesley's name wasn't on the door; perhaps a possible oversight he thought, so he just opened the door and went inside. A short, blond-haired lady was at the receptionist window.

"Can I help you?" she asked as he entered.

"Yes, I'm here to see Dr. David Wesley," he told her.

"Doctor who?" she asked, like she hadn't heard him correctly.

He inwardly sighed, but said patiently, "Dr. David Wesley."

"I'm sorry," she said politely, "There is no doctor here by that name."

"What!" he exclaimed in disbelief. "Are you sure? This is the right address, isn't it? The information board downstairs says room 204 for Dr. David Wesley."

"Okay, hold on hon, I'm fairly new here." The receptionist rolled around in her chair and yelled to the other lady in the office.

"Shirley, do you know a Dr. David Wesley?"

"Oh yeah girl, he used to work here," came a voice from the back somewhere.

"Oh, okay. There's someone here looking for him."

"Hold on, I'll be right there." The other lady's voice became louder as she walked to the front of the office.

"Hi," she greeted Cleabo pleasantly. "Are you looking for Dr. Wesley? He doesn't work here anymore."

"Damn! I've traveled so far to see him. We're old friends, could you tell me where I can find him?" he asked, trying his best not to show his frustration.

"Not really, I'm not supposed to give out that type of information."

"I've come too far to find this out." Cleabo's disappointment was evident in his voice.

"Where you come from sugar?" she asked.

"L.A."

"I'm sorry. Perhaps you should have called first?"

"No, I wanted to surprise him."

"I'm sure he would have been. But you know," the lady hesitated, then continued. "If you really are his friend, you'd probably want to check with the police to see where he is." She leaned across the desk and whispered to him. "They locked him up last month."

The lady stood there waiting for his response. Cleabo's mouth was wide open, displaying his sign of shock. It seemed like his entire world had come to a shattering halt. There was no need to ask her what he was locked up for. It was clear; she knew that he had an idea why the doctor was locked up.

"Damn! Thank you for your time Miss."

"Oh, you are quite welcome," she said, then added, "Now, you didn't hear that from me; I could lose my job, you know."

"Oh yeah, don't worry. It's cool. Thanks for telling me so I wouldn't be wasting my time trying to find out where he lived."

"You wouldn't have had much luck there either, they seized his property."

"Damn! He really messed up, huh?"

"Yeah," she agreed then looked quickly at her watch. "I've got to get back to work now; you have a nice day, okay?

"Alright, you do the same and once again, thank you for your help." Cleabo said as he turned to go. He walked out of the building in disappointment, wondering what his next move would be.

The first part of his plan had failed. Now, he was in hot ass Phoenix, with little cash and no place to stay. He couldn't let it get the best of him. Cleabo needed time to think this one out. There was no need to walk all the way across town again. On the way to the doctor's office he noticed some rail road tracks. It wasn't too far away from that park he had stopped at. The park was located close to downtown. "That would be a nice place to relax and get my head together," he thought.

In the park, he noticed the local transients, and it seems as though they all had a certain resemblance. There was a vendor selling ice snow cones. Cleabo bought one for fifty cents. The strawberry flavored ice cone really quenched his thirst. He was half tempted to rub some of the ice over his hairy chest and let the cold chunks find it's way to his unmentionable area to really cool himself off.

Sitting on the park bench, he could easily see all of the stores that were in line with one another on the streets of the downtown area. Placing his backpack closer to him on the bench, Cleabo began to search inside with one hand, while the other hand held his ice cone. He wanted to get his binoculars out and get a better view of his surroundings. There were people in the park walking their dogs, and kids roller skating and playing numerous sporting activities. A perfect scenery for a painter; he thought. With his binoculars, he zoomed in on a perfect creature as she walked the sidewalk across the street.

Oh, she was beautiful! Smooth skin, everything about her was perfect. She wore a beige, silk, two piece suit and her figure was outstanding. Her long brown hair hung to her shoulders as it lay from underneath her summer hat. Her dark shades kept him from seeing her eyes, but even from where he was sitting, he could tell she was stunning. The way she strutted, her walk seemed to be a familiar grace of pace; however, it was one he couldn't remember or place. Without a doubt, the way this woman walked reminded him of someone; he guessed senility was starting to set in on him.

As the woman continued to walk, his eyes and the mini-binoculars continued to follow her. Cleabo was really getting upset with himself trying to figure out who this woman was. The long brown hair threw him off considerably, but her fineness was indeed someone he knew he had encountered in his past. Then it finally dawned on him who this lady was. If he was to remove the long brown hair, the hat and the sunglasses, he'd be damned if this wasn't the same woman he bumped into at the lake in L.A.!

"No, it couldn't be!" he tried to convince himself, as he continued to follow this woman who had such a beautiful stride.

"What the hell is she doing here, and disguised like that?" he wondered out loud.

The woman turned the corner with a sexy, fashionable walk. Cleabo had to pick up his backpack and run to the other side of the park to continue watching her. After almost running into the water pond with its beautiful overflow, he was able to continue to watch this beautiful creature. She entered the bank across the street from the park. Cleabo's instincts were always almost right during his lifetime, and something was telling him that this was the same lady who stood in front of his nude body just a couple of days ago. But, what she was up to now? He had no clue.

After about fifteen minutes, he saw her coming out of the bank. With his mini-binoculars he could see her lips moving as though she was talking to someone. He couldn't see a microphone, only her lips moving for a period of about thirty seconds.

"Damn, could she be fifty-one fifty?" he thought. "No, she's too swift for that; besides she is too fine! She's disguised for some reason."

From the bank, he followed her to a jewelry store about four stores down. Through the glass window he could see her every move. Out of curiosity, he glanced back at the bank. It was at that time he noticed an older woman walking into the bank, then two younger dudes. Turning back to the fine woman he could see her asking the lady if she could try on a diamond ring that was in the showcase.

It was pretty obvious what was going on; this woman was into something hi-tech. The sales lady handed her the ring, and the woman received the ring with her right hand, but in a cuffed fashion. All of a sudden, the bank alarm went off and people were running out of the bank like crazy before the doors of the bank were closed. The excitement distracted the sales lady for just a split second as she glanced at the window to see what was going on. While she glanced away just for the moment, the fine lady bent her left arm in a horizontal position to try the ring on, but she kept her right hand cuffed. With her left palm facing the floor, Cleabo could only assume a thin metal mechanism ejected from the area of her elbow.

The thin metal device scooped the ring from her right hand and he could see her moving her fingers from the cuffed fashion and a duplicate ring appearing as she placed it on her finger, pretending to be trying it on. How smooth and quick were her moves; it was done in a split second. The sales person had only glanced away for a moment and the diamond ring was swapped. The fine lady must have known the sales woman would have looked at the excitement from the bank.

It was easy for Cleabo to assume she was a part of the bank robbery. She must have cased the joint, then called it in through a mini microphone alerting them that the coast was clear; then she pulled a heist right down from the bank. Cleabo was unable to see the two guys leave the bank because he was too busy watching her; but he knew they were connected.

The moves were sweet; and he knew they had their stuff together. Earlier, with a camera of some sort, she must have been able to take a picture of the diamond ring, then had a duplicate made of glass or cubic zirconium or something. The excitement from the bank allowed time to substituted the fake ring and an easy get away.

Cleabo watched her walk out of the jewelry store and into McDonalds. When she came out she looked exactly like the girl he had met at the lake. This time she had on a short set and she stepped on the city bus making a smooth get away. Her timing was flawless and obviously pre-planned.

"Damn, that was sweet!" he thought to himself.

It probably took the jewelry store a couple of days to figure out the ring they now had was fake. After the enormous amount of planning required for both of those heists he could easily believe that the ring was expensive. How much was taken from the bank was unknown, he only knew they were in and out in a matter of minutes. She had to belong to a unique organization. The toys they used were high tech.

Cleabo had to put his mini-binoculars down. With all of the excitement going on, he knew that he had to get the hell out of there before the police come into the park asking questions. The two guys must have left in a getaway car. He noticed the police speeding down the street with their siren on as if they were in pursuit. But he knew this group was too smart for them.

Although his day of not meeting the doctor had gone bad, it was pleasant to have seen a little excitement. He was aroused by this young, pretty lady; she was indeed sexy and exciting. Now, it was time for him to find his way to the train tracks.

"Shit," he thought. "I hope no one tries to pin this one on me, suppose they saw me with the binoculars?"

His pace became faster as he made his way to the train tracks. He was determined not to ride in the compartment of an eighteen wheeler going back. Cleabo needed to see his surroundings; at least he could see and know when to jump off.

The tracks went through a secluded area; there was a switch handle located close to the fence line of a quiet neighborhood. The switch handle was used to switch the tracks. Cleabo knew then that the tracks were shared with Am Track and the freight line. Although the switch was done automatically, the handle for manual switches was a good indication that the freight liners would slow down there, making it easy for him to hitch a ride in one of the compartments.

Everything went well and he felt more comfortable on the train as opposed to the truck. Cleabo couldn't wait to get back to tell Cliff about his day. It had certainly been a peculiar one. While riding on the train and eating his potted meat he couldn't help but to think about that woman. "Damn, she was fine."

The train stopped in so many small towns, each time he had to get up and stand behind the sliding doors to stay out of sight. Fortunately for him no one came to his car investigating and he made it back to L.A.

"Maybe I could just hitch a ride like this if I had to do it again," he thought, as he walked away from the train yard.

CHAPTER XIII

CRIME ACADEMY

The sun was setting in L.A. and despite the sound of the police and firetruck sirens, Cleabo was feeling at ease. It was nice to be back home and on familiar grounds. A long walk was still ahead of him though, but he didn't care; just being able to put his disguise on would make him feel more comfortable than ever.

Back at the *"A.O."* things were quiet. It seemed like everyone had gone out somewhere handling their business. Cleabo's feline friend, Lucky, greeted him at the door with the look of, "Where the hell have you been?"

After calming his little happy butt down he fed his little furry friend. Keeping the mice away was how Lucky paid for his room and board. Cleabo slept comfortably that night, with not a fear of mice or anything else. The thought of meeting that fine lady at the lake again sped fast across his mind.

"I have to see her again; this time I wouldn't be shy. If I was down at the lake again and she stumbled upon me, I know now for certain she wouldn't scream rape. I should have known this from the beginning or not have been so scared and just talked to her," he thought to himself.

The next few days, he went to the lake looking for her each day as he bathed; unfortunately she never appeared. At the junction, Cleabo told Cliff what had happened. Cliff thought that Cleabo was a fool for not saying something to her on his first encounter.

"I guess I'm losing my touch in communicating with the finer aspects of life," Cleabo said to Cliff.

A week had passed and he was back into his normal routine. Cleabo finally managed to push aside the thoughts of the fine lady and what had happened in Phoenix. After panhandling and selling cans all day, he had made enough money to get him a bottle of cognac. Hennessey, his favorite, was out of the question, so he had to buy an off-brand for eight ninety-five a pint. He wouldn't share this top shelf liquor with anyone.

It was a sort of celebration for him, but for what reason he was still puzzled; perhaps it was a just because day. Cleabo stayed later than normal at the junction, shooting the breeze and drinking. Knowing he had to travel a few blocks to get to his *"A.O.,"* he told Cliff and the crew he would see them later. It was around ten o'clock or so; everyone knew that this late on a Friday night it was best to take the lighted path home.

Transients were constantly being mugged late at night, if not drive by targets. Therefore, he made sure he walked where there were streetlights. Between Hobo Junction and the boulevard, the hookers would come out at night.

"Walking the same path as they do will be safe," he thought.

With his hobo clothes on he passed by a nightclub that seemed to be jumping. There were cars lined up on the street and people were all outside talking, trying to pick up a female or vice verse. "Damn, they are having a good time," Cleabo mumbled to himself.

An elegant female, dressed in some skintight shiny black pants and a halter top came walking out of the nightclub. Her purse clinched underneath her armpits, she strutted away from the nightclub and made a right turn. Her face was beautifully made up; the eye brow's were even shaped to a T. Gracefully she walked; she was a total enticement. Cleabo had seen it before. It was her! This time he wasn't going to let her get away without saying something, regardless of how he was dressed.

"Maybe she'll remember me from the lake," he thought, and he was going to find out.

She turned the corner and to his surprise, he discovered he wasn't the only one following this beautiful creature. Two assailants grabbed her from behind around the corner. She continued to clutch on to her purse, while one of them tried to grab it. Quickly Cleabo ran across the street to her rescue. With swiftness, his knee plunged into the small of the assailant's back; the one that was holding her. Then he slammed an elbow to the base of the man's scull at the top portion of his neck; a temporary knock out. Such a blow could leave a person damaged for life.

The assailant fell to the ground, and the other fellow pulled a blade out. He swung at Cleabo, but with a circular motion, Cleabo curled his hand around the man's forearm, snatching it hard and forcefully. Crack! the sound of broken bones were heard.

The knife fell to the ground and simultaneously Cleabo pulled the injured thug closer.

"Aw!" the assailant screamed with his disabled arm in the air; leaving his rib cage available and a vulnerable target. Cleabo delivered a solid blow to the man's ribs with the heel of his left hand. The assailant's ribs crumbled and cracked, Cleabo knew they were broken.

But Cleabo wasn't finished; Cleabo's blade shaped hand quickly hit the thug in the throat, crushing the wind pipe and forcing the man to pass out. Then Cleabo helped the woman up from the ground.

"Are you all right?" Cleabo asked as he helped her up.

"Yes, oh man, thank you!" she said as she recognized him. "Oh, you are that guy from the lake, huh?"

"Yeah, that's me," he confirmed. "Hey, you should be more careful in this neighborhood."

"I sure will. Thank you very much. You move so quickly in combat."

"Yeah, you've got to in this neighborhood. If they recognize you, they come back after you, so I have to move quickly and destroy. Lets get out of here."

They walked away from the area, but his senses made him feel that there was something wrong. Cleabo looked around his surroundings and could only see the guys on the ground as they began to make their get away. The feeling he had at guerilla warfare training came over him. Instantly he felt the need to look up. There, on the top of one of the buildings stood two guys with night vision binoculars. It was difficult for Cleabo to see who the guys were from the distance, and being nighttime didn't help either.

He knew the woman was on a job at that point. But why she was casing a nightclub he had no idea. For sure, this woman was exciting and glamorous. If those guys were her partners they knew he had come to her rescue and they seemed to be calm with the situation.

While walking with his new friend, they introduced themselves. Her name was Trish. At first he thought it was short for Patricia, but later he found out it was just Trish. Just gazing into her light brown eyes was truly hypnotizing to Cleabo. How anyone could look this woman square in the face and not continuously commend her on her beauty, was beyond his belief. She was flawless; with the skin color and glow of an Egyptian. Her body was toned in every aspect; she was fine.

They continued to walk down the street and she received some stares because of him walking with her. She didn't seem to care though. This woman had the ability to tune the world out, and she made him feel like there was only the two of them in total existence. Cleabo felt as though they were walking in slow motion. They talked about everything except him being a transient, and whatever it was that she did.

"I normally don't let strangers see where I live." Trish said.

"Trish, I don't want to break your routine, you know. I can stop walking right here, if you like." He stopped for a moment, and held his head to the side waiting for a response.

"No, no C, I don't feel that way with you. There is something different about you. After all I did meet you at the lake."

"Yeah, but if we are going to be friends, I want you to feel comfortable with me. Trish, there is something that I ought to tell you."

"What's that C?"

"Not only did we bump into each other tonight and at the lake. But, last week I was in Phoenix and I saw you downtown."

"Oh really C? Why didn't you say something?"

"It looked like you were handling some sort of business, then you got on the bus. I just didn't think it was a good time, you know?"

"Oh no, C, you should have said hello at least. I guess that means that we aren't strangers then; so come on, you can continue walking me home."

Trish stayed in a high-rise that had security at the front entrance. The guard looked at Cleabo in a strange way, but common to most of the treatment he'd received dressed in his Sunday's best. They took the elevator up to her suite and Trish continued to talk, she was acting like a little girl in a candy store. She was indeed happy that he had come to her rescue.

Cleabo was around thirty years old by now and Trish looked as if she just had her twentieth birthday. Cleabo knew there was a significant difference in age between them, but with this young lady, age really didn't matter to him. From the glow that was flourishing off of Trish, he really didn't think it mattered to her either.

Trish's suite was immaculate; neat and clean. He had already checked out her shoes and he could see they weren't run over. Now he had the opportunity to inspect the rest of her life style.

When Trish opened the door, her golden retriever met them cheerfully, as he jumped up and down on her. Her suite was ready for a white glove inspection. The sweet fragrance of potpourri met them at the door. She picked up the leash of the pretty retriever and asked him to accompany her while she walked her dog Troy. Once again they found themselves by the lake. Fortunately, this time he wasn't totally nude. They laughed about their first encounter at the lake. Cleabo also told her he noticed how she just stopped and stared like she was hypnotized as he stood buck-naked. She said she almost was, and that she had liked what she had seen.

They returned back to her place and she put Troy in his room. He seemed to be trained well; he sat down and looked at them through his doorway gate. Trish offered Cleabo a little wine while they sat on the sofa. A few minutes later he asked her if he could use the bathroom. Her bathroom was clean and it had a garden tub.

"Impressive," he thought.

Hopefully, one day he would get a chance to view her closet to see if she was messy. As fine as she was it didn't matter at this point if she was untidy; he would clean up behind her, if he had to; after all what did he have to offer?

Sitting back on the sofa, Cleabo watched her stroll back from the stereo system after putting on some Sade. Such nice music with an elegant woman! "I must be in heaven," he thought, as he watched her cross her legs in her classy manner.

Trish continued to thank him for what he had done earlier. Then she asked if there was anything she could do for him. Cleabo didn't want to be rude by asking for mere pleasure; that would have just insulted her. She was the type of woman that didn't give it up the first time they meet someone; another quality Cleabo stressed on for a soul mate. So, he told her he would love to take a bath.

"Is that all?" Trish responded.

"Yes, a bath."

"Okay C, let me run your water and get things ready for you okay?"

"Okay Trish, and while you are doing that, do you have anything stronger than wine?"

"Yeah, there is some Hennessey behind the bar; help yourself." Trish pointed across the room towards the bar.

"Thank you Trish."

Cleabo's mouth turned dry, and his lips began to pucker from the thought of having the smooth tasting cognac running down his tongue. Just the thought of it flowing down his throat and esophagus, making it's way to his stomach leaving that warm sensation, sent chills throughout his body; he just couldn't wait. Having some Hennessey in his mouth felt like Christmas. It had been so long since he had tasted any of this top shelf liquor.

While Trish was in the bathroom, he took a couple of straight shots; she knew he must have, because he was extremely calm when she returned. She told him everything was ready. The bathroom had an intercom system built into the walls and Cleabo could hear '*The Sweetest Taboo*,' being played on the stereo.

The suds in the water were like mountains of bubbles in the oversized garden tub. It had steps to walk into and it was surrounded by fruit flavored smelling candles of some sort. Whatever they were, they smelled good. Trish knocked on the door as he stood admiring the bath he was about to take. In her hands she had a king sized bath towel and a robe, along with the bottle of Hennessey and his glass.

"Throw your clothes towards the door C. I will wash them for you while you clean yourself up. Here is a robe for when you come out."

"Thanks Trish, you make me feel like I'm in Heaven."

After he finished bathing, he could smell the scent of the sweet smelling soap all over his body. It made him smell like a woman; but he didn't care. Cleabo even used her deodorant on his furry armpits. As the last little bit of water ran out of the tub, he noticed a huge black ring around the rim of the tub.

"Damn, I've got to clean that out," he said.

After cleaning the tub with her sweet smelling soap he went into the living room and sat down. Trish came and sat down beside him with her drink and they began to talk again. However, this time the conversation went to another level. Cleabo knew that he had nothing to offer, so he didn't have shit to lose. At this point, sitting there wearing only a robe, he was game for anything she wanted to do.

"C, can I ask you a question?"

"Yeah, Trish, go ahead."

"What type of woman do you like C?"

"Why, of course the ones that are breathing Trish."

"Damn C, you are so funny! You know what I mean."

He laughed. "Yeah I know what you mean Trish. To be honest, I've had a few relationship before. But, I'm still looking for that special woman with my soul qualities."

"Your soul qualities?" Trish asked, frowning slightly with concentration. "What's that C?"

"When you and everyone else look at me, you see a bum; but Trish, I have lots of acceptable qualities, and this is only a temporary condition for me."

"Oh really? Tell me about this soul quality; the reason you haven't had a long serious relationship."

Cleabo had never before vocally voiced the qualities so important to him and he was careful to be clear. He took a few moments to consider his answer.

"I like a woman that is petite, attractive and toned. Smart, witty and with a good sense of humor. Neat, tidy, and meticulously clean. No drug user, I've seen enough of them in my days. I cannot rehabilitate someone, it's only a waste of time. I prefer a woman who doesn't do the club scene. It lets me know she has class and don't need to display her beauty in a night club environment. She isn't insecure with herself or her beauty, and knows that there is more to life to do and enjoy; you know what I mean?"

"Yeah I hear you, but go on."

"Someone that isn't influenced by her friends, and makes me her own world and isn't easily persuaded. Someone who has a strong mind and can concentrate on loving me totally. You see, I believe that justice, truthfulness, loyalty and honesty all define love. But, I believe that when I find that special someone I'm not going to be waiting for the word love. I'm going to be waiting for her to look me deep into my eyes, whereas I'll feel it. I've got to feel it Trish! I want her to look me deep in my eyes and say, I'll never hurt you. Those words are extremely important to me Trish." Cleabo turned his head sideways illustrating the deliverance of meaningful words, then he continued.

"Then I'll know that this is my soul mate, because she will gear her life towards never hurting me and I'll do the same. We'll make each other happy because we'll know what makes each other unhappy, so we won't do hurtful things. That's what love is about to me, Trish. A lot of people use the word love loosely; they don't mean it because they would never hurt the other person. And Trish, some don't even remember the words they repeated and swore to God at their wedding; what they would do for one another. Once, this young lady told me she loved me after we had sex for the first time. Now, what does a person think a man is suppose to say after he know he just slung some good sex on a lady and her response is she loves him? Shit, either she is delusional or just plain old fashioned whipped for the moment; you know what I mean Trish?"

"Damn C, that's pretty deep. At least you know what you're looking for; huh?"

"Oh, no doubt, everyone should. I've just got to get my shit straight first."

"I hear you C, and you know what? I like my men built like you C, and *mad* cute like you are underneath that beard. Everything else you said I agree with, but, also having a goal. I think the woman should have a goal too. Everyone needs a direction or they become complacent; don't you agree, C?"

"I sure do baby; you sound like my kind of friend."

"Hey C, it's getting late now and I have to get up early. I really enjoyed your company. Let me get your clothes out of the dryer."

"Okay, it sure has been a pleasure."

After he put on his clothes, Trish gave him her card and a nice hug at the door. Cleabo was glad she hugged him after he was dressed. It had been too long since he'd been with a woman and he knew for sure that he couldn't have stopped his nature from rising in that damn robe. But he displayed himself to be a true gentleman. Cleabo treated a lady like a lady.

The next couple of days went by slowly and he was back to his normal routine at the Junction and on the Boulevard. Cleabo told Cliff about what had happened and again Cliff called him a fool for not making any type of advances. Cleabo too started wondering if he was getting soft. Now Cleabo was certain; Cliff had no idea what he was talking about. He felt that he did the right thing in order to gain respect. He could have jacked off anytime, but to lose respect with a woman of such beauty was out of the question. He wanted her, true, but lets face it, he didn't own a Mercedes or any car of stature. Hell he didn't even have a home! Somehow, he felt that it really didn't matter with Trish. He had to win her trust and then she would know who he was. Cleabo made her laugh when he told her some of the things that had happened to him in New York as a child. Trish thought that his life style was interesting but mischievous.

After a week and a half had gone by, he found himself each day with her card in his hand spinning it round and around. He was indecisive whether to call her.

"What do I have to offer her?" Cleabo questioned himself.

Around lunchtime, he tucked the card away. Sitting against a building with his coffee can for all of his donations, he noticed himself being watched by some guys that were far from being either transients or the police. Not wanting it to be obvious that he knew they were watching him, he pretended he didn't see the men across the street or the other one at the corner.

As he turned away from looking at the men at the corner, he looked directly into a pair of binoculars from the rooftop. He knew their eyeballs connected, but he played it off casually. Slowly Cleabo gathered his things and stood up, wondering where this adventure was going to go. He wondered if they could have been stalking someone else? "That would be impossible," he thought; he was the only one out there other than the people walking the streets.

"Damn, they weren't any good; or was it that they didn't care if they let their presence be known?" Cleabo questioned himself.

Cleabo started walking away as the men wearing dark shades started to follow him. The men were dressed in baggy pants; sort of in a hip-hop type of fashion. They were easy to detect, because they never changed location and were always putting their fist to their mouths when they talked to each other. He began to walk at a fast pace as he noticed the men starting to come after him.

"Surely, if they had wanted to kill me, they could have by now," he thought.

Cleabo knew that his life wasn't what they wanted. Finally they approached him straight out.

"C, we need you to come with us," a short haired, physically muscularly built gentlemen said to him. He acted as if he was in charge. The man's voice was deep, and this without a doubt was an order and not a request. But still Cleabo had to inquire where he was going and why.

"What for and who are you?" Cleabo asked.

"Don't worry about that," the man retorted. "You just need to come with us, or we'll be forced to take you."

"You haven't killed me yet, so I guess you aren't going to, and I have no choice in the matter. From the way it looks, you just want to ask me a bunch of questions. Look, I haven't seen shit and I ain't heard shit."

"Just shut up and get in the car!" the leader said.

A black limo pulled up and they shoved him into the car. Cleabo dared not resist; thinking that as long as he remained cool, his life wouldn't be harmed. The three men sat in the limo with him and handed him a black suit jacket and a black pair of pants; telling him to put them on. They arrived at a restaurant in the lower portion of downtown L.A. From the way it looked he could assume Italian was its specialty. They walked around the restaurant and entered through the back. The other two guys were in back of him and they were consistently looking around to see if they were being followed or watched. Through the kitchen and into one of the freezers, they went.

While inside the freezer, the lead guy used a device and opened one of the wall panels. The panel opened at his command like a revolving door. There were steps leading downstairs. Cleabo thought, "For sure this is some hi-tech stuff."

There was another door they had to enter by way of this same electrical device he had. They entered a long hallway that had many rooms. The hallway was as shiny as the Army's barracks, with cameras that monitored their every move from the ceiling. They took him into a room and told him to have a seat. The lead man then gave him a cigarette and a light. Then he walked towards the door, leaving the other two guys standing by the wall in silence.

"What am I into now?" Cleabo thought.

The lead man made his exit and the door was opened wide enough for Cleabo to make eye contact with a lady as she walked by. She glanced at him and they recognized each other. It was Trish; she rushed into the room almost knocking the lead man down.

"C! How you doing? Don't worry, everything is going to be okay. You just got to go through the intro, and in two weeks or so you will be allowed to walk in public again, so don't trip! And listen to everything they tell you okay? It's cool, I promise you."

"Okay Trish." Cleabo said relaxing somewhat because he trusted her. "It's cool, I trust you. How have you been?"

"I've been fine, C. I've just been waiting for you to get here. Everything about you must have checked out okay."

"Oh really?"

"Yeah, they've probably been following you for a while and they only let their presence be known to you when it was time to bring you in."

"Hey Trish, you need to get out of here, Luther is on his way!" the lead man told her.

"Oh, okay see you in a few C."

"Okay, bye Trish."

Trish left and Cleabo felt more relaxed now; knowing that whatever this place was he was going to see a lot of her.

A heavyset man with a beard made his way into the room. He walked around the room and turned his back to Cleabo. With one hand in the pocket of his expensive looking designer suit, he turned around, looking Cleabo up and down. With a conceited sneer, he began to talk.

"Welcome to Crime Academy. You have a choice: join us or die. No one will miss you, so make your decision."

"Not too much of a choice is there?" Cleabo said.

"You got that right. We selected you, and you don't choose us. You were selected because of your self-defense tactics and being on the streets, you're expendable."

"Oh okay, you mean like I can get killed and it will be all right?"

"Not really, here at Crime Academy we try to avoid that."

"I see."

"Mr. C, or whatever your real name is, frankly I don't care, in a few days you will be given a new name; a code name. Your fingerprints will be cosmetically redone, along with receiving a new I.D. and passport. This is part of your in-processing, a new life Mr. C. Fortunately for you, it will be with Crime Academy. In your room you will get shaved and cleaned up. Your day will come early tomorrow. Since Trish recommended you, she will be responsible for you. She will come by your room and give you more details." Luther said sternly.

His room was equipped with all the clothing that he needed; from gym clothes to suits. The pants were folded in half on the hangers evenly and in line. All of the zippers were facing the wall and all of the butts to the pants were all spaced about a half-inch apart. His shirts were folded as if they just came out of the package, although he knew they weren't. Inside the dresser, his under garments were neatly folded and also in line; resembling a military style. There was a refrigerator, stereo and a stacked bar.

Some literature was on his bed; he assumed it was left there for him to study. It contained details about breaking into a safe. The information was elaborately detailed, from listening to the tumblers of different types of safes to the different types of explosives that were used to blow them up. To include the different types of material they were made out of; like metal or steel.

Lessons on welding and the different ways of entering a safe were his first lesson. He could hardly wait for Trish to stop by to fill him in on what was really going on. There were a lot of things he needed to know about this Crime Academy that he was drafted into. Trish finally knocked at the door.

"Hey C, what up?"

"Nothing Trish, but you can tell me what's this you've got me into?"

"Hey C, they probably said I recommended you, but honestly I didn't. They choose who they want whenever there is a shortage; just like they chose me. I'll have to tell you about that one day. You see, there were two other people there the night you saved me. They were on the roof and they saw how you handled those two guys. They knew you came back with me to my place and from that point on, they've been tracking your every move. C, they even told me about your cat." She then plunged her cute self on the foot of his bed acting so glad that he had become a part of Crime Academy.

"Yeah, I noticed those guys on the roof that night, I thought they were with you, just as in Phoenix, right?"

"Yeah C, I was on a job then; you know just handling my business. C, if you were smart enough to figure all of that out, that's the reason why you're here. You're going to like it C, and the pay is *hella* good. They train you on everything you do prior to a job. The only thing you have to do is remember all of the lessons; you will be required to use them again. There is no killing involved, we're thieves, but upscale thieves. There is nothing petty though, and a few bank jobs. We have connections all over the world and some of the jobs are abroad. That's the reason why I haven't seen you in a while. I've been away; my dog Troy was at the kennel."

"Oh, okay Trish, if I get to see you everyday it can't be all that bad, huh?"

"It's truly what you make it, and I could use the break from the jobs. I'll always be close to you doing your training and I may go with you on your first few jobs. You're the first person that I've ever sponsored, so I have to do a good job at this. Now I'm saying these things openly, but I want you to know that you should always be aware that someone is listening and watching you all the time. In about two weeks we can celebrate your graduation. I look forward to that C. It might make some folks here kind of jealous of you C, 'cause I didn't give them any play; but I like your style C. I can see who you are and I'm definitely overdue for being in the arms of a man like you. I hope you feel the same about me; but I do know how to separate work from play."

At that point; if the plan was for Trish to reel Cleabo in, it was working. She had him like a fish on bait. He couldn't wait to have her in his arms, no matter what the price he had to pay. After thinking about it, the deal no longer sounded bad to him. He would receive the new fingerprints that he originally wanted and he would be able to try and make Trish his lady. Why not?

Cleabo answered her, "Overdue is an understatement!"

Trish told him some things about Luther; he was considered the commander of the academy. People were sent to Luther's Crime Academy from all over the world; he had some serious connections.

In the hallway Cleabo saw about twelve other candidates walking with their sponsors. Trish also told him about the lead man that had brought him into the academy. She tried to warn him that this man would definitely dislike him. She said that he had always liked her but she had repeatedly told him he wasn't her type.

"I don't normally mix work and pleasure together," but you're different and I met you before you were a candidate of Crime Academy." Trish paused for a moment then continued. "If the people from Crime Academy hadn't found you I would've gone on a hunt for you myself."

He thought it was flattering that this fine young lady felt the same way he did. She told him again he would complete the training in two weeks, then they could celebrate. Cleabo could hardly wait for that, but he couldn't show how anxious he was either. Trish lifted herself up off the bed as he admired her figure eight shape. "How was it possible to have created something this beautiful?" Cleabo thought to himself.

"C, study the material on your bed, you will be tested on it tomorrow. I'll see you then. Meanwhile get acquainted with your room, okay?"

"Okay Trish, I will see you tomorrow."

They hugged each other and she felt so soft and smelled so good. His eyes followed her as she walked down the hallway. After shutting the door he noticed there was a black doctor's bag on the other side of his bed. It contained training aids for his first subject on breaking into safes. There were gloves, oil, a pick and something that looked like a doctor's stethoscope, but more hi-tech. He knew it was a listening device by looking at the headpiece. There were other gadgets which he was sure his lessons on the bed would tell him what to do with.

Cleabo's food was delivered to him shortly after Trish left. He guessed they didn't want him wandering the halls. Although the door wasn't locked, he could easily assume they didn't want him to come out, so he didn't. He just studied his lessons until he became sleepy. The information was fascinating; it seemed they had supplied all of the necessary information that he would need to open up this particular safe. The safe was timer controlled and he had a lesson on replacing the timing device in order to open the safe. His first lesson wasn't on blowing up the safe; just cracking the safe by way of distinguishing the sound of the tumblers.

There was a device inside of the black bag that was used to connect to the timing device. In the lesson, it stated that there was a sensor that would detect when the timer was tampered with, and the safe wouldn't open. He had to bypass the timer and connect the alternate timing device. There also was a section for the security alarm control box at the safe. However, all of that information was missing. It stated for him to just be aware of the alarm; someone else would be handling that portion of the job. The lesson also taught him breathing techniques to use while picking the safe.

There was a special type of polymer oil used to single out the ticks from the tumblers while searching for the combination. The lesson indicated the ways of determining which direction to start turning, and the way of knowing when to skip a turn.

"Oh, this lesson is deep," he said to himself.

With his listening device on his head he started practicing what it said to do; even the timing device was challenging. Cleabo had to strip some insulation from the correct wire without cutting the wires, then solder the new timer on within a thirty-second period. After the timer was set he had to pick the safe.

It was difficult waiting for his next day to come; his eyes were becoming heavy so he curled into the fetal position to get some rest. What a day he thought, restless with all of the criminology stuff on his mind. Surprisingly, the thought of getting caught never entered his mind. Counting sheep wasn't working at first, but finally he was able to get some rest.

At six in the morning Trish was at his door. She said it was time to start his day. "So early," he thought; so he knew they meant business. After his shower he slipped into a pair of the silk boxer shorts they had put in his dresser drawer. "They must have cost at least twenty dollars a pair," he thought, as he realized how smooth they felt on his rough and abused body. Breakfast arrived and again, so did Trish. She watched him as he swallowed his last bite, then she put his lesson on his bed and said, "I remember that one." She left Cleabo with the feeling, that no doubt, there were many more lessons to come.

Around seven she escorted him and his black bag to room number one. She told him she couldn't go in with him, but she would see him later. There was a chair, similar to the desks one might have in school;

a chair desk type with a piece of paper on top. On the chair desk was his instructions with time limits for each particular task. On the wall to the right of him, there was a safe door built into the wall. It was identical to the one in the lesson he'd been studying. To the right of the safe was a clock, much like a time clock for the twenty-four seconds clock in the NBA games. To the left of the safe was the timing device.

Although someone else would have taken care of the alarm aspects of the job, Cleabo had to ensure that the right wire was connected to the simulated timer that created a continuing loop. Reading his instructions told him he would have five minutes to take care of the timer and crack the safe. When the clock started his time would begin; then the clock would display stop at the end of the five minutes. Just as he finished reading the instructions a gentleman walked in. He was an older man with a gray beard, and he stood approximately six feet tall. The gentleman stood in the corner and didn't say a word, his stern look and demeanor indicated to Cleabo that he was strictly business. Cleabo tried to talk to him but he wouldn't say anything; not even good morning.

The gentleman watched as the start light came on. It was then that Cleabo had to take the timer out. He remembered which wire he had to strip and solder to his timing device. Somehow, he must have touched another wire when he attempted to strip it. The lights similar to the lights on top of a police cruiser started flashing and the sound of a siren filled the room. "Damn, I flaked up!" the word "Stop" appeared on the clock. He had failed within the first few seconds. The man looked at him and he raised his eyebrows in disappointment.

The older gentleman then went to the clock, reset it and walked over to the timing device to inspect it. After seeing that Cleabo merely touched another wire, he indicated for Cleabo to get ready again. The start light came on and he was at it again; this time Cleabo didn't touch another wire. However, when stripping the plastic insulation from around the wire he accidentally cut one of the copper wires. The siren, lights and the word stop appeared again. Cleabo was getting frustrated at this point, but the older gentleman just smiled and shook his head, then he replaced the wires and reset the clock.

The next time Cleabo inserted the loop timer, the older gentleman seemed impressed. Cleabo knew he could do it, because he had studied it deeply last night. He just needed to have his hands and mind in unison. Now, he was at the safe. With his head piece on, he used the spray oil with only two minutes remaining, he was trying to remember everything he had read. He knew that what had taken some folks a life time to learn and become proficient, Crime Academy was testing him and making him an expert in just one day.

Cleabo began to sweat profusely as he concentrated and listened so closely. Now he knew why Trish kept saying all he had to do is just listen. Cleabo was able to distinguish the sounds and skips to include the start directions. The chambers of this heavy, six foot wide, steel door were tricky. It's handle was similar to the steering wheel of a huge boat; the kind with numerous handles on it to turn. "The last number," he thought to himself as he stepped away from the combination dial to open the door of the safe. When he pulled on it, the stop sign, siren, and all of those lights came on again. "Damn!" Cleabo shouted. The gentleman in the back laughed at him and told him to go down the hall into the break room and come back in fifteen minutes.

During his break he had time to think about what he was doing wrong. Trish stopped into the break room and told him he was doing good. She said that most people didn't get to the safe until after lunch.

"C, no one can tell you how to pick it except the lesson, but, you've got to feel it. Perhaps you should treat the dial like you would treat me on our first encounter. Make love to the dial, don't be rough on it and make sure you have it smooth enough to hear it. You can do it C."

Trish left the breakroom after those few inspiring words. He was glad she had confidence in him, because he was about to give up on this task that reminded him of taking a hearing test. His ego was uplifted now, knowing he had someone in his corner. After the break he went charging back to the room. The moment he entered, the clock started, as the man stood in his corner with a note pad and pen. While digging in his bag of goodies for his necessary items, he notice a pen and a pad had been added to the bag. Although he knew that by pulling on the handle and the door didn't open in real life, he could try to pick it again, provided the alarm was taken care of. However, here at the Academy they were teaching him not to depend on the other man's job. He would only have one shot at it because of time, so it had to be done right the first time.

Swiftly he implanted the new timing device and made love to the tumblers of the huge safe. He wrote the numbers down with the pad and pen as he went through them, practicing as if he was on a real job. "Voila!" the heavy steel door opened. Quickly the man said, "Don't open it yet, have a seat again." He disassembled Cleabo's timer and rewired the old timing device. The older gentleman opened the door to the safe and changed the combination.

Cleabo couldn't see what was behind the door. His curiosity grew and he could hardly wait to see what was behind this heavy steel door. He made him do this continuously and each time the combination was trickier. After successfully completing the task numerous times; about seven to be exact, he sent Cleabo to lunch. Trish was there and she was grinning from ear to ear. With her lunch tray from the kitchen area she walked over to his table.

"I knew you could do it C!" she exclaimed enthusiastically.

"Hey, thanks for believing in me Trish."

"Sure, you're lucky though C."

"Oh really? Why?"

"There are only about twenty people on the west coast that can break that safe."

"Oh really?" he said, feeling even better.

"Yeah, the instructors, me and six other people here. You will probably meet them later today. You had the veteran instructor with you, and he likes you; that's unusual, C."

"I'm glad it worked out for me. I feel comfortable doing it now."

"There is still more to do, take care and listen. I'll be around."

Trish left him once again with puzzling thoughts of what extraordinary criminal task lay ahead of him. He finished his lunch and returned back to room number one. The instructor was there and again he had to perform the task of breaking into the safe. Cleabo felt confident enough to the point that he began thinking he could do this with his eyes closed. Fearing to become cocky, he professionally performed the task within minutes.

This time when he opened the safe the instructor told him to step inside. He followed him inside what he thought would be the inside of a vault, but it turned out to be another classroom. There were six desks and five other vault doors. The other vault doors opened up as students came inside the room. Apparently they all had partaken in the same training, and the instructors were also being judged on their accurate timing of getting them into the room around the same time. At their desks were their names with an equal sign and a code name. His desk had the letter C and then the word Seal; his new name. The six of them had different jobs on their desk, which was to break the same type of safe they had been tested on. But, their jobs were at different places in the world.

There was a package on their desk with more details of rendezvousing with a team; and the instructor continued to lay out the details of what they had to do. "Damn, this is serious!" he thought. His package was set for Brazil, and he had two more days of training before he'd meet up with the team at the hotel. The instructor questioned them about their missions. After about thirty minutes of studying the package they were sent to Cosmetic for fingerprints, pass ports and a new I.D. Only a few lines of the fingers were laser altered, making the healing process faster.

For the next couple of days they rehearsed endlessly. During this period Cleabo was not allowed to listen to music or watch T.V. They wanted to preserve his hearing for the job. On his second day he asked Trish why they just don't blow the safe open, as indicated in some parts of the lesson plan. She said that they only do what is required. "You may go into the safe and not take any money at all Seal." Seal, he had to get used to being called that! His name had changed from Clean Boy to C, and now Seal. A code name such as that could possibly reach popularity, he thought.

The afternoon of his second day he was taken to the range. Seal was being prepared for his next job before his first was completed. He was issued weapons and a vest. The weapons ranged from Tech Nines to Ooze's. All were equipped with silencers and automatic firing capabilities.

They also issued him a weapon called the Puff gun. It was a chamber fed weapon, firing rounds that were about the size of his thumb. Inside each round were chemically formatted dirt and a tiny durable microphone. The dirt covered the microphone upon impact, and a conversation could be monitored as clearly as day through wood, glass and even brick. Target practice with the other weapons was done basically by aiming at center mass and making head shots at the silhouettes. With the Puff gun, however, the corners of window sills were his target. His aim had to be precise; the rounds dispersed upon impact and camouflaged the microphone. Continuously he practiced until finally his aim was on target each time with the simulated rounds. His issued rounds were for his other "Soon to be job."

After his third day of training, Seal was on the plane en route to Brazil. At the hotel he met his team, two Italians and an Asian fellow. All of them spoke fluent English with additional other languages. The plans were simple and they paved the way. He would crack the safe as he had been trained to do after attaching the timing device, then they would walk out leaving no indications of ever being there. Everything went smoothly for that job. Seal was amazed that the safe he cracked was identical to the one he had been practicing on. The execution was performed in such a timely manner, he knew he had reached pro status. The leader of the team kept the money. Seal stayed in his room as he was instructed to do. His job was completed and the next morning he was on his way back to the United States.

Trish gave him a big hug at the airport. She seemed to be so proud of him. Little did she know he had been scared shitless the entire time. Seal was so glad it was over, but he knew that soon it would happen again. After that he thought that Trish might go ahead and reward him good, but, she was a woman of her word, and when she said two weeks, she meant just that. After the small little smack on the cheek and all the shit he had just gone through, he was hoping for more. Nevertheless, he knew the time would come and when it did, he would handle her the way she needed to be treated.

Trish took him back to the academy and to his room. He was still on lock down; it seemed as if he hadn't proven anything to them. They still didn't trust him. His pay for that one job was five grand. Trish gave him a credit card with the name Seal Smith on it. She also gave him information to a Swiss bank where an account had been set up in his new code name.

"Five grand for one job; not bad," he thought.

Trish explained to him that after two weeks he had to find a place of his own, but she would help with that. That was cool with him, he wanted to get out of there at that moment; but he couldn't. The next day his entire morning was spent at the range with the puff gun. Continuously the instructor was perfecting his aim. They thought he picked it up exceedingly fast. Seal merely thought that with a scope on the rifle, how could anyone miss the corners of the window sills?

After lunch he was introduced to another task, which he knew would soon be another job. Seal was escorted to a garage like area. There were brick walls from one end of the garage to the other. A black van with tinted windows sat at the end of the garage's rolled up doors. He was told to get into the van. Inside the van there were three computers and a camera video monitoring system, with a camera mounted on top of the van.

The camera had the ability similar to that of a submarine's telescope. One computer controlled graphic designs of all sorts. After entering certain information into the computer, it controlled a high-powered masonry chisel machine. The machine was small, about waist level; but it was powerful. The high powered chisel worked so fast it was amazing. With it, either the bed joints or the head joints of the bricks could be cut within seconds. His instructions were to cut the mortar, (the material in between the bricks) into a specific design. There was another machine inside the van; it too was on wheels. This machine had high pressure suction cups that looked like toilet bowl plungers, built in the same design as the graphics of an uneven plus sign. He had to carve out the plus sign design into the bricks, then pull it away from the wall with the suction cups.

The machine was lowered down out of the van in the way handicap wheelchairs are. After putting the masonry chisel in place, he was taught to run the program on the computer to cut through the bricks. After a perfect shape was obtained without cutting any of the other bricks, he had to position the vacuum suction couplets. The suction couplet gripped the mass block that had been cut and held it as he rolled it out of his way.

After being trained on removing the brick, his torch cutting training started. The material was also on a rolling cart. Acetylene and Oxygen tanks were mounted. Chalk sticks, torch head and striker were available too. Another suction, with a telescope extended pole attached to it, was also on the cart. Later he learned it was to pull the money cabinet back into place.

Two days of training on this particular task passed, then he was sent on another job. A Puff gun mission, Seal had to take six shots to place microphones all around this huge house in a New Jersey, high-class subdivision. His job was done quickly and an easy three thousand was made.

After five days of training to cut into the safe, it was time to do the third job. Trish had been encouraging him during the entire ordeal. Now it was time to complete his next task in Atlanta. The area which he had to draw his diagram on the bricks was identified with a Puff gun earlier. Someone else had that task; he guessed it was the same job he had done in Jersey with his Puff gun, except that he had planted microphones.

Eighteen inches on all four sides, centered from the Puff gun mark. As the team moved quickly to loop the alarm system, he began to set up his equipment. Knowing the safe would be behind the wall, the signal was given to him to go ahead with his part of the task. The brick wall was cut in seconds, with the welding equipment Cleabo began to cut a square into the safe large enough for the team to enter. There was a cabinet in front of the hole he had created. Cleabo was told he would have to push it out of the way, so he did.

A human chain was formed and they passed the money to one another until it reached the van. With the telescope suction pole, similar to a large plunger, he pulled the cabinet back. Once again, another successful mission. Leaving the vault in its normal state was just to throw them off temporarily, until they counted the remainder of the money and found a lot of it was missing. Some important documents were also taken. Cleabo didn't know what they were, neither did he care.

There was plenty of training he endured the remainder of his first two weeks. Then Trish came into his room and told him it was time for him to go to his new place. She had found him a nice little Villa in south L.A. After settling in, Trish and Cleabo made plans for dinner at six that evening. Everything was set for him, first a bank account and now a place to live. They even had a convertible Mercedes in the garage for him and the refrigerator was stocked.

"What a life!" he thought.

Cleabo could hardly wait for six o'clock to come so that he could be with Trish. She told him that it was a black-tie dinner and that he would find something to wear in the closet, just as he did at the academy.

Trish was on time and dressed to impress. She must have known that he was going to select the black velvet dinner jacket, with the white banded collar shirt and the black tux pants. Her dress was also velvet and tight. It was so tight that he could easily tell Trish didn't have on any panties. She was ready for sex, but she still conducted herself as a lady with a whole lot of class.

They ate at a high rise restaurant, the view through the glass window overlooked the city. The Vault was the name of the place. The tab alone was over four hundred dollars, and he watched Trish pass the guy a fifty dollar bill just for seating them. Everything was on her; she had the tab, the tips and the looks to die for. They ate and then danced closely to soft music; she was beautiful. They returned to his Villa and he put on some music to continue their celebration. After a little wine and soft music, her nakedness was exposed to him just as he was on their first encounter. They made love continuously for three days. After the third day the Academy called both of them, it was time to go back to work.

Trish and Cleabo fell in love and were inseparable. He waited impatiently for her return from her missions, as did she when he went on his. They moved in together along with her dog Troy and his cat, Lucky, which Trish had surprised him with when he moved into his place.

As she had warned him, the team leader she worked for didn't like it. During the course of the year Cleabo's performance had established a reputation; a good one. He was detail-oriented and they knew it. Cleabo received a promotion to training, now he was preparing the missions for the new recruits. While preparing some of the missions he could observe how Trish's team leader was trying to give her the difficult tasks; some that could subject her to failure. Cleabo would change some of her duties since it was so obvious what the team leader was trying do. When Trish's team leader and Cleabo had a little confrontation about the matter, the team leader's case had no validity with their boss Luther. Luther told the team leader that Seal was doing a fine job, and to stop tripping.

Crime Academy started to change some of their missions. Some of the recruits were being trained to do hits and Cleabo knew that this was something that neither Trish nor himself wanted to get into. He also knew her team leader would be putting her to the test one day. Trish finally told him how she became connected with Crime Academy. She had been married to a batterer; he was Italian and the only child. After beating her up one night he walked away from her. As he was getting into his car in the driveway she ran up on him from behind and stabbed him.

One of the neighbors saw the incident and Trish became a fugitive. She took what money they had and fled to Europe. The FBI was on her trail and so were the Italians that were supposed to have been connected. Their son was their only child, he was rich and had plenty of women on the side. After spending all of the money she had in Europe, she returned to the U.S. by boat. On the boat she met her current team leader and he brought her into the Academy. She said she thought at first that he just wanted to help her, but later she knew it was more.

While preparing a mission for New Orleans, Cleabo came across a picture on the computer with the code name Luke.

"Damn, it's my old First Sergeant!" Cleabo said at a low tone, trying to keep anyone from hearing him. "Now I know how I was set up. It was a Crime Academy mission. He is high ranking in his district and now I know how we have so much access to military equipment."

He researched some more on the computer and also found a couple of his ex-soldiers, the ones that preformed the hits and took the money. It had been a sloppy job but effective, he guessed, because he had taken the blame. Cleabo shared his findings with Trish including the fact that she would be coming down to do hits. They were both upset. He wanted revenge and she wanted out; but they couldn't see the way to accomplish either.

An armed, bank robbery mission came down for Seal during this time period. It was in Alaska, so he had to construct the mission to include cold weather training. In the mission plan it stated that if they were walking in an area where there were no trees or bushes, they were probably on a lake. They had to be careful because the rendezvous was in a cabin outside of town. At thirty below zero they hit the bank dressed in white to include their white ski masks and the job proceeded smoothly.

They tied the people in the bank up and their snowmobile waited for them behind the bank. He was amazed at the connections Crime Academy had; everything seemed to always go so smoothly. He still had Luke, his old First Sergeant on his mind as he rode with his crew at top speed to the cabin.

As they rode their snowmobiles in a line type of formation, they slowed down as they approached an area that had a flat plain view. There were no trees or bushes in view. Without a doubt he knew this was a lake. They watched a teenager as she walked across a hill portion on the side of the lake. The ice broke and she fell in. She screamed as she glided downward, with her back breaking more ice as she fell. All the men knew they had to go to her rescue. One of the men retrieved a rope from the side of his snowmobile and quickly tied it around a near by tree.

The rope was not long enough to reach her, so they instantly formed a human chain. Cleabo found himself to be on the end of the chain reaching for the girl as he clutched his team member's hand. The ice broke and he felt himself falling into the treacherous cold waters. Letting go of his hand, his team members ran to save their lives.

As the cold waters drenched his body, he could feel his insides starting to feel numb. Down he went and he knew that if he were to go under the ice he would be dead. He pushed himself to the surface of the ice, knowing that he would have only one shot to save his life. To his right he could see the girl struggling for her life on her back in the broken ice. He reached and grabbed her with his right hand, as he watched his team members running up the slope.

With his left hand he reached for the hard ice to try and pull himself and the girl up, but it crumbled and they went down again. Quickly he pushed himself up again, reaching for anything solid. He felt the same feeling he had when that truck in New York hit him when he was only twelve; he knew he was dying.

Again he reached for the ice while holding on to the teenage girl. This time he felt a hand grabbing hold of his hand. It felt as if it was the size of a baseball mitten. The hand was large, strong and firm. It had to have been the largest hand he'd ever felt before in his entire life. The hand pulled him up as he held onto the girl. They were out of the water as he gazed into the eyes of what must have been a ten year old boy. He had blue eyes and his skin was tanned like the Eskimos of the region. Cleabo shivered as he watched this boy just walk away from him. The boy walked across the lake and diminished into the horizon. With dazed mind and numbed limbs, he thought many hours had to have passed, yet he could still see his team members running along the slope indicating the passing time had only been seconds.

"How could this be?" he asked himself. He dragged the girl to safety and his team members returned, rushing them to the cabin. At the cabin they stripped all of their clothing off and shared sleeping bags with them to bring their body temperature back to normal. While they were trying to prevent them from dying of hypothermia, he shared with the men what had happened to him and they looked at each other like he was crazy. Then one of them said, "Seal, you are probably a little delirious right now. We didn't see a little boy, you fell in and then you grabbed the girl and climbed out. I looked back at you and saw you doing this as I ran off the lake."

It was then that he realized that they didn't witness the miraculous work of a higher power. Cleabo could only assume that it was meant for his eyes only. For sure, he wasn't going crazy. Although they didn't see what he saw, perhaps it was not meant for them to see this little boy with the glove-size hands and eyes of gentle serenity. Cleabo remembered trying to say thanks but his lips couldn't move. Cleabo didn't know if it was because of the boy's presence or if he was just too cold. It seemed as if the boy understood what he wanted to say. The boy had tilted his head to the side, glanced at the girl, then back at him and smiled. Then he walked across the thin sheet of ice that had broken on the teenager and Cleabo. His presence wasn't of this world, that's for sure. What had seemed to be a long time to Cleabo, apparently was a short period of time. Cleabo was the only one who had seen him. The boy was radiant and delivered the same warm, peaceful feeling Cleabo had when he was twelve and lying on the hospital bed after being struck by the truck.

The teenage girl was given some hot chocolate and dressed in some of the men's clothing. With a blanket wrapped around her, she sat in front of the fireplace and her body temperature came back to normal. The money was disguised in suitcases; there was no way she knew what they were doing. If the men thought she knew they were robbers they probably would have killed her. Cleabo felt that someone wanted this young lady alive and he was the earthly person to use. The girl was quiet; perhaps a little too quiet for him.

Checking their timepieces, they anxiously waited for the chopper to arrive and take them away from this cold world that seemed separated from society and left in the midst of a primitive and remote state of being. The blades of the schnook helicopter shook the small cabin as it whipped up the snow. The effects from the blades were similar to a snowstorm, but they had to get the snowmobiles and all of their gear onto the chopper. The thought of being wanted by the authorities was far from their minds as they boarded the schnook. The little girl was left in the cabin.

From the schnook, they boarded an aircraft heading back to L.A. Cleabo didn't know what to think anymore; apparently no one else had seen what he had gone through, except for the boy and himself. He was puzzled, continuously wondering if this was a calling. He knew there was nothing religious about himself, perhaps the boy was sent to save the girl? "Then why didn't he do it himself?" Cleabo questioned himself.

At the house he couldn't wait until Trish came home; he wanted to tell her everything. When she opened the door she was mad, yet excited when she saw him. Trish was overwhelmed with disgust from the news she wanted to share with him. Trish had come down on a mission and it was for a hit; Cleabo wasn't surprised at all. She was selected to take someone's life, but not in self-defense. Such a cruel way for anyone to die, he thought.

Chills ran through his body as he held Trish in his arms and tried to aid her discomfort. They sat on the sofa and he began to tell her about what had happened to him. She was in a state of shock, as she saw how his entire body shook as he relayed to her everything that had happened. If there was anyone that would believe him he knew it was Trish. She was the only one that he could trust and a few times he was even tempted to tell her about his old life; but he dared not to. At that point they were fed up with Crime Academy; they wanted no more part of it. The money was good, but too many things were beginning to happen.

Trish knew she was slowly going down and would someday probably end up in prison. Cleabo couldn't let that happen to her, he was in love with her. After his incident he knew there was more to life than what he was seeing with the naked eye. He felt as though God had given him his last chance at life and the opportunity to save Trish and others lives.

"What a weird feeling," he thought.

Trish and Cleabo decided to take the money they had saved up and get away from Crime Academy. They knew that if they were found, they would be killed. Cleabo told Trish that the next day he would go into the computers and get enough information to take all of their asses down and that is exactly what he did. Cleabo gathered up all the documents to put Crime Academy out of business; especially his old First Sergeant and his two side kicks. He never could find information on the third soldier, but what he had was good enough. Cleabo had names, location, salaries, position and the history of missions. Without a doubt, he would be history if he were caught. They made him prepare Trish's mission while he was there. It was a diplomatic hit; he knew he was doing the right thing at that point. Murder was what the First Sergeant had set him up for. He was innocent then and he would stay that way, was the thought going through his mind. Cleabo may have been a thief, but he was no murderer.

Trish received her mission and they nodded at each other, knowing it wasn't going to happen. She had no choice, however, but to go through the motions. That afternoon she had to go to the range for target practice for the rest of the day. Her airline tickets directed her one way, but that night she and Cleabo fled in a different direction. With Crime Academy on their backs they made their way to Africa. In a missionary, they sought refuge, thinking that Crime Academy wouldn't find them there. They had no reason to come there, he thought; the land was too poor and as long as they pretended to be husband and wife they would be taken in by the people of the village. They were able to be a part of their new community. Cleabo read the Bible a lot and he started teaching to some of the village kids and soon to some of the adults.

When he found time, he wrote a letter to the one person he felt he could trust, the former prison guard and author that had published his life story. It wasn't hard to find his address.

"Dear Clayton,

Since I escaped I have been jotting down these little notes in my journal. Now it is time for you to amend your book with the rest of my story. Perhaps you can help me to clear my name and get immunity for Trish. Here are all the necessary documents to put Crime Academy away. Now, after the reprint of your book, Crime Academy will be coming after you also, to find us. Here is ten thousand dollars to help you hide and stay under cover until it's all over. You proved your friendship a long time ago.

Now if you're really my friend, you will help us. In thirty days Trish and I will return to the United States to get married. I'll contact you then. Forward your mail to a P.O. box when you receive this box. Inside the box is a self addressed envelope; write your P.O. box address on it and mail it back. I'll send you my P.O. Box number when we return to the United States. We'll keep in touch through the Post Office. List your telephone under the name Jack Jones.

Here is the driver's license and social security card for the name; all you have to do is put a picture in the license and seal it with the lamination I have provided. I lifted them from the Academy when I put together these documents you have in the box. I look forward to hearing from you in about thirty days. Peace man, and thank you so much. Trish and I really need your help. You must understand my position. I don't have anyone else I can really trust. I really don't mean to interrupt your life and what you have going on, but from the way I feel, this is beyond my doing to do alone. I feel like I was chosen to save that little girl's life I mentioned in my journal and I think that you are chosen to save Trish's and my life. Thanks again, your forever indebted friend, Cleabo."

CHAPTER XIV

EPILOGUE

"Damn," Clayton the ex-prison guard trembled after reading what had happened to Cleabo. "*Shit*! What a life!" he shouted. Clayton had really thought that Cleabo's life before prison was interesting, but after reading Cleabo's journal from the box that sat between his legs on the floor, he realized Cleabo's life after prison was even more exciting. Cleabo needed his help; never did he recall him ever asking for help. He remembered him as always being independent, but he was a changed man now. Cleabo was in love, helping the needy, praying and teaching the word of God. All he wanted now was some help to clear his name and be pardoned.

There was no way in hell he wouldn't help him out. Besides, Clayton needed the money that was in the box to hide out and rewrite the letters. Cleabo was right, he couldn't write that well. His handwriting had to be deciphered a great deal. It would take Clayton a few days to do this. Once again Cleabo's timing was right on the money. Clayton was getting pretty tired of his cubicle and the boring ass stories his boss wanted him to write. However, while working for the newspaper company, he met some influential people with his press pass. Clayton knew that some of these people could help Cleabo.

At that instant it dawned on him that Perry Poe, a congressman friend of his, could possibly help. Perry befriended Clayton; he was friendly and seemed to be straight and narrow and not tainted by regular politics. Perry was a middle aged man with droopy eyes and his hair was beginning to go bald. He was slightly overweight, but with the look of a man that works out periodically.

After flipping through his Rolodex, Clayton picked up the telephone and dialed Perry's number. After about three rings Perry finally answered the telephone.

"Hello," his deep voice vibrated through the fiber optic lines.

"Hey Perry, this is Clayton man. Been a long time huh?"

"Oh, what up Clayton? Yeah its been a long time. So what can I do for you?"

"How did you know I wanted you to do something for me?"

"Come on, it's normal. Most people call on politicians for something they need. You know what I'm saying, no offense though. But, go ahead lay it on me man. That's why I gave you my private line so that if you ever needed something I can help you out."

"Okay, thanks Perry. First I want you to read my novel so that you can be familiar with what I'm going to be laying on you."

"Yeah Clayton, I've been meaning to do that, but I've been so busy with the re-election and everything, I'm sorry man."

"It's okay Perry, but what I'm about to tell you may help your re-election out, if you help us out."

"Us? Who is us Clayton?"

"My main character is a real person. His name is Cleabo. Take the next few days to read the book Perry. I'm going to send you some important information."

"Okay," Perry said with curiosity, wondering what he could possibly be getting himself into.

"Can I send it to your office? That's the only address I have, it's on your card?"

"No, get a pen and send it to my home address. I'll give it to you now."

Clayton retrieved a pen from the small stand that supported his telephone. He carefully listened as Perry gave him his address.

"Got it!"

"Okay, I'll be waiting for it Clayton."

"Cool man, and make sure you read the book. I'll get in contact with you. Right now I have to quit my job and hide out somewhere."

"Damn man, this sounds like some heavy shit."

"It is man, have you ever heard of Crime Academy?"

"No man, I haven't."

"That's who my friend is in trouble with."

"Sounds like you may need the help of the Feds."

"Perhaps, but make sure it's someone you trust. They have a lot of connections, to include the bureau as well, and man they are dirty as shit."

"If you are talking about taking some heavy dudes down, your friend may have to come forth and be placed into protective custody in order to testify."

"That's cool, I trust you and I'll stay in contact."

"Not only your friend, but you too Clayton. After all you'll know too much and I wouldn't want anything to happen to you or anyone else that's involved."

"Perry, right now Cleabo and his wife Trish are safe, but Crime Academy is on their ass. I'm the only one that has contact with them."

"We better get off of this phone. Send me the documents and I'll read your book to get familiar with this dude. Give me a week, alright?"

"Okay, I'll be in touch Perry." Clayton placed the telephone on the receiver. "What kind of shit did Cleabo get me into? Oh well, what are friends for?" he thought to himself out loud. "He's just lucky I didn't have a new woman. Maybe a new life will come from all of this?" he questioned himself.

Clayton paced the floor of his small one bedroom apartment, scratching his head and mumbling to himself, trying to prioritize what he should do next. "It's a good thing Max is at my cousin's house. He'll be alright there," he pause for a moment, then continued to think.

"I've got to get me some clothes together and get a room with the money Cleabo sent me." Pacing the floor some more he glanced into his small kitchen observing the piles of dishes and empty wine bottle on the counter. He knew the kitchen would smell after he departed; however, at this point he really didn't care.

"I'd better empty my bank account. Don't know how long I will be undercover, I also need to pick up a cell phone and send Cleabo the number when I write him. Yeah, that's what I'll do."

Clayton packed all of the contents that Cleabo had sent him into a back pack, along with three days worth of clothing. From his bedroom he retrieved a portable electric typewriter, the same one he had used to type his book with. After clamping the typewriter case down he ensured that he had sufficient amount of paper to accompany him. He decided to leave his car and take a cab to a local motel. There he could retype Cleabo's hand written journal and send it to Perry. As he thumbed through the yellow pages trying to find a motel, his hand began to shake out of nervousness.

Clayton was trying to find a motel on the outside of town with restaurants near by. "The Best Western, I know where that's at, there is some eat out places there too." Clayton said to himself as he began to look for a cab company.

Eagerly he waited for the cab; constantly peeping out of his dirty blinds that were desperately in need of curtains and a good dust job. Just like a crackhead staring between the blinds of a window looking for the police as paranoia sets in, Clayton was waiting for the cab. The cab finally arrived and he locked the door and dashed down the stairs. Impatiently the cab driver blew his horn as Clayton expeditiously ran with his back pack on his back and the briefcase typewriter in his hand.

"Here I am, hold on!" Clayton shouted towards the cab driver.

The driver was Mexican, with the inside of the cab fully decorated with every color a person could imagine. The steering wheel was covered with a soft carpet like material. There were purple dumbbells on a lace hanging down across the upper portion of the windshield. The rear view mirror had a Mexican flag hanging down and the rear door panels were decorated with purple carpet. It seemed as though he was riding in a cab that was going to a parade or perhaps the Mardi Gra.

The driver was a middle aged man, around thirty five or so. Clayton could easily tell that he was short, his seat was pushed so far up it had to have been on the last notch; judging from how close the driver was to the steering wheel. With his beaded eyes and the thick mustache he looked in the rear view mirror at Clayton.

"Where to amigo?" he wiped the sweat from the side of his face, pushing his baseball cap upward out of his face in order to see.

"To the telephone company on Broad, and I want you to wait for me." Clayton said, as he recognize the cab had all of it's windows down, indicating there was no air conditioning.

"Okay," he answered, then clicked the meter on and drove off.

Traffic was as congested as normal in L.A. Clayton leaned his head close to the window to remain cool as the wind from the speeding cab rushed his face. At the telephone company Clayton purchased a cell phone and returned to the cab. "One more stop and I'll be out of this dreadful cab," he said to himself.

"To the Best Western on San Bernardino Avenue please," said Clayton.

"Okay," the driver said, as he started to drive and sing the Mexican song that was playing on his radio. The cab driver noticed the fare increasing to a large amount and he glanced in his rearview mirror, inspecting Clayton to see if he was the type to try and run from a fare. Clayton easily assumed the cab driver felt at ease when he tried to pick small conversation with his broken English accent.

"You heard about the little boy that got shot last night?" the cab driver said, as he moved his head carefully watching the traffic.

"No, I didn't, what happened?"

"He was only six amigo, got hit by a stray bullet from a drive-by."

"Damn that's a shame."

"I know amigo, we used to be able to let our kids go out to play, but now, we have to watch them like hawks. You know what I mean amigo?"

"Yeah, I hear you. Too bad times are changing for the worst."

"I know amigo. Here we are."

"Thanks man." Clayton looked at the meter that had thirty dollars on it. He also observed the driver sliding his left hand down the side of his seat as though he was reaching for a weapon.

"Here is the thirty and a five dollar tip amigo."

The driver brought his hand up and smiled at Clayton.

"Okay amigo, adios."

"Yeah okay, and thanks for the ride."

Clayton paid for a week in advance at the motel. He plunged his body onto the bed to take a nap before starting to type Cleabo's letters for Perry. He also needed to send Cleabo a letter informing him that he received the box and give him his cell number.

Ordering food and working day and night, Clayton managed to put Cleabo's story together for Perry. In precise detail, all of the jobs Cleabo participated in and the role Trish played was passed on to Perry. In his letter to Cleabo, Clayton explained they had to trust someone and Perry was his friend. Clayton assumed that Cleabo would feel the same way and believe and trust in him.

Perry received the letters, and after reading Clayton's novel, he couldn't believe the character he was going to help out. His attitude towards helping Cleabo was out of his character, he thought. But, after absorbing what kind of person Cleabo had turned himself into, Perry questioned himself if he was in a position to be judgmental. A single politician with a seven thousand square foot home, five bed rooms and no one to share it with, truly his elaborate life style also had some issues. It was two days later when Perry contacted Clayton with further instructions. With the letters in his hands, while sitting in his lounge chair outside of his pool, he picked up the old fashioned telephone made of ivory and trimmed in gold to call Clayton.

"Clayton, I've got the ball rolling. I need to bring you, Cleabo and Trish in though, trust me on this man."

"Okay Perry, but I have to wait until Cleabo calls me; we only have mail contact."

"When he does, here is what I want you to tell him."

"Okay go ahead." Clayton waited patiently for his instructions.

"Tell you what, this line might be tapped. A lot of people are trying to figure out what I'm doing that is so hush, hush. Let me get dressed and I'll call you back in about thirty minutes." They said their goodbyes and once again Clayton was pacing the floor, waiting for Perry's call. Finally while he was in the bathroom shaving, the cell phone rang. Knowing it had to be his friend, Clayton picked up and said, "Yeah Perry, what up?"

"When Cleabo calls you," Perry instructed, "I want you to set it up so that all of you can be picked up. The Feds will be picking you up, but they are afraid that Cleabo will not come if you are not present. He trusts you." Perry stopped for a moment to sip his ice tea. "When he calls, tell him to go to the Southland Mall and wait for you in front of Foot Locker at one p.m. the following day he calls you, okay?"

"Alright, I got it."

"Now you are going to have to call me as soon as you let him know this, so I can have all three of you picked up safely."

"Okay, hey, how did it go with the information I sent you?"

"Everything was right on time, and a lot of things have been checked out. Your boy was into some serious stuff."

"Yeah, I know." Clayton said.

"But I believe he is worth all this effort. I believe we can clear his name and also grant immunity to Trish, if she is willing to testify. I'm sure she will."

"I'm glad it's going to work out."

"Oh no doubt, we have the surveillance going on and the raids are about to start.

"Sounds like someone is going to have a good election for busting this organization up, huh?"

"Yeah, thanks man. Just thinking about those words, '*He was instrumental in the destruction of Crime Academy,*' runs chills through my body. I hope he calls you soon. The sooner the better."

"Don't worry, he will, then I'll call you."

"Yeah Clayton, and all you have to do is say '*tomorrow*' when you call me and I'll make it happen on this end."

"Cool, later man."

"Later Clayton."

Cleabo and Trish had returned to the United States and were staying near the P.O. Box number he had sent to Clayton when they arrived. The post office was just a few blocks over, near a donut shop.

Cleabo opened up the letter from Clayton and began to read it. Trish was still in the bed at the hotel room.

"Ouch, man!" shouted Cleabo as the hot coffee from the donut shop spilled on his hand while he was trying to read the letter. He put the donuts down, his hands were too full.

"What's the matter honey?" Trish woke up from the excitement.

"Oh nothing baby, just being stupid trying to read with both of my hands being full, that's all."

"Aw, poor thing, maybe next time you'll get ice coffee." She teased as she rolled back on her side.

"That's funny sweetie. Hey, we got a letter from Clayton."

"Really?" she threw the covers off and jumped out of bed. "What it say?"

"It says that he has a politician friend that's going to help us and I need to call him at this number."

"He wants us to trust a politician?" Trish questioned.

"Baby I trust him; I'm sure he screened whoever he's going to use."

"Guess it's a first time for everything. Hey, why not?" Trish said, sounding like she was exhausted from being on the run.

"I'm going to go to the pay phone and call him. I'll be right back, okay baby?"

"Be careful sweetie." She kissed Cleabo and he gave her a huge hug.

The pay phone was right around the corner from the motel. Within minutes Cleabo made it there, anxious to hear Clayton's voice.

When Cleabo heard Clayton's familiar voice he relaxed a little.

"Hey, nice to hear your voice again CO."

"What's up Cleabo? How you been? Been waiting on your call dude."

"I just got the letter Clayton. So what's the deal, can we trust this cat?"

"Yeah man, he's straight. Here's what I need for you to do tomorrow Cleabo."

Clayton informed him where to go and what time to be there. Cleabo felt comfortable with the deal. As long as he knew Clayton was going to be there, he could ensure Trish that it was okay. Trish was a true skeptic. She found it hard to trust anyone, but, she gave all her love and trust to Cleabo.

"Okay Clayton, we will be there."

"Alright, see you there. Peace."

By the time Cleabo returned to the hotel room, his coffee was cold and the taste for donuts was long gone. He went over the plans with Trish. He knew how she was going to react, but he had to convince her to do it.

"Cleabo, I don't know about this. How can we be sure?"

"We just have to pray on it baby."

"Okay we can pray baby, but I hope you don't mind me using some of my skills to check it out?"

"What did you have in mind Trish?"

"First of all, if they come to put us in protective custody, there will only be two or four Feds at the most, right?"

"Right."

"Clayton and the politician should be there together also. Right?"

"Okay." Cleabo waited to see where this was going.

"I'm going to find you a wig shop first of all. Then I'm going to buy you a dreadlock wig for a disguise, and I'll be a pregnant woman."

"Oh, I see where you are going. We get there about an hour and a half early and check the place out, huh?"

"You know it. If we spot more than four funny shoe wearing Feds, something isn't right. They shouldn't be raiding us."

"Okay." Cleabo had to agree with it.

Southland Mall was quite a busy place at eleven thirty A.M. Trish had on a brown wig and a balloon taped to her belly, looking as though she was about seven months pregnant. Cleabo stood distantly away with a long, dreadlock wig on. They pretended not to know one another. After casing the area for about thirty minutes, they took turns eating lunch. It seemed to them that everything was cool and a threat didn't prevail. At twelve forty five, Clayton entered the mall and Perry came from a different direction. They met and stood directly in front of the Foot Locker and waited for the Feds, Trish and Cleabo.

Cleabo was inside of the store with his back turned to them, pretending to be looking at some shoes.

"Perry, good to see you man. Where are your people?" Clayton said excitedly.

"What's up man? They'll be here. Any sign of Cleabo and Trish?'

"Not yet, but I'm sure they will be here."

Two federal agents entered the mall and placed their arms on the banister over looking the ice skating ring down below. Trish instantly spotted them, then turned and established eye contact with Cleabo while he was in the store. She nodded twice, indicating to him that she saw two. Trish continued to look at baby items in the store adjacent to the Foot Locker. She turned to her left and noticed there were two more. Once again she sent Cleabo the signal.

Cleabo purchased a pair of sneakers and with his bag in his hand he walked out of the store. He stopped and tapped Clayton on the shoulders and spoke with a Jamaican accent.

"Hey man, long time no see."

"Cleabo! How you doing man." Clayton hugged him and introduced him to the politician. "Hey man, this is Perry."

"Oh, the politician. Hey man." Cleabo extended his hand, and gracefully Perry shook his hand.

"It's a pleasure to meet you Cleabo, C or is it Seal?"

"Hey, Cleabo will be fine, and thanks for all of your help, dude."

"Cleabo, thanks to you we have about seventeen raids in the making. Some are probably happening as we speak. Where is your wife Trish?"

"Glad to be of service." Cleabo turned his head around looking for Trish. "Oh, she is around here somewhere, you know how women love to window shop and buy stuff."

Two FBI agents approached them.

"Thank you Mr. Poe, we can handle it from here. Gentlemen, I'm Agent Sawyer and this is Agent Taylor."

Perry departed the area and waved goodbye. Agent Sawyer stood about six foot two and around two hundred and twenty pounds. With his hazel blue eyes it would be difficult to determine if he could see his feet due to the beer gut he had. The sleeves of his suit didn't come close to his wrists, it looked as though he'd been sleeping in it for weeks. His comrade Agent Taylor, was short and had more of a waddle like walk, similar to a duck. He was a bit neater than Agent Sawyer and he constantly moved his head around as if he was looking for trouble.

"Where is the woman?" asked Agent Sawyer.

"She will meet us at the entrance door." Cleabo responded.

"Okay lets get out of here." Agent Sawyer said.

"Pow!" the sound of a bullet, as it ricocheted off the walls of one of the stores in the mall screamed in their ears. Quickly the two agents grabbed Cleabo and Clayton, rushing them to the exit door. The other two agents that were at the banister squatted down looking around to see where the shot came from. Along with the crowd of people in panic, Trish dashed for the exit to join Cleabo, Clayton and the agents.

"Trish, come on!" Cleabo yelled as he grabbed hold of her and they rushed out of the mall.

The other two agents watched as the local authorities apprehended a youth with a bandanna wrapped around his head. They were pleased to know that it was just a gang punk that created the chaotic atmosphere and not a member of Crime Academy. Agents Sawyer and Taylor took Cleabo and Trish to a house where they were guarded until the day of the trial. Clayton was placed in a different location with the other two agents. Clayton could no longer communicate with Cleabo, but he knew that they both remembered how to reach one another after the ordeal was over. There was no way the FBI would let them communicate with each other again by regular means.

After a couple of weeks and numerous raids on Crime Academy, it was time to go to court. The courtroom was packed; filled with people and reporters, as the prosecutor made his opening statement. Federal agents guarded the front and the rear of the court room. It was standing room only as Clayton made his way into the congested courtroom. He couldn't recognize any of the members of Crime Academy, probably because he didn't know any of them; he only knew Cleabo and a brief informal view of a scared disguised pregnant woman, that was supposed to have been Trish.

The people that sat in the courtroom stared Clayton down as he entered with armed agents at his side. Out of the corner of his eyes he could see one of them with his novel in his hands, pointing and whispering to the person next to them, "There's the author." Clayton's only thoughts at that moment was how he could collect the royalties for the reprint of his novel with a new identity.

A few minutes after he took his seat, Cleabo and Trish entered the courtroom. The armed agents were pushing the mob-like crowd away from them, as the flashes of the numerous cameras continued to flash in the hall. The doors closed, and Clayton noticed Cleabo glancing around the room and walking as though he was in a trance of some sort. The men in the defendant box turned and whispered to each other. Cleabo just stared at them, displaying no sign of having a scared bone in his body.

"Trish was fine, as Cleabo stated in his letters." Clayton thought to himself, as he looked upon them.

Cleabo was well groomed and it was hard for Clayton to believe he could have been a transient at one point of his life. His beard was no longer than a quarter of an inch thick and his salt and pepper hairs were trimmed neatly. Cleabo sneered as he looked at the men in the defendant box, then he established eye contact with Clayton and gave him a gentle nod. Cleabo and Trish sat down as the FBI brought more escorted witnesses in for the prosecution side. Things weren't looking too good for Crime Academy.

Most of the new witnesses were also members of the notorious organization. They were also granted immunity for testifying against the leaders of the criminal ring. Clayton noticed Trish establishing eye contact with one of the gentlemen that sat in the defendant box. Clayton could only assume that he was her team leader that Cleabo described in his letters. The trial lasted for about two weeks. Continuously each defendant's lawyer tried their best to either plea bargain, cut a deal, or have their client set free. But, the prosecution wasn't going for it. There was too much evidence against this underground criminal organization.

After two weeks, verdicts were delivered, and it wasn't in favor of the Academy representatives. Most of the higher ranking like, Luther and Cleabo's First Sergeant, received forty years to life. Twenty years were issued to most of the team leaders, and the instructors received five to ten.

The members that conducted hits were set for first-degree murder trials. All types of big wheels in the political arena were taken down and forced into prison or retirement for any affiliation with Crime Academy. Cleabo and his friends were glad it was finally over.

As for Clayton, the FBI set him up nicely. They gave him enough money to start his own business on an island with white sand beaches. Clayton bought a publishing company that had Internet access, and he published several famous authors. With a new name and identity he was living large, making much more money than he did at the newspaper firm in L.A. Clayton gave up writing though, too many people may have recognized his style of writing and he couldn't risk being traced. Clayton was extremely grateful to Cleabo for letting him be a part of his exciting world. It really changed the way that he thought of the different people that exist in our judgmental society. Although the FBI wouldn't tell him where Cleabo and Trish were, he knew one day he would see them again, as he did when Cleabo fell on top of the hood of his car as a transient in L.A.

After a few years, things finally started to die down, and the Crime Academy scene seemed to faded away. It was then that Clayton felt that he should try to contact Cleabo, his forever friend. It had been years since they talked; his only hope was that Cleabo remembered the code name he told him to use for his identification years ago. Clayton used that name as the name of his new business and it was on the Internet. Jack Jones Publishing; a fictitious name of course.

After a few days of thinking about him, Clayton received a message on his computer. It said, *"I knew the game, and I had to play it by the rules. Church of Christ, 876 Dawson St. Queen City."* The state wasn't listed, but he knew it was Cleabo. Clayton made arrangements to go back to the United States.

He arrived on a Saturday, in the midst of one of the South's largest cities. Sunday he went to the Church of Christ after obtaining the correct address from the telephone book. He found a large, white wooden church that was packed with people inside. It's tall steeple seem to be swaying, as the choir rocked the building with their tambourines and loud musical instruments. Clayton peeped over everyone's head and shoulders, trying to see a familiar face. A lady turned around, looked him square in the face and smiled. She was plump with a cute face. Her skin was tanned from the southern heat. "Damn, it's Trish!" Clayton said to himself. She waved for him to come and sit on the front row with her.

As the choir quieted down, a man came out with a white robe on and a glow that just smoothly shimmered down the entire church. His white/gray hair was like snow and his words flowed like a whisper. It was Cleabo, and when he spoke a pin drop could be heard. His sermon was truly motivating. Clayton didn't know he had it in him, as he stared in amazement.

Trish was still pretty; but chunky and round now. She was beautiful and still madly in love with her husband. People flocked over Cleabo like flies on honey, but he managed to have Clayton at his side after church was over. He told Clayton the FBI had arranged for him to go into the ministry and he had finally earned his Doctorate of Divinity. He felt that the ordeal in Alaska was his wake up call, and he needed to touch others with the word of God. Clayton wasn't much of a religious man himself, but the way Cleabo glowed, it was easy for him to see there was something different about him. His long time friend had truly found himself, and Trish was his true love. They invited Clayton to dinner and he saw how well the church was taking care of him. They shared tears as Clayton said his final goodbyes to his long time friend. They knew a visit like this could never happen again, not for a while anyway.

As for Cliff, Willie and Angel, they are probably doing the same old thing, on the streets of L.A. Sara and Jonah married and she read the novel, so she knew what had happened to Cleabo. She was relieved that he was safe. Grandma Sadie Bell is still talking shit and telling folks like it is.

Clayton was relaxing one day at home on the island where the sand is white and the water is as clear as drinking water; when the door bell rang at his huge house. Opening his door he saw a woman standing there with neat, short, sandy hair and a figure that was out of this world. She was beautiful.

"Hi," she greeted him, reaching out to shake his hand. "Cleabo and Trish told me to look you up while I was on vacation here. My name is Sunshine." He turned his head away from her and murmured to himself, "This life has perks too."

Clayton later sent Cleabo and Trish a post card saying that he received 'Sunshine,' and it's all good.

So, if you know a preacher in your town that has a certain glow and a chubby, pretty faced wife, pay attention. His story and life could be far beyond what you could ever imagine. He may not ever share it with you, but his heart is genuine; believe that.

ABOUT THE AUTHOR

Clayton F. Brown is a native of Orangeburg South Carolina. He now resides in the subdivision of Charlotte, North Carolina, after traveling throughout the United States and abroad.